INTRODUCTION TO SOFTWARE MANAGEMENT AND QUALITY ASSURANCE

WA 1069902 3

D0514355

19.95

THE McGRAW-HILL
INTERNATIONAL SERIES IN SOFTWARE ENGINEERING

Consulting Editor

Professor D. Ince
The Open University

Other Titles in this Series

INTRODUCTION TO SOFTWARE PROJECT MANAGEMENT AND QUALITY ASSURANCE

Darrel Ince
Professor of Computer Science
The Open University

Helen Sharp
Lecturer in Computer Science
The Open University

Mark Woodman
Lecturer in Computer Science
The Open University

McGRAW-HILL BOOK COMPANY

London · New York · St Louis · San Francisco · Auckland · Bogotá
Caracas · Hamburg · Lisbon · Madrid · Mexico · Milan · Montreal
New Delhi · Panama · Paris · San Juan · São Paulo · Singapore
Sydney · Tokyo · Toronto

1069902   3   004. 068
                INC

Published by
McGRAW-HILL Book Company Europe
SHOPPENHANGERS ROAD · MAIDENHEAD · BERKSHIRE SL6 2QL · ENGLAND
TELEPHONE: 0628 23432
FAX: 0628 770224

British Library Cataloguing in Publication Data
Ince, Darrel
   Introduction to Software Project
   Management and Quality Assurance. –
   (McGraw-Hill International Series in
   Software Engineering)
   I. Title   II. Series
   005.1
   ISBN 0-07-707436-X

Library of Congress Cataloging-in-Publication Data
Ince, D. (Darrel)
   Introduction to software project management and quality assurance/
   Darrel Ince, Helen Sharp, Mark Woodman.
      p. cm. — (The McGraw-Hill international series in software
   engineering)
   Includes bibliographical references and index.
   ISBN 0-07-707436-X
   1. Software engineering—Management.   2. Computer software-
   —Quality control.   I. Sharp, Helen.   II. Woodman, Mark.
III. Title.   IV. Series.
QA76.758.I53   1993   92–34360
005. 1′068′4—dc20   CIP

Copyright © 1993 The Open University. All rights reserved. No part of this publication
may be reproduced, stored in a retrieval system, or transmitted, in any form or by
any means, electronic, mechanical, photocopying, recording, or otherwise, without
the prior permission of The Open University.

1234   CUP   943

Typeset by the authors

and printed and bound at the University Press, Cambridge

12.10.93

CONTENTS

One of the most striking features of the publicity materials that are circulated by computer science book publishers is the paucity of material on software project management. While there seem to be many books on programming in languages such as Pascal, Ada and COBOL, very little appears to have been written on software project management. This book is an attempt to remedy this deficiency.

We also hope that it will remedy another deficiency which we have noticed about those software project management books that have been published: the fact that they often consist of rather uninspiring lists of the tasks that a project manager carries out. In this book we have attempted to give a flavour of what it is like to be a software project manager—both the positive and negative aspects. We have, however, to admit that some of the book will contain lists of managerial activities that have to be carried out—this is unavoidable in any project management book. However, we hope that you will see these lists in the context of what software project managers actually do.

Another feature of this book is that we have included material—either interviews or descriptions—concerning important advances which we feel will affect the software project manager in the nineties and beyond. These include:

- Software metrics: numerical values of quality which can be used to characterize how good or bad that product is in terms of properties such as its proneness to error.
- The cleanroom technique, an approach to software development which has very many analogies with the production methods that are used to make simpler artefacts such as cars, domestic products and ball bearings.
- External software quality standards: standards developed both by national governments and pan-governmental organizations such as the CEC. Such standards will become increasingly important in the nineties, and we felt that the reader should at least have a flavour of what is in such standards.

The audience for this book is quite wide. We would suggest that two categories of reader would benefit from the book. First, technical staff who are currently carrying out tasks such as programming or design, and who wish to consider a career in software project management. Second, students on computing courses who want to read an *introductory* textbook on software project management and quality assurance. Typically, these students would be studying at the HND level or in their first or second year in a university.

This book owes its origins to an Open University course, M355 *Topics in Software Engineering*, which contains a similar treatment of project management and quality assurance. As in the course, we have included throughout the book a number of questions with the acronym SAQ. This stands for 'self-assessment question'. These questions can be used by the reader to judge whether he or she has understood the text preceding the SAQ.

Darrel Ince, Helen Sharp and Mark Woodman
Milton Keynes

ACKNOWLEDGEMENTS

The photograph (Fig. 8.2) is reproduced with the permission of EDS Scicon (Chapter 8).

IBM and Mike Dyer for the Cleanroom Experiment interview (Chapter 16).

BSI QA and John Souter, Head of the Software Engineering Department, BSI Quality Assurance for Registered Firm/Pascal Validation Service Interview and PVS samples (Chapter 17).

BSI Standards for permission to reproduce extracts from various draft standards (Chapter 17).

MoD: Interim Defence Standards 00-55 and 00-56 (Drafts) (Chapter 17).

UNIX is a trade mark of Digital Equipment Corporation.

ACKNOWLEDGEMENTS

SOFTWARE ENGINEERING AND SOFTWARE DEVELOPMENT

AIMS

- To introduce the developmental techniques used on a software project.
- To introduce the validation and verification techniques used on a software project.
- To describe the central role of the system specification in software development.

This introductory section describes how a software system is currently developed by the software industry; this process is summarized in Fig. 1.1. It is important to point out that this section of the book describes the development of bespoke software, for example it assumes the existence of a single customer or group of customers with a relatively consistent set of demands upon a software system.

In this chapter we shall assume that the reader is familiar with elementary software concepts such as programming.

1.1 REQUIREMENTS ANALYSIS

The starting point of any software project is a document which is prepared by the customer for a system and is known as *the statement of requirements*. This document, which is usually written in natural language, can be a few pages in length, or can consist of a number of volumes of text.[1] Normally, the less experienced a customer is in computing, the smaller the statement of requirements will be. In the document, the customer details what the proposed software system must be able to do, together with the constraints upon the system and upon the development process.

An important point to bear in mind is that the statement of requirements is usually couched in terms of the customer's business rather than in computing terms. Thus, in a hospital application, terms such as *bed*, *consultant*, *patient* and *appointment*, would be used rather than terms such as *communications interface*, *indexed sequential file* or *subroutine call*. A fragment of a statement of requirements might be as follows:

---

[1] The size usually depends on the degree of computer sophistication of the customer.

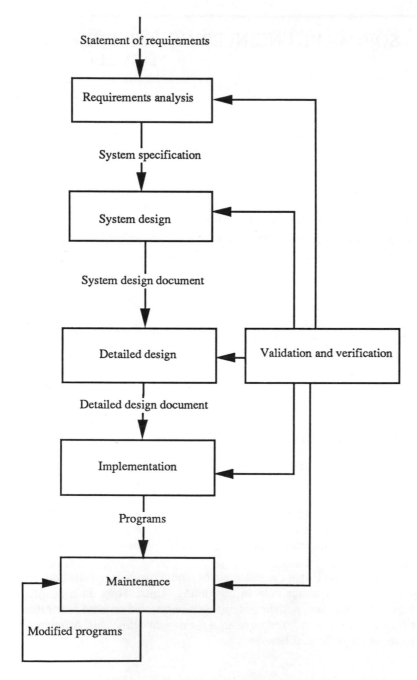

Figure 1.1 A model of software development.

> When the UPDATE command is typed, the system will prompt the user for the name of the flight to be updated and the new flight plan. The user will then type in a series of pairs of digits. Each pair represents the coordinates of the flight plan and is stored in the flight plan database. If the user mistypes a coordinate, then the system will respond with an appropriate error message. The flight plan database should be updated within two seconds of the command being completed.

This fragment is part of the statement of requirements of a system for storing the route (flight plan) of an airliner. There are two major points which are important to notice about it. First, it includes information about what the customer wants the system to do: to update the flight plan database in response to the UPDATE command. This type of information is known as a *functional requirement*. Second, it includes information about a limitation upon the system, i.e. that the response of the command must be two seconds. This type of information is known as a *constraint* or *non-functional requirement*.

Non-functional requirements govern either the characteristics of a system, for example by specifying response times or the amount of memory that a system should occupy, or they govern the developmental process. An example of a non-functional requirement which governs the developmental process is an insistence on using a particular programming language for implementation.

> SAQ Examine the fragment of a statement of requirements shown below. Identify the functional requirements and the constraints.

> > The monitoring system should monitor and display the temperatures in a series of reactors, detect any hazard conditions from these temperatures which indicate a reactor malfunction, and periodically write temperature data to a database which is used to provide information about the day-to-day running of the reactors. Since other systems have already being implemented on the host computer only 60K of memory is available for this system. All the file handling that the system performs should be implemented by means of calls on operating system procedures. The system should also periodically archive the temperature database to magnetic tape or else the file store used for the database would become exhausted.

> SOLUTION There are five functions, they are:

> - The system should monitor the temperatures in a series of reactors.

> - The system should display the temperatures in a series of reactors.

> - The system should detect any hazard conditions from the temperatures which indicate a reactor malfunction.

> - The system should periodically write temperature data to a database.

> - The system should periodically archive the temperature database to magnetic tape.

> There are two constraints:

> - The developer has to ensure that the system fits into 60K of memory.

- All the file handling that the system performs should be implemented by means of calls on operating system procedures.

The first constraint is a constraint on the system, the second is a constraint on the development process.

Given a statement of requirements the developer has to carry out the processes of requirements analysis. Requirements analysis consists of analysing the statement of requirements and extracting and clarifying the functions and the constraints. It involves a period of considerable interaction with the customer, and is probably the most difficult part of the software project.

One of the reasons that requirements analysis is so difficult is that the two main parties involved are divided by quite a considerable 'culture gap'. One of these parties is an expert in information technology who often has little knowledge of an application (the developer) while the other is an expert in a particular application but with a scant knowledge of the capabilities of information technology systems (the customer).

A second reason is that the statement of requirements exhibits a number of properties which make requirements analysis difficult. The extract used in the above SAQ illustrates one of these properties, i.e. the functions and the constraints are not gathered together in one place;[2] other properties are described below.

Functional and non-functional requirements are intermingled

Very rarely will you find a statement of requirements that is structured neatly into constraints and functions, with the constraints partitioned into those specifying system performance and those dealing with development practices.

The statement of requirements contains ambiguities

This arises from the use of natural language and will occur in even the best organized and most technically up-to-date projects, since natural language is the only medium which the customer is able to use to communicate with the developer. Although natural language is an ideal medium for novels and poetry, where ambiguity plays a major role, it is ill-suited for the level of precision required in a software project. It leads to sentences such as:

> Whenever the system detects that the operator has typed an error, a warning screen will be displayed with the type of error displayed in the first line of the screen. It will be displayed using flashing red letters.

This is taken from the statement of requirements for an airline booking system. The ambiguity here arises from the use of the word *it* in the second sentence. Does *it* refer to the warning screen or to the first line of the screen?

The statement of requirements contains platitudes

Probably the best and most common example of this is the sentence:

> The system should have a user-friendly interface.

---

[2] This is one of the major problems with validating a system specification.

which really means nothing at all! In a well-written statement of requirements this sentence should be replaced by concrete details about facilities such as menus and help facilities which provide the naive user with assistance, and details such as the use of long and short commands.

The statement of requirements contains design and implementation directives

A design directive is a statement that tells the developer what to do during the design phase of the software project. The following are examples of design directives:

> The main file which contains salary details of staff should be an indexed sequential file whose key is the salary number.

> The system should be partitioned into four subsystems....

An implementation directive is a statement that tells the developer what to do during the programming phase of the software project. For example, specifying which programming language should be used is an implementation directive.

Such directives should not appear in a statement of requirements. The major reason for this is that the customer, who has written the directive, is not normally an expert in the capabilities of software. If the customer were an expert there would be no need to ask a developer to produce the software in the first place! Consequently, it is unlikely that the solution suggested by such directives is the most appropriate. For example, the design directive above states that a file should be an indexed sequential file. It might very well be that a simple sequential file would achieve the functions asked for by the customer. Since such a file would occupy less space, this would be a better choice to make.

> SAQ In what circumstances would it be appropriate for design and implementation directives to appear in a statement of requirements?

> SOLUTION Often a new system has to interface with other systems which have already been implemented. When this occurs, design and implementation decisions made during the development of the latter impinge on the development of the former. For example, a new system for providing financial reports of sales of commodities might use the same indexed sequential file which is already employed by existing financial systems.

The statement of requirements is often incomplete

When describing large systems it is extremely easy to leave details out. For example, the following paragraph is part of the statement of requirements for a system which administers examination results:

> When the examinations clerk types the SUMMARY command at the keyboard of a VDU it should be followed by a school name and an examination number. In response, the system will display, either on the VDU or on a remote printer, the result statistics for the pupils who were entered for that examination from that school.

It contains two significant omissions.

> SAQ What are these two omissions?

SOLUTION The first omission is that there are no details about how the examinations clerk should notify the system where the statistics should be displayed, i.e. on the printer or on the VDU. The second omission is that there are no details about what should happen if the examinations clerk makes an error, say, by mistyping a school name or an examination number.

Functions are described at different levels of detail

Functions are often expressed at different levels of detail in a statement of requirements. For example, you might find in a statement of requirements for a stock ordering system functions such as:

The system should keep track of all orders for products which the warehouses keep in stock.

intermingled with functions such as:

The function of the OUTORDER command is to display, on the originating VDU, the stock numbers of all those products which have been recognized as having unacceptably low stock levels.

The first of these is at a high level of abstraction while the second example is quite detailed.

These, then, are some of the properties of the statement of requirements that make the task of requirements analysis difficult. The underlying features which are important are the functions and the constraints; however, these are clouded by vagueness, ambiguity, platitudes, design and implementation directives and omissions. In addition, it is very rare to find a statement of requirements with neatly partitioned sections marked: 'functions', 'constraints', 'design directives' and so on. Usually, the functions and constraints are intermingled freely with the less desirable features.

The aim of requirements analysis is to write down, in an unambiguous way, what a proposed system should do, i.e. its functions, and what the constraints are upon the developer. The document that is produced is often known as the system specification; it is the key document on which all subsequent activities in the software project depend.

Apart from functions and constraints, the system specification will also contain other details. These include:

- A specification of hardware to be used.
- A description of any training that the software developer is to offer to the customer in the use of the new system.
- A description of support from the software developer, for example in rectifying errors that occur during its operational use.
- A description of the criteria for acceptability of the software product: those tests, to be carried out by the customer and developer, which determine whether the customer will accept a product.

The last point listed above, the criteria for acceptability of the software product, is a major component of the system specification.

In this book we will concentrate mainly on the specification of functions. This is not to say that we regard the constraints as unimportant; indeed, in many systems, particularly those used in real-time applications such as avionics and process control, time constraints are vital. A longer than expected response in adjusting the wing flaps of an airliner or in opening an escape valve could lead to catastrophe.

The part of the system specification which details the functions will usually be the largest of its sections; it is known as the *functional specification*. It should have a number of properties, which are listed below. In describing these properties it is worth stressing that other documents used in the software project, and described later, should possess many of these properties.

The functional specification should be unambiguous

You have already seen that statements of requirements usually contain vague statements about system functions or system constraints. If such statements were allowed to pervade the system specification, then since the functional specification is a key document on which all subsequent activities in the software project depend, whole development teams might carry out expensive design and implementation tasks on false premises, only to discover that when the software is demonstrated to the customer it is not what was required.

The functional specification should be free of design and implementation directives

As discussed earlier, the statement of requirements should not constrain the software developer, but it should leave as many options open as possible in order that the developer can choose the best design which implements the system functions and satisfies the system constraints. Since the functional specification is derived from the statement of requirements, it also should not contain any such directives. In fact, during the process of requirements analysis, directives present in the original statement of requirements may have been removed after some discussion.

The functional specification should be in a form which enables the developer to reason about the properties of the system it describes

During the requirements analysis process the developer will be continually developing the system specification and checking that the properties of that system match the customer's view of what it should do. For example, in carrying out requirements analysis for a chemical plant monitoring system the developer will ask questions such as:

- If the escape valve is open and the system is in emergency mode will an alarm sound at the main control console?
- If the operator types a chemical reactor name and that reactor is closed down will the system notify the operator of this?

These questions would be extracted from the current version of the functional specification, an answer obtained from the customer, and this answer checked with the functional specification. If the answer is different then the functional specification should be amended. In order to derive an answer from the functional specification the developer will have to carry out a process of reasoning: identifying premises such as 'escape valve open' from the functional specification, and seeing whether conclusions such as 'an alarm sounds at the main control console' are described, in the functional specification, as following from the premises. The functional specification should be written so that such a reasoning process can be carried out soundly (so that one may be confident of the validity of its results) and effectively (so that the required results may be reached with an acceptably low effort).

The functional specification should be partitioned

Information in a functional specification should be partitioned into self-contained sections. This allows the analyst and customer to read the specification a section at a time. An example of this partitioning, representing part of the functional specification for a car-hire system, is as follows.

1. Financial information. The system should provide financial information for the company accountant. This is obtained by typing the following commands.

   1.1   The DAYSUMMARY command. This produces the receipts for a particular day. The day is to be typed in after the command.

   1.2   The REFUND command. This produces the total refunds given to customers on a particular day. The day is to be typed in after the command.

   1.3   The MONTHSUMMARY command. This produces the total receipts for a particular month in the current financial year. The month is to be typed in after the command.

2. Car usage information. The system should provide information on the use made of cars in the company's fleet.

   2.1   The CARMILE command. This command produces the total mileage travelled by a car. The car's registration number is to be typed in after the command.

   2.2   The AVERAGEMILE command. This command produces the average mileage travelled by cars in the company's fleet.

The functions are split into two separate areas: those functions concerned with car use and those connected with financial information. Notice that in this example each function is split up further into more detailed functions. For example, the function concerned with car mileage processing is split up into functions concerned with total mileage and functions concerned with average mileage.

SAQ Why should functional specifications be split up in this way?

SOLUTION   There are two reasons. First, by using a hierarchic decomposition scheme it enables the staff carrying out the process of requirements analysis to concentrate on small tractable parts of the system specification. It is really for the same reason that the code of a software system is organized in a calling hierarchy: it enables the top-down design process to be carried out in such a way that the staff involved can concentrate on small tractable units of software.

Second, it makes interaction with the customer, or the customer's staff, easy. Normally, for a large system development, there will be a number of the customer's staff involved in the requirements analysis process. For example, in the car hire example in this SAQ the company accountant would be interested in functions associated with financial information, while a service manager would be interested in car mileage information. Both of these members of staff would normally be interviewed during requirements analysis. By organizing the specification into functionally related areas, the process of interviewing can be made smoother, with the interviewer not having to swap over pages continually.

An important point to make about this partitioning of the functional specification is that it provides the main mechanism for handling complexity in the software project. It enables the description of a large system to be split up into tractable portions which can be reasoned about and processed individually[3] but which can also be combined together and reasoned about and processed as a whole.

The functional specification should be free of extraneous detail

By this we mean that it should contain only the information relevant to the task of requirements analysis and to the later task of system design (see below).

For example, the functional specification for an airline booking system should not contain details of the character sequences that need to be typed when querying a database of information about stored flights; this type of detail can be dealt with during the later stages of design. Properties which are important to the customer must be easily identifiable and not hidden by too much detail. A good analogy for this is the British Rail Intercity route map. Such a map is shown in Fig. 1.2. The map represents a model of the Intercity rail system: it does not show the geographical layout of the tracks, the location of public conveniences, where tickets are collected, where the wastebins are or the exact position of lamp standards. What the route map does show is a stylized description of the topological relationships between stations and connecting lines—the only information required by the rail traveller. Any information about wastebins, pedestrian walkways and so on would only clutter the map and make the task of finding a route through the system more difficult.

In the same way a functional specification should not be cluttered with irrelevant detail.[4]

The functional specification should be understandable by the customer

Once the system specification is complete, it is read and approved by the customer and agreed. In the contract for a system there is normally a clause which states that the system specification must be agreed by both the customer and the developer,[5] and that once this agreement is reached, no more changes may be made to the specification without the developer's permission. This means that the customer or the customer's staff must check the system specification thoroughly and ensure that it represents the required system. Once agreement is reached the document is formally 'signed off' by the customer, indicating that it does represent the required system. Often, a percentage of the developer's fee (for example 20 per cent) is paid at this point.

An important point to make about the specification that is produced is that it is a contractual document. Also, there are a number of possible contracts that can be negotiated between a customer and a developer. The two main ones are a fixed price contract whereby the developer undertakes to produce a system for a fixed sum of money and a cost+ contract

---

[3] A strategy known as *divide and conquer*.
[4] This is one of the major problems when using natural language as a specification notation.
[5] The system specification is normally a contractual document.

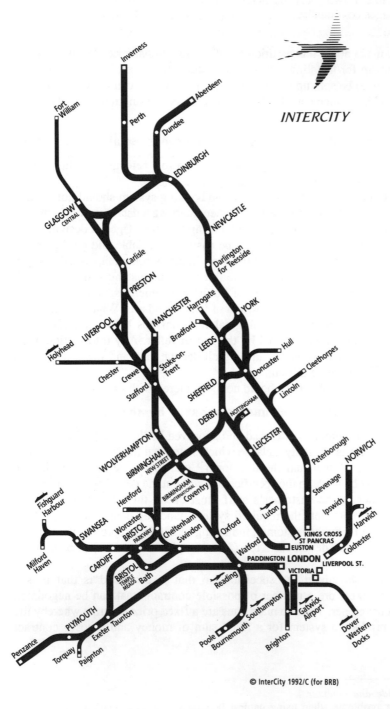

© InterCity 1992/C (for BRB)

Figure 1.2   The British Rail Intercity route map, reproduced with permission from Train Lines of Britain, license number TLB/92/1911.

whereby the developer undertakes to produce a system for the cost of producing it plus a profit figure. There are a number of variations on this basic model, for example, arranging for staged payments or paying a short list of potential software developers to carry out some preliminary work such as producing an outline specification, as an aid to judging the competence of the developers. The vast majority of contracts these days are fixed price.

1.2 DEVELOPMENT OF THE SYSTEM AND ACCEPTANCE TESTS

When a system has been developed, it is not just handed over to the customer. The cost of a software system can now run to many millions of pounds, so the customer, quite rightly, expects a demonstration that the developed software meets the system specification. This is the role of the *system tests* and the *acceptance tests*.

These two sets of tests are carried out after a system is complete and should explore thoroughly every function of the system as described in the system specification to ensure that the software satisfies the customer's requirements. The system tests are conducted first, usually at the developer's premises, and act as a preliminary check for the acceptance tests which are carried out in the operational environment where the software is to run. Usually, the acceptance tests are a subset of the system tests. The point about system and acceptance tests is that they are one or more tests which prove that the final system meets some or all of the agreed specification and that the staff who carry out the tests are not allowed to test features which are not described in that specification.

It is often necessary for some of the operational aspects of the developed system to be omitted or simulated for the system tests. For example, in system testing software for monitoring a nuclear reactor, it is clearly impractical to construct such a device at the developer's premises, and so it must be simulated either by software or special-purpose hardware.

System tests are performed because it can be very expensive, and embarrassing, for acceptance tests to fail.[6] In the example above, it is fairly clear what catastrophic effects may result if acceptance testing were to fail, however there are less spectacular potential penalties. One reason for the expense when an acceptance test fails is that the customer has every right to ask that the whole set of acceptance tests up to the point of failure be re-executed.

SAQ Why do you think '...the customer has every right to ask that the whole set of acceptance tests up to the point of failure be re-executed'?

SOLUTION When an acceptance test fails the developer has to discover the reason, and then modify the system so that it passes the failed test. However, in modifying the system, a further error in the part of the system which has been successfully acceptance tested could be created. Hence, the customer is completely in the right to demand a re-run of all the acceptance tests from the beginning.

Specification of the system and acceptance tests begins during the latter stages of requirements analysis and specification and is carried out by the developer in conjunction with

---

[6] It is also highly expensive to rectify errors.

the customer. Normally the tests are expressed in outline form initially, and are then fleshed out during the rest of development.

The tests for anything but the most trivial system will occupy many volumes of text. In order to illustrate why this is so, consider the description of a function taken from the specification of a chemical plant monitoring system:

> When the INFORMATION command is typed in by a process worker the system will return the average temperature and pressure for a reactor for a particular day. The command line typed should include the day and the name of the reactor.

If the system specification stated that all errors in commands should be notified to the process worker, then this one function would give rise to a series of acceptance tests, the first few of which are shown below:

INFORMATION command

Test 1   The system should demonstrate that when an invalid date is typed in, an error message indicating this is displayed.

Test 2   The system should demonstrate that when a date is typed in for which the specified reactor gave rise to no temperature and pressure data, a message is displayed indicating this.

Test 3   The system should demonstrate that when a date outside the limits of operation of the reactor is typed in, an error message indicating this is displayed. The limits of operation are a period starting 30 days before the date on which the command is typed and finishing on the day previous to the one on which the command is typed.

Test 4   The system should demonstrate that when an invalid reactor name is typed, an error message indicating this is displayed.

Test 5   The system should demonstrate that when an invalid year is typed, an error message indicating this is displayed.

Test 6   The system should demonstrate that when a valid reactor name is typed and a valid date is typed, the correct average temperature and pressure are displayed for a database containing average values supplied by the customer.

Test 7   The system should demonstrate that when a valid reactor name is typed and a valid date is typed, the correct average temperature and pressure are displayed for a database containing high values supplied by the customer.

Test 8   The system should demonstrate that when a valid reactor name is typed and a valid date is typed, the correct average temperature and pressure are displayed for a database containing low values supplied by the customer.

Test 9   The system should demonstrate that when a valid reactor name is typed and a valid date is typed, the correct average temperature and pressure are displayed for a database containing a mixture of high and low values. The high values being in the first twelve hours of operation, the low values being in the last twelve hours of operation. These values being supplied by the customer.

If the system specification contained constraints such as a maximum response time, and the use of short and long versions of the command (for example INFO and INFORMATION) then there would be a substantial number of tests for one seemingly straightforward command. For medium to large systems there will be many thousands of acceptance tests.

1.3 SYSTEM DESIGN

When the system specification has been completed the next stage in the development process is that of *system design*. This is the process of defining the architecture of a system in terms of the operations that are to be carried out by the system and the data which is to be processed. This architecture is often expressed in terms of discrete chunks, which we shall refer to as *program units*. A program unit is a self-contained collection of code and data that can be invoked in a software system and which communicates with other program units by means of parameters. An example of a program unit is the Pascal procedure. In the literature you will often find program units referred to as *subroutines*, *packages* or *modules*.

Program units implement operations on the stored data of the application. For example, in a banking application, program units extract customer records, modify these records and write them back to the area of backing storage where they reside. As in the functional specification, the description of the program units will be partitioned: a unit may call on another one in order to carry out its task. For example, a program unit for scanning the items in a queue of messages in a computer network may first call another unit which retrieves the queue before the scanning process is carried out.

System design also involves specifying the organization of the data which is used in the application. For example, a set of salary records, which might be referred to in a system specification as a file might be designed as an indexed sequential file. In developing a system design the developer uses the system specification as the base document. No other documents are used.

> SAQ Why do you think that the only document used is the system specification. Could the developer use the statement of requirements? This, after all, represents what the customer wants from a system.
>
> SOLUTION The system specification is the only document used because the statement of requirements contains ambiguities, platitudes, design directives and other features which will all lead to a system which stands only a faint chance of being what the customer wanted. The requirements analysis stage is specifically intended to clarify all of these points, and it would therefore be a waste of time and effort if the designer then reverted to using the original statement of requirements.

The system designer attempts to derive an architecture which satisfies the functional specification and any constraints that are described in the system specification.[7] All the functions of a system must be implemented correctly, yet at the same time constraints such as a maximum response time and amount of available memory limit the number of suitable design alternatives.

---

[7] The designs produced from a system specification often miss the desired response time and tuning has to take place after implementation.

The important point to notice about a system design is that it expresses how a system is to implement a series of functions in *computing* terms. This is in contrast to the system specification which is a description of what a system is to do in *application* terms.

At the end of the system design stage, the developer will have specified the function of each program unit and will have chosen a structure for the data which those units will operate on. An example of an individual specification of a program unit in a system design is as follows:[8]

```
LOOKUP (Planetable, Found, Plane)
Parameters
   Planetable: ARRAY of plane identifier
   Found: BOOLEAN
   Plane: plane identifier
Global   variables   affected
   None
Description
   When executed, this procedure will look for Plane in the
   table Planetable. If it is found than Found is set to true,
   otherwise it is set to false. On entering the procedure the
   parameter Found will be undefined.
```

This is relatively straightforward. It gives the name of the program unit LOOKUP and a description of its parameters. It also shows that no global variables in the software system are affected by the execution of the program unit and terminates with a description of the function of the unit.

The system designer is also concerned with the structure of the data which is to be manipulated by the system. If the functional specification is good, then there will be few, if any, directives about the way data is to be stored. All that the specification will contain is a description of what is intended to happen in an application, and descriptions of the entities which make up the application. For example, part of the functional specification for a booking system for an airline might state:

When the booking clerk types the BOOK command, the name of the passenger, the flight number and flight date are stored by the system.

Here the function of booking a seat is described and the data to be manipulated (flight number, flight date, passenger) is specified. No mention is made of whether this information is to be stored in a file or in main memory, and, if in main memory, what sort of data structure is to be used.

The system designer takes the functional specification, which will contain statements such as the one shown above, and decides on how the data is to be stored in the system. The factors which determine this choice are the constraints described in the system specification.

For example, an enquiry system for a warehouse, where the clerks are continually answering queries about stock availability, may have stringent constraints on response time, but have generous constraints on memory. In this case the system designer may well decide on a hashed table implementation to hold details of stock. On the other hand, the system may have stringent memory constraints and a generous response time. In this case the system designer may well choose a table which is ordered, and adopt a binary search mechanism for

---

[8] Although this is expressed in a notation which has a flavour of Pascal, it is capable of being implemented in any programming language.

extracting stock details. Choosing this data design will result in a system for which the operation to insert details of a new stock item will be relatively slow, since a table arranged for a binary search has to be kept in order.

Thus, the process of system design involves a progression towards implementation concerns and a reduction in the number of choices open to the developer. The system specification should give the developer as much choice as possible in the way that a system is developed. The design cuts down that choice, because the system designer will have specified the operations that are to occur in the system, and will have decided on the structural details of how data is to be stored.

Before we leave system design it is worth examining the properties that a system design document should have; they are very similar to those of the functional specification.

The system design document should be unambiguous

Obviously, any errors in interpretation of a system design will result in errors which might remain undetected until the end of a project, hence the system design document should be unambiguous.

The system design document should be free of implementation directives

Such directives get in the way of the design process and should be deleted. A designer wants to concentrate on the process of developing an architecture which meets a system's functional specification without being overloaded with detailed information about how screens should be displayed, the number of decimal places to be displayed and details of the input devices that are used in the application.

The system design document should be in a form which enables the developer to reason about the properties of the system it describes

This is similar to the property required of the functional specification. However, there is one subtle difference: the reasoning that is carried out during the design process involves the properties of the architecture of the system, rather than those issues which are important to the customer.

The system design document should be partitioned

Again this ensures that we are able to cope with the massive complexity of software systems. It enables the system to be partitioned into tractable chunks which can be coped with one at a time, and then recombined into larger chunks. In the case of the system design these chunks will be the individual operations on the application data. Operations will be expressed in terms of other operations, and so on, until some acceptably 'primitive' (requiring no further decomposition for computational understanding) level is reached.

The system design document should be free of extraneous detail

The principle is the same as that described earlier: a document which is used for a particular activity in the software project should contain no more information than is necessary for the efficient execution of that activity.

SAQ One of the properties that a system specification should have is that it should be understandable by the customer. Should this be a property of the system design document?

SOLUTION No. The system design document is a technical document which normally contains software-related information rather than application-based information. It is a document used on a project which addresses technical issues. Therefore there is no need for the customer to understand it.

SAQ What choices are still open to the designer after the system design stage? Remember that after system design has been completed the system will be specified in terms of the operations that are to be carried out and the way data is to be stored. The operations are specified by the effect they have on the stored data.

SOLUTION One important set of choices concerns the processing that is to occur in each of the operations. Although the system design will specify what is to happen when these operations are executed, it will not contain a description of the detailed processing that is to occur. For example, it will not have specified that a 'for' loop or a 'while' statement is to be used. It need not even specify the algorithm by which an operation is executed.

Another decision which has not been made involves the detailed storage of data: although the system design might specify a storage mechanism such as an ordered table, or an indexed sequential file, it will not include details such as the number of bytes to be allocated to the table or the maximum file size that is available.

After the system design has been developed the major development task that remains is programming or implementation: devising the computational algorithms that are initiated when an operation is executed.

It is worth pointing out that in this section we have described system design on pure software projects. If a project has a hardware element then a major task to be carried out would be the partitioning of the system into its hardware and software components.

Another important point to make is that there are levels of system design. In a large, complex project the system designer may initially produce a system design which only describes subsystems, this would then be expanded into subsubsystems and expanded again into descriptions of the modules in the system.

1.4 DETAILED DESIGN

The next phase after system design is *detailed design*. After system design the software system will be partitioned into a number of program units together with a description of what each unit is to do. The system design specifies only what processing is to occur, it does not specify the algorithms to be used. Detailed design does this.

The function of detailed design is to fill in the gaps in the system design. The processing that is to occur is specified in terms of a language known as a *program design language*. It contains all the control constructs associated with a programming language. An example fragment of a program design language might be as follows:

```
i := b[0]; s := 1;
while  i < 11 do
    i := i + 1;
    s := s + b[i]
od
```

The first line sets the variable i to b[0] and the variable s to 1. The second line is a loop which is executed while i < 11. Inside the loop are two assignment statements: the first increments the variable i by 1 and the second adds the ith element of the array b to s.

The advantage of using a program design language is that it provides a programming language-independent representation of the processing that occurs. The fragment above could easily be translated into Pascal, FORTRAN, assembler or COBOL. The advantage of using such a notation is that it provides a common notation across projects for a company that employs a number of different programming languages.

Rather than have one detailed design notation for COBOL, one for FORTRAN and one for Pascal, a common notation saves on training costs, and enables the developer to have a language-independent version of the software system; this would ensure that if the software were implemented on a new computer, using a different language, then minimal work would ensue. It is fair to point out, however, that a number of software developers, particularly those where one or two languages are used for implementation, choose not to use a detailed design language, and employ the programming language to express the processing that is to occur.

The information generated during the detailed design stage is captured in a detailed design document. Notice that when detailed design has finished, the choices that are open to the developer are very small. The processing has been fully defined, the data structures which are to be manipulated have usually been specified. All that remains for system production is implementation.

1.5 IMPLEMENTATION

The *implementation*, or programming stage, consists of taking the operations that were defined during the system design stage and implementing the algorithms which were defined during the detailed design stage using a programming language.

Once a unit has been programmed, the process of *unit testing* is performed. Unit testing is the test of a program unit which implements an operation. The programmer will have coded a program unit in some programming language, and will need to check that it carries out the functions expressed in its detailed design. This checking is carried out by executing the program unit a number of times, each time with a different set of test data. After each execution the programmer checks that the results given by the unit are correct.

In selecting the test data, the programmer has to ensure that all the cases that the program unit is to handle are correctly executed. For example, a program unit which sorts a sequence of data into some order would be tested with normally distributed data, with data which consists of just one number repeated a number of times, with one number, with no input at all and so on. The unit testing process is usually terminated when the programmer believes that all the branches of a program unit have been traversed.

Integration testing is the process of testing a partially built software system. During implementation, program units which have been adequately tested will start to emerge. The software developer takes these units and gradually builds up a system. Each time a unit, or small number of units, has been added to the partially built system an integration test is performed. The major function of such a test is to check that the added unit(s) has (have) no deleterious effect on the rest of the system which has already been constructed.

Integration testing is designed to detect errors, such as one program unit passing data to a second program unit which is outside the range of data that the second unit either expects or is programmed to process. While a programming language such as Pascal, which has strong typing, would not allow such an error to occur, there are a number of popular languages where this is not the case.

A developer integrates a system together gradually, rather than constructing the system all at once (a technique known as the 'big bang' approach), because there are usually errors in the program units which have not been detected during unit testing since they are concerned with how the units interact.

If all the coded units are added together and testing is started, then these errors will certainly manifest themselves in erroneous output. Tracking down the faults that caused such output, in a system of hundreds or thousands of units, would take considerable intellectual effort. However, if one or two units are added at a time, the developer would have a high degree of confidence that any error that arose during an integration test could be traced either to the body of the program units being integrated or to their interfaces. Because integration testing does not require that all coded units are available at the same time, it overlaps in time with implementation.

Integration testing also has other uses. It is often used as a type of preliminary system test. After a series of integration tests have taken place, the developer may find that the partially built system completely implements some of the functions found in the system specification. For example, in integration testing a system for controlling the defence of a warship, a developer might find that all the units designed to implement the functions of monitoring radar signals for the presence of a potential aggressor had been integrated and tested. If so, then the next series of integration tests that are performed, could contain elements of the system tests designed to test this monitoring function.[9]

It is also useful during integration testing to check that constraints, particularly of response time, are being satisfied correctly. One of the most difficult tasks in a project which implements software with time constraints is predicting the exact time responses from a design. If the response times of a system are out of the range specified in the system specification, then the developer must know as soon as possible during a project so that avoiding action can be taken, e.g. by selecting faster algorithms and different data structures. Integration testing is the first opportunity for the developer to gain an accurate impression of response time, so it is often worthwhile to include some timing tests in the integration tests.

When all the units have been integrated into the system and have been tested, the process of system testing begins. Once the developer is confident that the system will satisfy the acceptance tests, the software is transferred to the customer's premises, if necessary, and

---

[9] A careful developer will plan to cover a large number of the system tests during integration testing.

acceptance testing is performed. When the customer is satisfied with the system's performance, the remaining balance of the developer's fee is paid.

1.6 VALIDATION AND VERIFICATION

The important point that we stressed at the beginning of this section is that a software system has to meet a set of customer requirements. The processes that are applied by the software developer to ensure this are known as validation and verification. *Verification* is the process of ensuring that the product of an activity in the software project satisfies the product constructed by a previous activity. For example, the product of system design is the system design document, the process of checking this document to ensure it adequately implements the system specification is an example of verification: the document produced by an activity (the system design document) is checked against the document produced by the previous activity (the system specification).

Validation is the process of checking that a document or piece of software accurately reflects the customer's requirements. System testing and acceptance testing are two examples of validation.

A useful way to remember which is validation and which is verification is to think of validation as being 'a check on whether a developer is building the right system, i.e. one that meets the customer's requirements', and verification as being 'a check on whether the system is being built right, i.e. whether the output from an activity accurately reflects the input'.

SAQ Is the process of checking the system specification against the statement of requirements an example of validation or verification?

SOLUTION It is an example of validation since it checks whether the developing system matches the customer's requirements.

A number of validation and verification techniques are available to the developer. Some of these are described below.

1.6.1 Prototyping

This is the process of producing a quick version of a software system early in the software project. Remember that one of the major problems in the software project is the difficult process of requirements analysis, i.e. checking that a system specification, which contains many volumes of text, matches the customer's requirements.

SAQ Why do you think the process of requirements analysis is so difficult?

SOLUTION First, there is a major cultural difference between the customer and the developer: the former is an expert in software development and the latter is an expert in an application area. Second, there is the sheer bulk of the documents produced: the specification for even a medium-size system can occupy many volumes of text, since it has to describe in minute detail what that system is to do.

Prototyping involves developing an early version of a system during requirements analysis and showing it to the customer for approval. Hopefully, this will prevent misinterpretations of the statement of requirements being carried through into later stages of development. When the prototype is approved, it is signed off by the customer and is used as a model to judge the development of the complete system.

Prototypes are developed in a number of ways. One way to produce a quick version of a system is to compromise on some of the constraints or functions detailed in the system specification. For example, the developer may not implement the processing part of the software, but just implement those parts concerned with communication with the user—the human-computer interface. On the other hand, the developer may ignore constraints such as response time and produce a slow version of a system which implements all its functions. There are now tools which enable the developer to do this. These include fourth generation languages, which include facilities for report writing and manipulation of stored databases, and very high level languages that enable large productivity increases to occur but at the cost of developing slow software.

1.6.2 Reviews

A review is a managerial technique that is used for both validation and verification. It involves a meeting of a number of staff on a software project to examine and check one of the products of the project. A typical review might contain four staff: a chairman, the designer or programmer whose work is being examined, a member of the developer's quality assurance organization, and a member of staff from another project who has knowledge of the broad application area for which the software is being developed.

The purpose of a review is to check part of a document or code produced for a system. For large systems it is impractical to examine the whole system design, or the entire code of the system, so only fragments are normally examined. The main purpose of a review is to determine the adequacy of a product with respect to its requirements.[10] For example in a system design review the designer must present a convincing argument for the adequacy of the proposed system design fragment being reviewed, and the reviewers must sign a document to the effect that they were, or were not, convinced by that argument.

Reviews are used continually throughout a project: system specification reviews check conformance of the system specification with the statement of requirements, design reviews check that a system design document adequately reflects the system specification, system test reviews check that the system tests adequately demonstrate that the customer's requirements are met and so on. Surprisingly, since the idea behind reviews is so simple, they have proved an extremely effective method for validation and verification.

1.6.3 Mathematical Verification

There are now a number of proof techniques which enable the developer to demonstrate that a system design, expressed in mathematics, satisfies the system specification, and that operations expressed in a programming language satisfy those parts of the system design which describe the operations.

---

[10] Other purposes for a review include checking adherence to standards and the feasibility of the project plan.

1.6.4 Testing

Testing is the process of exercising a software system with data to ensure that it performs as expected. It occurs in a number of guises, and forms an integral part of software development. You have already seen examples of testing: unit testing, integration testing, system testing and acceptance testing.

> SAQ Is unit testing, the testing of a module in isolation, an example of validation or verification?
>
> SOLUTION It is an example of verification. The output of the activity of programming (a coded program unit) is checked against the output of the previous activity (the detailed design of a program unit).

1.7 MAINTENANCE

Maintenance is the term given to the developmental activities that take place after a system has passed its acceptance tests, and has been handed over to a customer. At this point the customer will have paid for the software, and hence owns the system. It is not widely known that as much as 60 per cent of software development effort is normally expended on maintenance: the modification of existing software.[11]

There are two reasons why software has to be modified. The first is that a software developer will have made errors in development which will remain undetected by system and acceptance testing. These errors will be detected when the system is put to its first heavy use in its operational environment. This activity is considered to be part of the original contract to develop the system, and there is often a contractual obligation on a software developer to track down these errors and rectify them.

The second reason for maintenance, and one which gives rise to the majority of maintenance activities that a developer carries out, is due to the changing nature of the world. The world in which software is used changes at a rate which often invalidates many of the original requirements and often gives rise to new requirements, as the following examples illustrate:

- A system which administered the financial reports on the products sold by a company became invalid when that company was taken over by another, bigger company. The company which carried out the takeover reorganized the sales division of the smaller company, and insisted that the financial reports produced conformed to the format of the reports required by the accountants of the bigger company. During the takeover, company tax law was changed; this required further changes in the system.
- A system for tracking aggressor missiles and initiating countermeasures was installed in a number of warships. The system had to be changed when reports indicated that a new air-to-ship missile had been developed which had a faster speed than previous

---

[11] Recent surveys have estimated the cost to be as high as 85 per cent.

missiles, and was capable of non-linear flight. Consequently, the detection subsystem of the system had to be modified to speed up its response time.

- A monitoring system for chemical reactors took its data from thermocouples and pressure transducers attached to a series of reactors. These monitoring instruments were replaced by cheaper and more reliable instruments. Consequently, the system had to be modified to take cognizance of this fact.

Software systems are a major investment for a customer and rather than commit resources to commissioning a totally new system which incorporates any changes in requirements, a customer will often ask a developer to modify an existing system and provide a new version. This activity is not covered by the original contract, but the developer will often sign a maintenance contract with the customer so that modifications which are required can be carried out by the organization that developed the original system.

The problem of changing requirements is, in fact, more serious than the previous paragraphs have indicated. A software project which delivers medium-to-large systems often takes a number of years to complete. During this time the original requirements, which are cast in stone in the system specification, become out-of-date and the system delivered to meet this specification ends up being, at best, one which only approximately meets requirements and, at worse, unusable. Software developers attempt to overcome these problems by designing systems which are flexible, i.e. which can be modified easily. One approach is to try to anticipate where changes will occur, and to choose program units with these anticipated changes in mind.

1.8 SUMMARY

This chapter has described, at some length, the activities that make up the software development process. Many of these activities are phased, and are associated with an end-product. Some of the processes, for example verification and validation, occur throughout the software project.

Development starts with a statement of requirements produced by the customer. The developer analyses this statement and produces a system specification which carefully details both the functions and the constraints of the intended system; this process is called requirements analysis. This task is difficult because the statement of requirements will usually be written in natural language which is ambiguous and therefore lacks the precision required for system specification. In clarifying requirements, the 'culture gap' between the developer and the customer also hinders progress.

System design is the process of producing a system architecture based on a collection of program units, each of which performs a specific function on the system's data structures. A set of specifications which describes the processing involved in each unit is produced together with a specification of the data structures to be used. The document containing this information is known as the system design document.

Detailed design expands these descriptions by specifying the algorithm to be used in each unit, which can then be translated into a particular programming language during implementation. The document produced by this activity is called the detailed design document.

Throughout system development, verification and validation are performed to try to ensure that the system performs as expected. Remember that validation is 'a check on whether a developer is building the right system', and verification is 'a check on whether the system is being built right'. Usually, the software will be paid for after completion of the acceptance tests, which are a set of tests devised by the developer and the customer to ensure that the software meets its requirements. After the system has been delivered, the activity of software maintenance begins. This includes all tasks concerned with ironing out any remaining errors, and with modifying the system because of changing requirements.

1.9 FURTHER READING

An excellent textbook which describes software engineering with a particular stress on maintenance is Lamb (1988). A good introduction to software engineering in general is Pressman (1987). Kaner (1989) is a splendid book which describes virtually every aspect of testing. Rook and Wingrove (1990) is a good introduction to project management and control. This paper can be found in Rook (1990) which is an excellent handbook on software development. Although it is aimed at the developer of safety critical software, it can still be read with profit by anyone developing other types of software.

BIBLIOGRAPHY

Kaner, C. (1989) *Testing Computer Software*, TAB Books, Blue Ridge Summit, PA.

Lamb, D. A. (1988) *Software Engineering, Planning for Change*, Prentice-Hall, Englewood Cliffs, NJ.

Pressman, R. S. (1987) *Software Engineering—A Practitioner's Approach*, McGraw-Hill, New York.

Rook, P. (ed.) (1990) *Software Reliability Handbook*, Elsevier Science, Barking.

Rook, P. and Wingrove, A. (1990) 'Software project control and management' in *Software Reliability Handbook*, Rook, P. (ed.), Elsevier Science, Barking.

2

SOFTWARE PROJECT MANAGEMENT

AIMS

- To describe the functions of management.
- To describe the day-to-day life of a project manager.
- To place the functions of software project management within a software development environment.

2.1 INTRODUCTION

Good management of a project in any sphere is important because of the financial consequences of it being managed badly; if the project is completed late or fails to achieve its aims then this could cost the organization a lot of money. For software projects, management becomes a particularly important activity because of the intractable nature of the product being developed.

Many of the books on software development give the impression that development occurs in isolation, simply because they tend to concentrate on the technical aspects of software development. However, there is, in fact, a lot going on in parallel with the technical development of software, and indeed there is a lot of activity required before technical development can begin, i.e. before requirements analysis starts. This chapter describes the activities that are performed in parallel with software development and introduces those performed before software development can begin.

In order to set the scene for this discussion of project management activities, we shall introduce an extended development life-cycle for software. Figure 2.1 contains this extended life-cycle which shows the major tasks which need to be performed before technical development can begin.

The process is initiated when a potential customer asks a developer to compile a proposal document for producing a system. The customer provides an outline statement of requirements from which the developer produces an outline system specification and outline system design. Based on these documents, the developer also performs risk assessment and produces a cost figure representing how much the customer should be charged.

It is worth emphasizing that this is not the only way in which a customer can contract for a system. For example, an increasingly popular method of contracting involves the developer

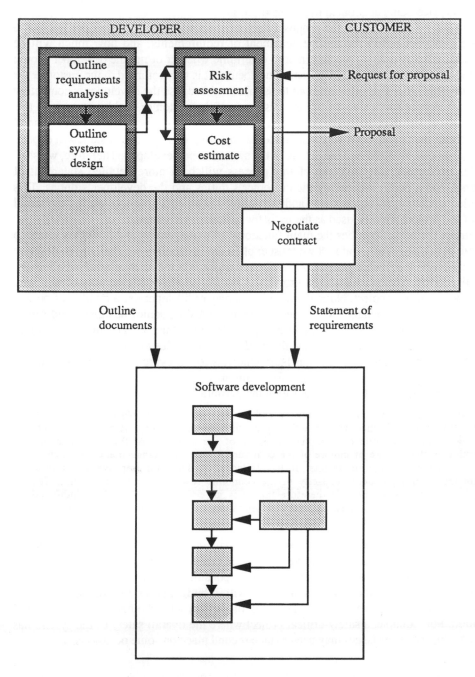

Figure 2.1 An extended software life-cycle.

producing an estimate for the total cost of a system, and then carrying out each stage for a fixed price with this price being negotiated for the next phase.

The information contained in the proposal document shows how the developer intends to achieve the goals set out in the outline statement of requirements, and how much will be charged for it, and it is used by the customer to determine whether or not the developer should be appointed to produce the required system. This document is then returned to the customer for consideration; this process is often referred to as 'bidding' because the developer is competing with other developers for business from the customer. If the customer decides to appoint this developer, then a period of contract negotiation takes place. It is not possible to make general statements about the negotiations which are undertaken during this process, since it will depend on the organizations involved and the details of the system to be developed. Therefore, we shall explore this no further. The outcome of this process will be a more detailed statement of requirements, and a contract detailing the customer's duties and the developer's duties. This more detailed statement of requirements and the outline documents produced during the initial planning of the project are then used as the basis for system development.

This part of the book describes the main functions[1] of management and how they relate to software project management, but first we must explain the vocabulary we shall use to describe the organization of a software project. A *senior manager* is a member of staff who has the responsibility for overseeing a number of projects. A *project manager* is a member of staff who has direct control of one project. Normally a senior manager will supervise a number of project managers, and a project manager will supervise senior analysts, senior designers and senior programmers who, in turn, will supervise analysts, designers and programmers. Different organizations are structured differently, and the matching of job titles to duties also differs from company to company, but we shall use this hierarchic view of software project organization, as illustrated in Fig. 2.2, since it is still the most common.

So what is management? Consider the following definition:

> Management must always, in every decision and action, put economic performance first. It can only justify its existence and its authority by the economic results it produces. There may be great non-economic results: the happiness of the members of the enterprise, the contribution to the welfare or culture of the community, etc. Yet management has failed if it fails to produce economic results. It has failed if it does not improve or at least maintain the wealth producing capacity of the economic resources entrusted to it.... The first definition of management is therefore that it is an economic organ of an industrial society. Every act, every decision, every deliberation of management has as its first dimension an economic dimension.   (Drucker, 1968)

This is probably the most naked definition of management that it is possible to make; it sums up the primary function of the manager, which is that of producing economic results. In a software context this means that the manager is responsible for delivering a system which meets functional and non-functional requirements within budget and on time. However, it is important to point out that there are some types of project where other factors enter into consideration. For example, a safety-critical project where the overall safety of the system has to be considered, economic issues may need to take second place on some occasions.

---

[1] The term 'function' is overused in software engineering, but it is used here because it is conventional to describe the activities which managers are involved with as functions.

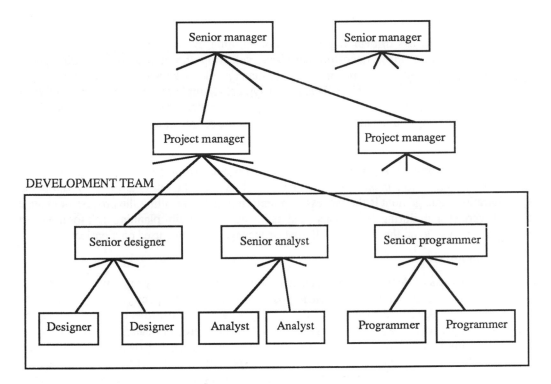

Figure 2.2 The hierarchic organization of a software project.

SAQ In the extract shown above, the terms *economic result, economic performance* and *economic dimension* are used. Is such an emphasis on economic concerns appropriate when considering management in a non-industrial context, for example when managing a charity?

SOLUTION Even in a non-profit-making environment such as charity work, economic results are important. Money is used to promote the activities of an enterprise, therefore the more efficiently that money is used, the more money there will be available to further that enterprise's primary objectives. For example, if the aim of a charity is to provide materials for drilling wells in areas of drought, then more money will be available to be spent on buying such materials if the charity is well managed.

2.2 MANAGEMENT FUNCTIONS

In order to manage a project, a manager will perform many different tasks. These tasks fall, broadly speaking, into the following categories: planning, organizing, staffing, monitoring, controlling, innovating and representing.

2.2.1 Planning

Planning is the process of deciding what to do, defining events which signal the end of a particular stage in a project, costing activities, selecting the means to meet objectives, subdividing large project activities into smaller manageable tasks and allocating appropriate staff with appropriate skills to carry them out. A typical example of this activity in a software project occurs during the planning of system testing. Here a manager divides the system testing effort into a series of individual testing tasks, specifies the source of data required for each test, specifies the expertise level of the staff who carry out each test and, finally, costs the effort for each test. Without planning and the consequent production of a plan there is no way to judge the progress of a project. A good example of the importance of planning involves a discipline known as *configuration management*, a topic which is described in detail later in the book. Configuration management is the process of monitoring and controlling the process of change to a software system during development and maintenance. A major planning task for a project manager is to decide on the level of configuration management to be used on a project.

2.2.2 Organizing

This is the process of deciding what kinds of staff are required to carry out a project and what the duties and responsibilities of each position are and of specifying clear lines of communication. A typical example of organizing in a software project occurs before the requirements analysis phase of the project begins, when the project manager establishes clear lines of communication between the customer's staff and his or her own staff. Organizing involves specifying communication not only within the software project but also between the developer's staff and the customer's staff. Project managers will need to establish which staff employed by the customer can be contacted in order to amplify the statement of requirements and the areas in the statement of requirements where they possess expertise. Project managers will also need to establish which members of their project staff will liaise with the customer, and the list of customer staff whom they are allowed to contact. In this way communicational complexity, both within a project team and between a project and the customer, is cut down to the minimum. It prevents events such as a junior programmer contacting the customer's senior director in order to resolve a minor problem!

2.2.3 Staffing

Organizing involves identifying the kinds of staff required by a project; staffing is concerned with selecting the right people to fill those positions. Staffing also involves promoting training and identifying and encouraging members of staff who have the potential to be promoted to more senior positions. Encouraging promising members of staff is a particularly important task since the continuing success of the company depends on there being senior personnel ready to take on responsibility as others leave or retire; this involves allocating more and more responsible or technically difficult tasks to them. An example of staffing occurs in a software project during its initial planning when available personnel are assigned to various roles such as chief designer or junior programmer.

2.2.4 Monitoring

Monitoring is the process of measuring progress on a project. During the planning process a manager will have set major objectives, and monitoring involves checking that these objectives are being met. An example of such an objective is to deliver the system specification to the customer by a particular time. In order to keep track of whether these objectives are being met the manager will need to monitor the activities of the project. Monitoring implies that the manager will have identified a set of measures and will be able to relate values of these measures to the major objectives of the project. By monitoring the progress of specifications, designs and tests a project manager can gain an idea of the progress of the project towards its delivery date. Monitoring may result in the need for action which falls into any of the other categories listed here. It is important to point out that monitoring not only involves staff and activities inside a software project but may also involve entities which do not lie within the direct control of the project manager. For example, an important task on large software projects involves the monitoring of progress made by subcontractors.

2.2.5 Controlling

The process of keeping a project on target so that it meets its objectives is called controlling. It involves activities such as reallocating resources when unforeseen circumstances occur. For example, the non-delivery of equipment may require the rescheduling of testing tasks, swapping those which require the equipment for those which do not. It also involves providing day-to-day directives and leadership for subordinates, telling them what to do and helping them do it. Planning a project results in directives which are of a long-term nature such as 'Design this system starting at week 10 and finishing at week 34'. On the other hand, controlling is normally a shorter term activity where day-to-day problems are solved and solutions found. Typical of such day-to-day problems on a software project are 'The test file for integration test 5761 is not ready yet, what alternative tests can I carry out while I'm waiting?' and 'My contact at the customer's head office has changed and the new guy doesn't seem to know much about the project; can you do something about this?'

2.2.6 Innovating

Innovating is the process of finding and applying new ideas, techniques and tools in order to improve the efficiency and creativity of the enterprise for which the manager works. Some examples of innovation in a software project are selecting a new design method and evaluating it on a small project, and buying a software tool which helps to ensure that project documentation is better organized.

2.2.7 Representing

The project manager must represent the software project in dealings with external agencies such as the customer and outside hardware suppliers. The manager must also represent specific projects in dealings with senior management. Examples of representing in a software project include meeting a customer to report on progress and meeting a technical director in order to ask for more resources for a project which has slipped.

The categorization introduced above is not intended to be a rigid one. The tasks performed by a manager are not independent of each other, and often interleave. These functions are also not peculiar to software projects since they are needed to manage any form of project.

SAQ For each of the above management functions, describe two tasks connected with the system design activity which fall into the relevant category.

SOLUTION Examples of planning include deciding that the delivery of the full system design specification marks the end of system design, estimating the designer time which is needed to design a subsystem and subsequently calculating the cost, deciding to employ simulation during design in order to check on timing, and splitting up the overall design task into subtasks which can be given to individual designers. Examples of organizing include deciding on the number of senior designers and designers required by the project, what their duties are, and how they should liaise with the analysts. Examples of staffing include finding the right senior designers and designers to work on the project, and training staff in the use of a particular design approach. Examples of monitoring include overseeing the production of function descriptions for program units, and checking that the system design document is produced on time. Examples of controlling include deciding what action to take if an important designer working on the job is taken ill, i.e. deciding on who replaces the missing designer, and deciding which part of the system should be designed next when technical information for one subsystem arrives late. Examples of innovation include introducing a new system design notation, and introducing a new piece of software for producing program unit descriptions. Examples of representing include meeting with senior management in order to discuss which senior designers are to be allocated to the project, and meeting with the customer to report on progress in producing the system design document.

SAQ The following is a list of activities carried out by a project manager. Identify which of the above functions is being exercised in each case.

(a)   Meeting the customer at progress meetings.

(b)   Selecting a different method of project organization from that normally used by the developer.

(c)   Costing a software project.

(d)   Hiring new programmers for a specific project.

(e)   Checking on project expenditure.

SOLUTION

(a)   Representing.

(b)   Innovating.

(c)   Planning.

(d)   Staffing.

(e)   Monitoring.

2.3 A WEEK IN THE LIFE OF A PROJECT MANAGER

The aim of this section is to give you a real flavour of what software project management involves in practice. Helen Sharp interviewed a senior manager, Tim Hadden, in order to ask him what a typical week in his life involves. His reply is given below.

According to our use of the terms, Tim acts as both project manager and senior manager in a very large British software company, since he has direct control of projects, but is also in charge of a number of projects. This situation is not uncommon in real software companies, but we have simplified the management roles in this context for the sake of clarity.

Tim's job is to ensure the smooth running of a project and to solve any problems as and when they arrive. In addition, keeping the customer and staff happy and informed, and attending meetings form a large part of his job. The purpose of the meetings is to inform or to be informed about the project's progress, and so they are largely concerned with the monitoring activity.

Helen: How does your week begin?

Tim: The week always starts off with coming in and catching up on the things that have gone on over the weekend.[2] This is particularly relevant to the work we have in the Middle East, because they work from Saturday to Thursday, with Friday as their day off. So there's usually a batch of faxes that have arrived over the weekend, telling me all the events. Then I will sit down and plan what I'm going to be doing through the week and catch up with the main projects that I have in the UK.[3]

Helen: Roughly how many projects do you have in the UK at the moment?

Tim: At the moment I've got five, one of which is a very large fixed-price project,[4] the others are for various clients, and vary from people working on-site for a client, to small implementations back here in Wavendon.[5]

Helen: So what would you do after you've worked out your plan?

Tim: I would then go and talk to the various project leaders who I have reporting to me and really catch up on progress. The prime concern is the fixed-price contract which is in its final stage of integration. So we always have a weekly review as to where we've got on that integration:[6] what the current problems are, how we're performing against plan, and what contingency or other action we're going to take to ensure that we stick to that plan in the coming week.

Helen: So, if there have been any problems on one of these projects, what would your role be in trying to sort out these problems?

Tim: I would start off by getting as much information on the problems from the point of view of my project leader.[7] I would then review any communication that I've had from the customer as to his perspective on the problem. I would look at where we

---

[2] An example of the monitoring function.
[3] An example of short-term planning.
[4] There was a history in the United Kingdom of some contracts, certainly those in the defence area, being paid for on the basis of the developer's costs plus a profit. However, the vast majority of projects are fixed cost.
[5] Wavendon is a village in Buckinghamshire where Tim's company has a large branch.
[6] The monitoring function.
[7] The project leader is the manager who is in direct control of a particular project.

are in terms of the next milestone[8] event that's required to happen, and look at first of all, given the nature of the problem, whether we have time, by working overtime, by rearranging things, to meet that deadline. If not, then I have to look for a minimum path of overrun and get the customer's agreement to do so. Now, I will take technical advice about solutions either from the project, or I'll call in consultants from outside. I have to then weigh the advice that I'm getting, and make the decision as to the path forward.

Helen: So you would probably say which way they should go to try to solve the problems?

Tim: Yes, indeed, that's always my responsibility, to make the decisions as to how we cope with the problems.

Helen: So what else would you be doing?

Tim: We're always looking for the next project, so we're working very closely with the client at the present time in putting a bid together for a system which is to be installed in the United States. Because American customers like everything down in absolute detail we have a stack of documentation 12 inches high which we have to provide.

Helen: That's a lot of documentation.

Tim: That's a great deal of documentation just for the bid. The documentation that goes with the project goes by the pantechnicon.[9]

Helen: How many people would be involved in producing this bid?

Tim: From our side we have three areas that are contributing. It's extended beyond the work that we've done for the initial project in the UK. So we're calling in assistance from two other groups in the company. I am coordinating that input, with the input that we're getting from our own people. But there's a balancing act here, between getting this bid together and minimizing the impact on the on-going project.[10] I'll undoubtedly have to go and visit the client.[11] If the M1 is kind the Dartford tunnel isn't, or vice versa.[12] It is a problem because I don't want to lose too much of the day. So it usually involves getting up at the crack of dawn to avoid the rush and then try and come back midday, or early afternoon, again to avoid delays in travelling. But of course these days you can never be too sure.

Helen: Would this involve visiting every client of the jobs that you have on?

Tim: Yes, indeed, the larger the project the more frequent the visits are. We have some people working on site in Barrow-in-Furness,[13] and I visit the client once every two

---

[8] A milestone is a significant event in the course of a project, such as the completion of the system design. Milestones are used to judge the project's progress.

[9] A pantechnicon is a term used in the United Kingdom for a very large lorry.

[10] What, in effect, Tim is talking about is a conflict between a function such as monitoring and the planning function.

[11] An example of the representing function.

[12] The M1 is a major arterial road into London and is a major traffic problem.

[13] A town in the north of England renowned for ship building.

or three months. We also have a client in the Middle East. I try to visit that client on a quarterly basis and he has trips over to the UK three or four times a year, so he'll come and visit us on those occasions.

Helen: Is this to try and sort out any problems from the client's point of view?

Tim: I'm looking at a number of issues. The current problem is that of replacing staff who have been out there for some time. So we have to select the most suitable people, the people who will survive in an overseas environment. We then have to pass the details of these people to the client. The client doesn't have the right under the contract to refuse people, but of course we are looking for on-going business with the client, so we will always try to come to an agreement that somebody is suitable, and if there are any areas of weakness, then we'll try and arrange training. The client's situation is that we have some systems which have been installed over the last four or five years. We currently are in the maintenance phase, and the client is looking to the future with those systems. As some of the hardware becomes obsolete he'll be looking to replace it. He's also looking to consolidate his information processing capability across his area in total. So it's a very interactive situation technically and we need to communicate regularly to ensure that we're up to date with the changing nature of what's going on out there.

Helen: So you would hope to continue the contract with the client?

Tim: Indeed, its been going on now for six years. The other reason for going and visiting is to see the staff, to talk to the staff, in the environment in which they work. That's particularly important for staff morale. The same of course is true of people working in Barrow-in-Furness. It's only 250 miles away, but from their perspective it's an awfully long way from the company. So it's important for the company to go to them.

Helen: Is that the only contact you have with the team?

Tim: We have contact by telephone. We encourage the people from overseas to come into the office if they are on holiday in the UK. For the people on British projects we often call them back to meetings. That's as much as anything to keep them informed about what's going on, how the company is progressing and so on. During the course of the week we do have to cope with a number of acts of God and other events. Through the course of a project we have a number of milestones getting progressively more and more compliant with the total requirements. Let me give you an example of one of these events. On our projects we have to take the source software, compile it, link it into an executable system and then transfer all that software from the machine onto magnetic tape. That includes all the source files, object files and the command files used to build the system. So that we know exactly what the software is, what its components are, and that is then formally released to the client. Its release is formally witnessed by our quality assurance organization and it goes out with a certificate of conformity that says 'this is compliant with the release stage that has been agreed'. So it's a major activity and it can take a long time. So we set it off on the computer, running on batch files.

	Unfortunately, last week, we had a thunderstorm which caused the power to go down in this area, and so we lost everything and had to start again.
Helen:	Oh dear.
Tim:	It happened after the resident computer operator had just left the site, so it was a matter of phoning around making contacts that we hadn't made for a while, and saying 'You remember me, can you do me a favour?' I now owe a number of people in the company a few drinks, but we did manage to get an engineer who was able to get the computer back and running for us.
Helen:	Does this mean that you are on call during the night?
Tim:	As a member of the management team, I do not really have a contractual day of nine to five thirty. I'm paid to fulfil a function, and that function can mean working late at night, working weekends and such. I'm not on call as such on any of the current projects, but there are people who have my current home telephone number, and if a problem arises, particularly with someone working on-site, then of course they'll call me and try to get a decision made, or try and get some action taken which they need urgently.
Helen:	So this problem with releasing some software took up a fair amount of your time?
Tim:	It took up a fair amount of time. Every time that we came to a problem, then that was referred to me and I had to contact the client and keep him fully aware of what the situation was.
Helen:	So he needed quite a lot of reassurance that everything was going all right.
Tim:	Absolutely. The problems were handled at our level, but we were both aware that if the problem became more difficult, and there was a danger of not being able to handle things, like not being able to get quality assurance or support for the computer over the weekend through the normal channels, then we would have to escalate it through our various organizations to a point where a senior director would make a decision.
Helen:	Do you report directly to a senior director?
Tim:	Officially I report through a divisional manager up the organization. However, along with all the project managers, if a problem arises, and needs attention at a given level, we will make the decision to contact whoever is necessary to get the action taken.
Helen:	Is that true of the people who report to you?
Tim:	It is true, certainly when I go on leave, then they will go to the divisional manager. Sometimes, if it's known that I'm taking leave for decorating, or such, that results in a phone call home, but the option is always there. If it's available, then the action should be taken directly through me, as indeed, if my divisional manager is available I will work through him.
Helen:	What else has happened in the week?

Tim: One of our employees is a football referee, and had been injured in a football match. He had been off for the previous week, and we got a phone call from the client on Tuesday, informing us that while he was very sympathetic the project that he was running was at a very critical stage, and he needed somebody available for the following Monday. I phoned the member of staff at home, he informed me that he was going to see the doctor on Thursday and he was fairly confident that he would be signed off fit for work, but he wasn't sure. So the thing we did in the meantime was to look around and find a member of staff who we could reallocate, if the case arose.[14] Fortunately, the doctor signed him off fit for work. Staff allocation is a major headache. Staff allocation assumes that people are going to finish the work that they are doing at a particular time, and for continuity we need to have other work for them to do. This is where the divisional manager and his senior managers have a role to play, because the various project managers will all be stating that their project should have the highest priority. The decision, therefore, cannot sensibly be made by the project managers. And so we have to have an independent arbiter, and this is why, whether its done officially, formally or otherwise, there is always a sense of a matrix organization between the staff and the requirements of the divisions and the individual projects.

Helen: You've already mentioned meeting with clients. Are there any other kinds of meetings that you have to attend in a typical week?

Tim: Yes, we have a quality organization in the company, and all of our projects are audited from time to time. There are various activities on each of these projects which are on-going, so at some time in a week, I will be interacting with the quality organization. Either at a liaison level, or as part of a quality audit.

Helen: Are these official meetings or formal meetings?

Tim: The quality audits are formal meetings. The quality control, or in other words the quality implicit in the product, is the responsibility of the projects within our company. The quality assurance organization is there to ensure, or assure, that there is quality implicit in the product. This starts off by us having to produce a quality plan initially, which lays down the procedures and standards that we will be adopting. The quality organization will agree that this is satisfactory. Then, during the course of a project, they will come along and actually inspect what we are doing, to ensure that we're using those standards and to ensure that we're applying them correctly.

Helen: So the plan will be set up at the beginning of the project, and then checked as you go through the project?

Tim: That's right. Our major projects are usually checked a minimum of once a year; if it's a very large project then each area of the projects will be checked on an annual basis. But at the end of the day, there will be a list of actions that have been noted where either we're not complying fully, or where the techniques that are being used

---

[14] Another example of the planning function in action.

could be modified to enhance the quality. That will end up in a report, and that report will be sent to me in a draft form and discussed with me by the auditor before it is passed up our organization. We will agree any actions and the time-scales for completing the actions.

Helen: Are there any other kinds of meetings?

Tim: Yes, we have divisional meetings on a monthly basis where we sit down and formally review the status of the projects: questions such as staff allocation, recruitment, training, and so on. And between that we have less formal ad hoc meetings to discuss the issues and they usually happen once or twice a week.

Helen: And what would your role be in such a meeting?

Tim: As an effective participant in stating where we are, the financial situation of each of the projects in turn, what our problems are, what our needs are, what our achievements have been and really taking a view forward. And then, putting cases forward as to why it's my particular project that needs priority, at that time, as opposed to somebody else's.

Helen: So that's a fairly high-level meeting?

Tim: Yes, that's between all the project and business area managers within the division.

Helen: So do you get involved in lower level meetings as well then?

Tim: Yes, indeed. I have regular weekly meetings with each of my project managers, separately. I also have formal monthly meetings on each of the projects where we review progress and deal with any problems. The monthly meetings, being formal, are minuted. The minutes are filed away and distributed to interested parties, including the divisional manager.

Helen: Is that just you and the project leader, or would there be other members of the project team involved?

Tim: It is me and the project leader, plus any other team members, either on call, or according to the particular situation at a given time. The project leader will decide to bring others along if he or she feels they have an input to make. I will call other people in if I feel that I need their input during the course of the meeting.

Helen: And what kind of problems might you expect to try and solve during these meetings?

Tim: Well, the main purpose of the meeting is to look at where we are in terms of progress of the project. Now that's both the technical progress and financial progress, so the points that we will be addressing are: whether we have achieved what we're required to achieve, whether we've done that within the price that we're supposed to, whether there is any opportunity to look for more money from the client if we're in a situation where we're overspending, because the problems are often not all of our own making, and sometimes they're caused by the client himself.[15] Really, it's just a case of monitoring where we are and deciding what actions, if any, are necessary.[16]

Helen: Well, you've given me an idea of what activities you might do in a week where you're switching from one project to another, dealing with crises when they arise. If you were describing to someone outside your business, how would you sum it up do you think?

Tim: I think I'd sum it up by saying that my job is actually to do nothing other than to ensure that what other people are doing is in line with what is required, and then to deal with problems as they arise; and above all, to make decisions which help us to get projects completed on time, and within budget.

Helen: And to keep the client happy?

Tim: And to keep the client happy, because if you don't keep the client happy he's not going to come back to us.

An activity which Tim referred to, but which we did not explicitly consider in the last subsection is that of forward planning, i.e. looking for future business for the company, bidding for that business and ensuring that appropriate resources are available to fulfil that bid. He mentioned this concern on a number of occasions, including the fact that he is involved in coordinating a bid for a project with an existing customer. Producing a successful bid, also called a project proposal, means that a lot of effort must go into developing an initial plan for the project, which can be used to estimate the project's cost, and hence its potential profit margin. It is very important that the proposal is accurate and reflects what the developer can actually accomplish, but planning for a software project is a difficult task.

Monitoring and planning for a project are difficult to carry out, and the consequence of failure may be financially disastrous for the developer. In order to illustrate this, some of the problems which might arise during initial planning and monitoring are discussed in the following subsections.

It is worth pointing out at this stage that the role of a project manager can vary widely. For example, in some organizations it is purely a coordinating and monitoring role.

2.4 THE INITIAL PLANNING OF A SOFTWARE PROJECT

In the interview, Tim mentioned that he was involved in putting together a proposal for a new project. Producing a proposal of this kind involves a period of initial planning which usually begins when a developer receives a request for a proposal from a potential customer. This will normally contain an outline statement of requirements for a software system together with contract details and, if the project is to be tendered, a document which describes how to organize and structure the tender.

At this early stage the project manager will be concerned with the high-level details of the system since these will be used to prepare the bid. The important points considered will be the

---

[15] For example, through the client making a requirements change in mid-project.
[16] The control function.

estimated project cost, the resources required and the project's compatibility with the company's overall business plan.

In order to cost the project, the manager must first identify what resources will be needed. The human resources which the project would employ are of particular interest, since developing a software system can occupy a large number of software staff with diverse skills for extended periods of time. An outline system specification and an outline system design document must be developed.[17] This is all that is necessary at this stage of the project, since if a company carried out a full requirements analysis during the bidding for a software contract they would be risking a large amount of resources on only the possibility of being awarded a project. From the design, the tasks required during the project must be identified and approximate costs must be assigned to each. These tasks must be scheduled in sequence and the project manager must ensure that enough resources are available for the tasks to be carried out adequately. For example, enough computer resource must be available for system testing during the period that this activity is scheduled.

How the cost is estimated will be explored in more detail in Chapter 7. If the project is one which is to be tendered then the cost figure will be used to produce a tender. If the software is to be developed under a fixed-price contract, then an outline cost figure would enable senior management to decide whether there was sufficient profit in the project to proceed. If the developer and the customer are part of the same organization, then the cost of the project will be evaluated against the company's business plan and the decision to proceed made on the basis of that evaluation.

Medium-to-large software projects now cost millions of pounds and errors in this process could lead to hundreds of thousands of pounds being lost. In other engineering disciplines, cost estimates are relatively easy to obtain because standard tables and a wealth of historical data to support the estimation process exist.

Unfortunately, the software project manager is not in this position. There are three reasons for this. Firstly, many companies do not keep historical data. Secondly, those who have built up a database of historical information which they know to be useful in cost estimation are unlikely to admit to its existence, let alone publish it. Thirdly, it is open to debate whether such historical data is useful when costing a software project anyway. Civil engineering products such as bridges have many things in common and their specifications are relatively simple: they have to carry certain traffic loads over an obstacle subject to certain limits of wind speed. Software developers are not in this happy position, however, since software has only been in existence a relatively short time, and its complexity has increased markedly over that time. Research is currently being carried out into historical methods of project costing, however this research is still in its early stages and, consequently, the software project manager has few tools for costing a project as compared with managers in other disciplines.

A software developer's activities will normally be based on a business plan. This contains the projected financial level of business over future years together with estimates of the staff requirements which are needed to achieve that level of business. Every project that is considered by a developer has to be evaluated against this business plan. In evaluating a future project the developer has to ask a number of questions which should be answered during this initial planning phase. Two important questions to be answered are: 'Have we the staff resources to

---

[17] This is done in order to identify project tasks.

carry out the project?' and 'Does the profit level from the project match the profit level required in our business plan?'

SAQ Describe two circumstances where the business plan and the staffing levels should not be rigidly adhered to when deciding whether to take on a new project.

SOLUTION The business plan and staffing levels should not be rigidly adhered to when it comes to speculative projects which respond to short-term factors. For example, a developer may feel that there are certain types of software project that currently offer little profit but which, in the future, will offer very large returns. If so, the developer may consider taking on small speculative projects. These projects may ensure that, in the future, the developer has expertise in a growth area that puts the company ahead of any potential competitors.

A second example is where a developer may take on a maintenance contract for an existing software system at a low rate of return knowing that he or she would be in a good position to win the contract for the eventual replacement of the system.

When bidding for a future project, a manager must perform enough planning to make an accurate estimation of the project resources required. Some common mistakes that are made during the initial planning stage are as follows:

- Failing to make adequate provision for perturbations in manpower. Perturbations in manpower are fairly common on software projects; a typical example is when a senior designer leaves a project half-way through. When planning a project, therefore, the project manager should ensure that any critical roles such as the senior designer position can be taken over by other staff in the event of that person moving. This could be done by ensuring either that reserve manpower is available during critical periods of development, or that a more junior member of the development team works in tandem with the critical developer. Using the former approach would mean notifying senior management who might then earmark another member of staff working on a less important project which is running at the same time.

- Underestimating support resources. We mentioned one example of such an error previously, i.e. that of underestimating the computer resource required for system testing. Many project managers have made the mistake of assuming that if they have been given access to a computer during system testing, then this phase will be adequately carried out. Often it is forgotten that if the computer is being used for running existing applications then the true amount of resource available for system testing may be quite limited.[18] The worst case occurs when system testing is scheduled during a period of peak processing for existing applications. This is a particularly common mistake when dealing with large mainframe systems such as a travel agent's holiday booking system. For instance, if the system testing for such a system is scheduled to occur during the first three months of the year, the computer power available is likely to be quite limited since this is a very busy time for holiday companies and so response time is likely to be reduced.

---

[18] This, of course, is really only applicable to mainframe and minicomputer projects.

- Overreliance on the successful completion of activities not under the developer's control. Another error made during planning is being too confident in assuming that events outside the developer's control will be carried out adequately and correctly. For example, hardware developed by an outside contractor may be late, and software produced by an outside company may be imperfect when first delivered. In order to forestall difficulties with outside bodies, a project manager has to ensure two things. Firstly, that if there is reliance on an outside activity, and that activity is completed late, then the project can proceed with little effect by internally rescheduling other activities in the project. Secondly, that compensation for lateness in an outside activity is obtained which at least matches the inevitable loss of resource suffered by the developer, i.e. the outside contractor suffers appropriate penalties if work is produced late. The subject of subcontract management will be returned to later in this book.

The activities involved in planning a software project will be revisited in Chapters 5 and 6.

SAQ Why are low-level details, such as who is to carry out detailed design and in what order program units are to be implemented, not considered at the outline planning stage?

SOLUTION For the very good reason that the software has not been defined in sufficient detail for this to happen. For example, during the initial stages of a software project system design will not have occurred and individual program units will not have been identified and, consequently, could not be assigned to staff.

SAQ Why is a software project manager at a disadvantage when it comes to the initial planning of a project compared to project managers in other engineering disciplines?

SOLUTION Other engineering disciplines have standard tables and a wealth of historical data on which cost estimates can be based. Unfortunately, the discipline of software engineering has neither tables, nor a collection of relevant historical data.

2.5 MONITORING THE PROGRESS OF A PROJECT

Tim spent much of his time on activities concerned with monitoring project progress. It is important for the project manager to be able to gain very quickly an idea of how far a project has progressed. The reasons for this are primarily economic:

- At the beginning of a project the manager will have planned which activities occur at which times during the length of the project. However, these activities rarely occur at those times; often they will be later than their scheduled times, sometimes they are earlier. If an activity is running late, then the project manager will want to know this as soon as possible so that the overall effect that it will have can be gauged. A good reason for this is that the developer will usually have contracted for a particular delivery date for the software. Lateness in delivering software means, at best, embarrassment and loss of reputation, and, at worst, stringent financial penalties being applied by the customer.

- Accurately knowing the progress of a project is important to the developer's senior management because of the impact it may have on other projects. Normally, software projects are scheduled in a company so that little slack resource occurs. This means that as staff leave a project they are normally assigned to other projects. Any lateness in a project will therefore usually have a knock-on effect for other projects.

- The customer will want regular progress reports. It is a very unusual customer who just wishes to be informed when a software product becomes available. Many customers rely on an accurate prediction of a delivery date; this date can be crucial to them. For example, knowing a delivery date will allow them to schedule training, and plan the release of key staff to learn about a new system.

For very small projects, progress can be judged by asking each member of staff how far they have reached in their current task. Unfortunately, most projects are too large and project teams are spread over too large distances for progress to be estimated using this technique. In fact, even for small projects this technique is dubious because staff are always optimistic about their progress and have a natural desire to please management. Consequently, a more objective measure has to be devised.

The measure usually used is the *milestone*. You will have noticed it mentioned during the interview with Tim Hadden. A milestone is a significant event which occurs during a software project and should normally be based on the production of some concrete entity which can be used to track progress during the project. Usually, a milestone occurs when a highly visible part of the system, such as the system specification, is planned to emerge.

Milestones can be used by both the developer and the customer to examine project progress. However, the customer is going to be interested in major events, while the developer is interested in both major events and relatively minor ones. Therefore, there are two main types of milestones, *internal milestones* and *external milestones*. Both types are used to monitor progress, but the former are used mainly by the project manager while the latter are used mainly by the customer and the developer's senior management. Normally, there will be many more internal milestones than external milestones. Internal milestones will not only include the external milestones but also significant events which happen between external milestones; these are used to chart progress towards the next external milestone. Some examples of internal milestones are:

- the integration of a subsystem;
- the design of a subsystem;
- the preparation of the test data for system testing.

A list of some external milestones in a project is given below. Remember that each milestone corresponds to a significant event that can be measured:

- completion of a draft of the system specification;
- acceptance of the system specification by the customer;
- successful completion of system testing;
- the system becoming operational.

As well as the main types of milestones, there will also be *informal milestones*, which are often personal to the individual programmer or designer. Every member of a project team, whether a senior manager or a senior programmer should have a set of milestones to judge progress. The senior managers in a project will use external and internal milestones. However, other team members such as senior programmers will have more detailed informal milestones to judge the progress of the staff they control. For example, assume that a senior programmer has the job of managing the programmers responsible for producing a series of packages for a subsystem. The senior programmer will use informal milestones such as the production of the detailed design of a program unit and the implementation of the program unit to judge the staff's progress.

One major task that the project manager has to carry out is to define a project's milestones; another is to use reports on their completion to measure the progress of a project.

SAQ Which of the following events are poor external milestones and which are good external milestones? For those which you consider to be poor external milestones, suggest what other kind of milestone they are suitable for.

(a)   The completion of the detailed design of a particular package.

(b)   Fifty per cent of the system has been implemented.

(c)   The completion of the system design document.

(d)   The production of the system tests.

(e)   The production of the design for a subsystem.

(f)   The user manual has been signed off by the customer's approved representative.

SOLUTION

(a)   This is a poor external milestone since it is too detailed for the customer to consider. It is probably a good informal milestone.

(b)   This is a poor milestone of any type. Although it seems to be measurable it is not quite certain what is being measured. Has 50 per cent of the functionality been implemented? Have 50 per cent of the program units been implemented or has 50 per cent of the estimated code been produced? There is no indication whether the 50 per cent produced was simple code or complicated code.

(c)   This is a good external milestone as it corresponds to the production of an actual document which plays a major part in a software project.

(d)   This is a poor external milestone, since the customer is unlikely to be interested in this event; the start of system testing itself is more likely to be an appropriate external milestone. The production of the system tests is a very good internal milestone, however.

(e)   This event is not significant enough for it to be classified as a good external milestone, although it is a good internal one.

(f)   This is a good external milestone as it corresponds to a significant event in a
        project which can be measured.

2.6   OTHER LIFE-CYCLES

Throughout this chapter we have assumed that the project that is to be managed is organized
according to the model described in Chapter 1, that is, as a series of non-overlapping phases
where the development effort is primarily driven by considering the functions of the system.
There are other types of software development, however, and the concluding sections of the
book describe how the management of these forms of project differs from the process presented
in the previous sections of this unit.

It should be remembered that the same functions described earlier in this chapter are still
exercised by the project manager.

2.6.1   Object-oriented   development

Object-oriented software development is a recent technique which has gained prominence
through the rise of programming languages known as object-oriented programming languages.
Such languages allow the programmer to describe an object, say an invoice, together with any
associated operations on that object, for example, the creation of an invoice, the amendment of
a file in the invoice, etc. The object would be implemented using the data structuring facilities
of the language while the operations would be implemented using some subroutine facility.
One of the advantages of object-oriented development is that object descriptions together with
their associated operations can be held in a library and re-used time and time again in different
operations. For example, a queue object can be re-used as a plane queue in an air traffic
application, a queue of files in an operating system application or a queue of messages in a
communications system.

An example of how a project might be structured to cope with re-use is shown in Fig. 2.3.
The use of object-oriented techniques in system development affects the management of the
project in a number of ways:

1.   The system specification will stress the objects and operations of the system, while the
     functions, which play a major part in the type of project described in Chapter 1, are
     relegated to being second-class citizens. This change in stress affects many of the
     activities in the project, for example, the software requirements review team will
     concentrate on questions regarding whether the operations and objects correctly model
     the application.
2.   The functional part of the system specification will often be delayed until a later part of
     the project after the objects and operations have been derived.
3.   In a company which promotes the use of object libraries a key activity will be the
     determination of which objects are to be re-used in a project.
4.   In a company which encourages projects to use object libraries actively a key task
     would be the determination of whether any object descriptions generated by a project
     should be deposited in the library.

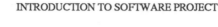

Figure 2.3 A simple object-oriented life-cycle.

While the life-cycle for this form of development is a little different from the rather simple one presented in Chapter 1 the project manager still has to carry out the monitoring, controlling and planning functions. For example:

- During the planning of the project the manager will have to specify standards and procedures which direct staff to ensure that the software withdrawn from the library is at least as well tested as the system into which the software is to be inserted.
- A project manager may be faced with a risk such as a key designer leaving. If this was a serious occurrence, for example, the only other designer available might be relatively inexperienced, then the project manager, in consultation with the customer may decide to re-use software which is not quite suitable rather than design from anew. This might entail some negotiation with the customer in dropping or modifying some functional requirements.
- During the final stages of the project the project manager may have to ensure that if the project is to donate software to the object library then it is at least as well tested and documented as the software that is already in the library. This may mean specifying extra testing standards during the planning stage.

2.6.2 Prototyping and evolutionary development

One of the common *cris de coeur* heard from software developers is: 'if only you had shown me the system at the beginning of the project'. This appeal arises late in the project—normally during system or acceptance testing—when the customer discovers that the system that has been built does not satisfy user requirements. Prototyping is an attempt to deliver such an early system. Three forms of prototyping have been identified: throw-away prototyping, incremental prototyping and evolutionary prototyping.

Throw-away prototyping involves the developer in constructing an early version of a system, and checking it with the user. When the user indicates that the prototype matches requirements, conventional software development starts, based on a requirements specification that has been constructed from a study of the prototype. The term *throw-away prototyping* arises from the fact that once a prototype has been agreed with the customer it is not used in the subsequent development that follows the prototyping process.

Incremental prototyping is really a euphemism for staged delivery. What this entails is the developer partitioning a software system to be delivered into sets of non-overlapping functions, with each delivered version of the system implementing a new subset of the functions. For example, a chemical plant control system would normally have four non-overlapping sets of functions: monitoring functions, control functions, user interface functions, and optimization and management information functions. The latter are used by chemical engineers who need to know about the detailed functioning of the system in the past, in order to optimize the operation of the plant in the future.

Incremental development is always a good idea. It leads to the establishment of small teams with little of the communicational overhead that bedevils large projects and soaks up valuable development effort—some large projects have had so much communicational overhead that adding staff to the project when the delivery date was becoming compromised has actually made the project later. As well as being a good idea in project management terms, it can also be used as a prototyping strategy. For example, a developer could decide on a delivery plan whereby those functions that were fuzzy or ill-expressed were delivered in the earliest versions of the system.

Evolutionary prototyping is in complete antithesis to the previous two approaches. In this form of rapid development a prototype is first constructed, agreed with the user, and then forms the basis for subsequent development. For example, a form of evolutionary development used in commercial data processing involves the developer producing a slow prototype and then devoting much of the rest of the project to the process of improving its running time.

Evolutionary prototyping is the most promising of the three approaches described here. It is an attempt to cater for change on the software project. Changes in requirements afflict software projects throughout their life and also during the maintenance of the subsequent system that is produced. Evolutionary prototyping provides a framework, and a number of mechanisms, whereby change can be easily accommodated almost right up to delivery.

Object-oriented programming languages lend themselves well to evolutionary prototyping: the development of an initial prototype, followed by a series of improvements applied to the prototype in order to make it meet user requirements.

In describing how to use evolutionary prototyping we shall assume that planning for a project that uses this technique has taken place. Given that this has happened, the next stage is to carry out a form of rapid analysis. This involves examining the statement of requirements of the system, and interviewing potential and actual users. The aims of the initial analysis are to gain a high-level view of the functions of a system, and also to identify any objects and operations required. Initial analysis is an important task to carry out, since it provides a base for the prototyping effort and ensures that the initial prototype will not be too off beam.

The product of the initial analysis will be a high-level system specification, usually no more than two or three levels—often just one level—and a list of the objects and operations that are needed. It is important to point out that initial analysis should not take too long—once it starts taking longer than a fortnight you should get worried. Remember if you do start spending a large amount of time on analysis, then there is the distinct possibility that large amounts of the specification you produce will be rendered obsolete by the prototyping process.

Once you think that you have captured the essence of the initial analysis, the next stage is to design and implement the first prototype. This consists of a number of activities:

- The existing database of objects and operations is scanned in order to discover any that match the objects discovered in the analysis. If the developer has previously carried out even a few projects using object-oriented technology, then this library will usually consist of general objects such as stacks, queues, sets, sequences and functions.

- The objects are brought in and stored in a project file, any obvious differences are catered for by modifying objects using the facilities of the object-oriented language.

- The system is designed in terms of a program design language, with the designer using the top-level system specification to drive the design process. The final level of the design will involve basic facilities such as input/output or calls on object operations.

- The design is then translated into program code and combined with the objects and operations identified in the first step.

- The final step is to create a test database of data which the first prototype, constructed in the previous step, can use.

The first prototype has now been constructed. The next step is prototype iteration. Here the prototype is demonstrated and changed until the user/customer is happy with what has been shown.

During this process the developer should ensure that the following criteria are met:

- The demonstration period is short. Normally one hour is advised. An hour is long enough for anyone to stare at a VDU. A demonstration lasting an hour will usually give rise to a large number of changes which often seriously affect the functionality and require implementation before further prototype evaluation can take place.

- Only one component, usually corresponding to a data flow bubble at the top level of a requirements specification, is examined at at time. For example, a natural candidate for an evaluation session for a purchasing system would be that part of the system which dealt with the back-orders queues.

- A script is produced which details all the functions that are to be invoked together with the order in which they are invoked. This will include descriptions of the function execution, the data entry procedures, any report writing procedures, and any error messages or error reports that are generated.

- The user should be allowed to operate the prototype. This encourages the user to think possessively of the prototype and leads to a much better rapport between the developer and the customer.

After a demonstration, the developer should issue a report form which details the important events and concerns that the demonstration gave rise to. This report should detail the following: what new functions were exercised in the demonstration session (usually this would be specified in terms of data flow bubble numbers); what functions were exercised during the demonstration which were left over from a previous demonstration, e.g. a previous demonstration may have given rise to some change requests and the demonstration being documented may have shown these amended functions in action; the development staff who were involved in the demonstration; the customer staff involved; and any suggested modifications that arose from the customer's unhappiness with a particular demonstration of functionality.

Prototype iteration—the process of modification, demonstration and elicitation of change requests from the customer—continues until the customer is happy with the system that has been shown. The time that this iterative cycle takes really depends on a number of factors: the experience of the developer with prototyping; the experience of the customer with prototyping; the tools that are used (some are quicker to apply modifications than others); and the quantity of requirements that are to be prototyped—a system where only a small number of functions are fuzzy will obviously take a shorter time to prototype than a system that requires full prototyping.

There are two important points to make about the modification, demonstration and elicitation of the change request process: first, the specification should be kept in step with the prototype. If this does not occur, then the developer will have major problems when further change requests are demanded by the customer—it will not be known what functions affect each other or what parts of the system correspond to the requests. The need for the requirements specification to be kept in step with the prototype virtually means that some form of CASE technology should be used in maintaining the requirements specification.

The second point is that it is optional whether the design that was produced during the derivation of the initial prototype should be kept in step with the prototype. This is less critical than keeping the requirements specification in step. Normally most companies who carry out evolutionary prototyping re-engineer the design from the final code of the prototype, merely by examining the code and discerning the overall structure.

After the customer has finally signed off the prototype, and if the design has not been kept in step with the prototype, the design is derived. The prototype is now at the stage where the developer has virtually carried out all the system testing of functionality that is required. The user has signed off the prototype and said that the functions that were demonstrated were those that were required. However, at this stage the developer may have delivered a prototype which, although functionally complete, has performance problems. The next stage in the development process is to tune the prototype.

Tuning involves the developer in examining the implemented objects and applying local optimizations. For example, the developer may have used a singly linked sequence for holding a queue and the application required the customer to traverse this queue backwards and forwards, hence requiring a doubly linked list. In this case the list would be augmented with a backward link as well as a forward link. Another example of a local optimization might occur in a table which was searched linearly. The developer might find out that only a few items were normally searched for. An increase in response time can easily be achieved if, when an item is found after a search, it is placed at the beginning of the table.

These are just a few of the large number of optimizations that can be carried out. What is important about the optimization process is that it should be carried out incrementally with the final set of stored data that the application will manipulate. By carrying out the optimization process incrementally—either an operation at a time, or a group of operations associated with an object at a time—the developer can ensure that if a programming error occurred during the optimization process, the location of the error can be discovered very easily.

When the optimization is complete, system testing starts. Now, as has already been stated, the prototype evaluation cycle involves the user signing off the functionality of the system. There is thus no need to test the functionality of the system during system testing: all that is required is to test for non-functional requirements such as response time and memory usage. The system testing will involve using real data for the application, both the data that is normally expected, and also data that occurs when the system is operating at peak load. When the system tests have been developed, the system can then be handed over to the user.

It is worth stating that, just as with conventional software projects, it is useful for evolutionary prototyping projects to have a number of reviews scheduled. Two useful reviews are, firstly, the rapid analysis review, to which a customer representative is invited. The aim of this review is to check that the products of the rapid analysis phase match, in concept, the system that is to be developed. Secondly, a review, or really a set of reviews, is the final prototype review, which occurs prior to the signing off of the final prototype. The main aim of this review is to ensure that all the functional requirements of the system have been demonstrated, and all the problems and changes notified by the customer have been taken into account by the developer.

This form of development is one of the most difficult to manage. The project manager of such a project has his or her work cut out to ensure that this form of dynamic development does not go out of control. For example:

- The project manager should select quality standards which ensure that he or she gets regular reports on the amount of prototype modification that goes on during the demonstration of the prototype to the user. One of the problems that occurs during this task is that the customer demands more and more functionality to the point where the final system would become infeasible because of poor response time or memory requirements. By receiving regular reports from prototype demonstrations the manager is able to step in and remind the participants of the effect of their changes.

- Many projects have what is known as a configuration management system: a series of procedures and standards which control the change to a system. On many projects the configuration management system is quite strict: changes have to be evaluated, validated and documentation issued. On an evolutionary prototyping project where the changes are so frequent the project manager will have to specify a much looser configuration management system for the early stages, or even dispense with it.

- The costing of such projects is very difficult. The project manager has to cost a project effectively where the requirements may be very fuzzy, and where he or she has little idea about the outline design of the system. In such a case the project manager may decide on a staged costing of a project with, say, a cost figure being produced for a prototype which is produced in versions; with each version including more and more functionality.

2.6.3 Parallel development

Parallel development involves splitting the system into subsystems and allowing each subsystem to be developed in parallel, each forming its own miniproject. Such miniprojects could follow the model described in Chapter 1, thus employing the techniques described in this chapter. For example, a chemical plant system may contain functions for monitoring chemical reactors, controlling reactors, maintaining a database of reactor readings and managing the interface between the system and the plant operators. Such a system could be divided into four subsystems, each of which is implemented in a separate miniproject which is executed in parallel with the other miniprojects. The major implication of this form of development for project management is that change control and communication between the miniprojects must be carefully controlled. For example, the staff responsible for configuration management must ensure that a change to any stored data is communicated to all the miniprojects.

Projects developing concurrent systems are ideal for this kind of development, since the system is divided into separate sections which communicate via well-defined channels, and can therefore be developed separately. The type of communication required between the processes must, however, be specified very tightly. This obviously has the following implications for the project manager carrying out monitoring, control and planning functions:

- In planning a project which involves parallel development the project manager has to ensure that there is regular communication between teams. This may mean the scheduling in of regular weekly progress meetings.

- Many commercial data processing projects have a central data design with each team implementing functionality. A common occurrence on such projects is for one team to demand a change in data architecture in order to support a function efficiently which impinges on another function implemented by some other team—usually by increasing its response time. The project manager will be actively involved with this form of change: in strengthening the configuration management system, in representing the project with the customer during the tricky negotiation process involving response times and in attempting to mediate between reasonable and unreasonable requests.

- The project manager must monitor such projects very carefully since a delay in a particular task carried out by one team may mean the whole of another team being idle for a period. When parallel working is adopted with a consequent shortening of project duration the impact of delay tends to be magnified.

2.6.4 Formal methods

The use of mathematics in the development of software is central to the idea of engineered software. Quality assurance will be much easier if formal methods are used since a mathematical representation of the system is constructed early on in the development process. The main implication for quality assurance is that mathematics provides a clear, unambiguous statement of what the system is intended to do which can be verified mathematically. Verifying documents should therefore be relatively straightforward, although this certainly does not imply that it will be easy.

Since a single formal notation is used during development, up until implementation, it is difficult to identify distinct phases and documents which correspond to the system specification, system design document and detailed design document as described in Chapter 1. This means that a strict phase-oriented approach is not appropriate. A more evolutionary approach can be used in which the system is developed in small chunks, each of which is isolated from the others. As with evolutionary development, as discussed above, this has implications for the project manager in the choice of project milestones, since the end of a phase is often seen as a major milestone in other types of project.

Since the technique of proof is used to verify project documents throughout development, the likelihood of errors going undetected until late in the project is slight. This is obviously a good thing, but the extra effort required to perform the proofs must be considered, and the project manager should assess the pros and cons of using formal methods when planning the project. Chapter 16 describes a particular project that involves this form of development.

2.7 SUMMARY

Managing a software project requires that many tasks be performed. These can be classified into seven categories: planning, organizing, staffing, monitoring, controlling, innovating and representing. Planning involves producing the overall plan for the project, i.e. identifying what to do, defining events which signal the end of a particular stage in a project, costing activities, selecting the means to meet objectives, subdividing large project activities into smaller manageable tasks and allocating appropriate staff with appropriate skills to carry them out. Organizing involves arranging the project team to enable the project to run successfully, i.e. deciding what kinds of staff are required, and the responsibilities for each position, and specifying clear lines of communication. Staffing is the process of finding the right staff to fill the roles needed by the project. Monitoring is the process of measuring the project's progress. Controlling is concerned with directing the project when problems or other unforeseen events occur, so as to ensure that the project meets its objectives. Innovating is the introduction of new techniques, notations or software tools for use on the project. Representing is the activity concerned with meeting outside bodies such as the customer and subcontractors.

The initial planning of a software project is important since a mistake here could be financially disastrous for the developer. However, it is quite difficult when compared to projects in other engineering disciplines, since software has only existed for a relatively short time, and there is little historical data available to help in the estimation process. Also, the complexity of software has increased dramatically over a relatively short period of time.

Monitoring the project's progress is very important because software is an intractable entity. Progress is measured, therefore, by examining a series of events called milestones, which are significant events in the project and are normally based on the production of some concrete entity such as a document. There are two main types of milestone, external milestones and internal milestones. External milestones are used mainly by the developer's senior management and the customer to monitor progress, while internal milestones are used mainly by the project manager.

2.8 FURTHER READING

One of the best advanced books that has been written on software project management is Humphrey (1989). This is an excellent book which describes what is necessary to carry out all the functions described in this chapter. An important point made by Humphrey in the book is that before you attempt to set up management and quality assurance standards properly you will need to identify the processes that make up your software projects.

BIBLIOGRAPHY

Humphrey, W. A. (1989) *Managing the Software Process*, Addison-Wesley, Reading MA.

Drucker, P.F. (1968) *The Practice of Management*, Pan Books, London.

3

THE INFORMATION NEEDS OF PROJECT MANAGEMENT

AIMS

- To describe the information needs of the software project manager.
- To illustrate the information needs of the software project manager by examining one software task: software testing.

3.1 INTRODUCTION

Information is vital for the project manager to manage effectively. Both information about current projects, and information about previous projects are important. The importance of the latter for use during project estimation has already been stressed. The importance of the former is clear from the interview with Tim Hadden, introduced in the previous chapter. In this interview, when asked about solving problems which arise during a project, Tim Hadden said that the first thing he would do would be to get information from the project team and from the customer regarding the problem. He would look at what stage the project had reached regarding the next significant milestone, and decide whether, given the current problem, there was enough time to meet that deadline, and if not, he would look for the path which would give the minimum overrun. In order to achieve this, Tim must have available to him information about the schedule for the project, and the planned resource usage. He must also have some idea of the impact of the necessary changes to the schedule.

A large part of the project manager's job is concerned with making decisions like this. In order to make sound decisions, and therefore to manage successfully, the following pertinent information must be readily available:

- In order to carry out planning, some historical data is needed which enables the resource levels and costs for a software project to be predicted. For example, if a project manager is asked to cost a software project which, in parts, is similar to a project that has already been completed, then cost and resource figures for that project could be used to cost the proposed project. Such information would have to be gleaned from documentation on that earlier project. As mentioned above, such historical data is difficult to find; often a manager will be using his or her own personal experience.
- In order to monitor the progress of a project, data must be available which reflects that progress, for example, data on problems, the results of reviews, and progress reports on activities such as testing.

- In order to control a project, ideally historical data is needed which enables the project manager to predict the effect of any changes in that project. For example, if it is necessary to reschedule a project activity, then the impact which this will have on the rest of the project must be clear.
- Data is also required when the project manager is innovating. When an innovation occurs, senior management is normally keen that it occurs in a small part of a company and that it is evaluated. This implies that data is required which not only reflects the impact of the innovation on a project, but also supplies information about equivalent activities with which the innovation can be compared. For example, if a manager wants to introduce a new software design tool into a company, it would be necessary to gather data on the amount of time spent designing on the project that used the tool, and on an equivalent project which did not use the tool.

SAQ Would the sizes of program units from a previous, similar project, and the time taken to unit test those units be useful data for the project manager? Explain your answer.

SOLUTION Yes, the sizes of program units and the time taken to unit test them would be useful for the project manager, since they could be used to predict the amount of resources required to unit test other program units of similar complexity.

The need for information and data about project activities is intimately bound up with prediction. The tasks of planning, monitoring, controlling and innovating all involve the manager in predicting future events. Examples of the type of prediction which need to be performed efficiently on a software project are as follows:

- How many system designers will be needed to design the system represented by this system specification?
- Given this frequency and occurrence of errors during implementation how many errors can the software system be expected to contain when it is released to the customer?
- Given this predicted error rate during maintenance how many programmers should be assigned to this activity?
- How much time will be taken by the programmer who implements this detailed design?
- Given this statement of requirements what will be the resource utilization of the project over its first 18 months?

SAQ How is prediction connected with the function of innovation?

SOLUTION When a manager innovates he or she must have some degree of confidence that the innovation will have a positive economic benefit for the enterprise. In order to have that degree of confidence the manager must be able to appraise the impact of that innovation on the enterprise and predict that it will have a positive benefit.

The mechanism used to satisfy the information needs of the project manager is documentation. During the course of a project, many documents are generated which contain vital information for later stages of the project, and for planning future projects. Documentation production is therefore an important activity in the software project. It is important to point out that the remainder of this chapter describes an example of the information needs of a project manager: while the example is that of system testing this chapter is not about testing *per se*.

3.2 SYSTEM TESTING

This section considers the production of test procedures as a means of illustrating the importance of documentation to the project manager. In this instance, the document being generated is known as the *test plan*, and it contains all the information necessary for planning and carrying out the system and acceptance tests. Both system and acceptance testing are vital to the success of a software project. If a software product fails a set of system or acceptance tests then the project's management should be questioned seriously. Information about the activities involved in testing is required by the project manager in order to estimate accurately the resources needed to carry them out; these activities consume a large amount of many resources and so errors in predicting their needs can cost a company a lot of money.

Generation of the test plan begins during the predevelopment stages of the software project, when management needs to estimate the amount of resource required to carry out the project, part of which will be for system and acceptance testing. Since the project is at the planning stage, detailed requirements analysis has not been carried out so only an outline of the system specification is at hand. From this outline, the project manager is able to extract a series of functions that need to be tested during system and acceptance testing. This list of functions is used as the basis for estimating the amount of testing resource required. Examples of such outline functions are as follows:

> We need to test that incorrect syntax for all the operator commands will be detected and the corresponding error messages displayed.

> We need to check that emergency conditions detected by the reactor monitor are handled correctly.

> We need to check that if the DEPOSIT command or the INSERT command is executed when the database is full then the correct message is displayed.

> We need to check that when all terminals in the system are busy the response times to all query commands meet the response requirements.

Notice that at this point in the project the functions that need to be verified are relatively abstract. This level of detail is usually sufficient for a good project manager to formulate a proposal to go either to a potential customer, or to management for internal review.

If the developer is asked to continue with the project by the customer, then the list of functions extracted above will be refined during the requirements analysis and system design phases of development. Some examples of the kind of tests that can be identified during the latter stages of system design are shown below. In the extract the LOAD command is an operator command which will load details of a new chemical reactor into a database of reactor temperatures and pressures.

> We should test that when the LOAD command is typed and the first parameter to the command contains an invalid character then the ERROR1 message is displayed.

> We should test that when the LOAD command is typed and the second parameter to the command contains an invalid character then the ERROR2 message is displayed.

> We should test that when the LOAD command is typed and the first and second parameters to the command contain an invalid character then the ERROR3 message is displayed.

> We should test that when a reactor monitor issues three malfunction signals in a row an error alert message is displayed on the master console.

> We should test that when a reactor monitor issues ten malfunction signals in a row a shutdown message is displayed on the master console and the subsidiary controlling computer issues a shutdown signal to all the offending reactor's valves.

These are more detailed than the outline functions listed above, but are clearly expanded versions of these original outlines. In a well-managed project this level of detail is normally achieved by the end of the system design phase, and certainly no later than the detailed design phase.

SAQ Which outline functions listed above are expanded by these more detailed tests?

SOLUTION The first three detailed tests which deal with the LOAD function are expansions of the first outline function:

> We need to test that incorrect syntax for all the operator commands will be detected and the corresponding error messages displayed.

The last two detailed tests which deal with malfunction signals from the reactor monitor are expansions of the second outline function:

> We need to check that emergency conditions detected by the reactor monitor are handled correctly.

Because of this level of detail the project manager is able to predict with greater accuracy the resources needed during the system and acceptance testing phases.

SAQ What type of resources should the project manager be able to predict will be needed during system and acceptance testing given the kind of test descriptions shown above?

SOLUTION The project manager should be able to predict the people, software, hardware, test files and computer time required. Probably the most important resource is people. They are required to carry out the testing process which involves copying data files, executing programs and examining test outputs. However, other resources need to be predicted, such as software tools, special-purpose hardware, test data files and computer time. Special software tools might be required to simulate hardware that is not available or to generate data automatically. Special-purpose hardware may be needed in a project which has a major hardware component such as an avionics project. Test data files will also be needed, since the bulk of acceptance and system testing is concerned with executing the computer programs on typical data. Finally, computer time needs to be estimated for acceptance and system tests. It is worth pointing out that many project managers often use a rule of thumb to predict overall resources needed for testing. For example, one typical rule of thumb for some projects would be that testing took up one-third of the overall resources of the project.

During the detailed design and implementation phases, the tests will be expanded even further to produce a number of test procedures. These detail the step-by-step instructions for carrying out a test. Each test procedure should specify what the test is intended to check, the data to be used for performing the test, the software and hardware configurations to be used, any software tools and any special test routines to be used, and a list of instructions for performing the test, including the expected test results. An example of a test procedure is given below:

TEST NUMBER

Func1231

TEST DESCRIPTION

This test checks that the command processor correctly processes the DEPOSIT command. In order to check this the command is executed with 24 different parameter values.

INPUT DATA

The input data is held in the file tests:func1231.

SOFTWARE CONFIGURATION

The configuration to be executed in this test is build12. This is the partial system which implements all the system functions apart from line monitoring. It will be found in the read-only file builds:build12.

HARDWARE CONFIGURATION REQUIRED

This will be the normal configuration ZONKPC with 256K RAM.

SOFTWARE TOOLS REQUIRED

The program examinedatabase will be required to examine the state of the system database after the tests have occurred. This tool prints the key numbers in the database which have been unaffected by write operations and will also print out the contents of those records whose fields have been overwritten. This tool can be found in the file tools:exdbase.

SUPPORTING SOFTWARE

The driver for this test will be contained in the file support:dr1231.

TEST ACTIVITIES

Attach the test data file tests:func1231 to channel 2 of the build program.

Execute the program.

Check that the message 'build12ok' has been displayed in the top left-hand corner of the VDU. If it has not, then fill in a problem report form.

Check that a file called 'results' has been created by the run, if not then fill in a problem report form.

Connect the file results to the examinedatabase tool and execute the tool. A file called 'monitor' will have been created. Print this file out.

Using the file monitor check that the commands have been executed correctly. In order to do this carry out the following steps.

(a) List the file tests:func1231. Each line of the file will contain a record key and a name.

(b) Check that each record in monitor corresponding to a record key in tests:func1231 contains the corresponding name from tests:func1231.

SAQ Why do test procedures have to be expressed in such detail?

SOLUTION The reason is that the person carrying out the test will almost certainly not know the system and may never have even seen the statement of requirements. Also, by specifying the steps to be taken explicitly, the project manager can be sure that the tests are performed exactly as intended. Another reason is repeatability. Often tests need to be repeated, for example, after a change to a software system which might occur when an error is discovered. The existence of test procedures allows tests to be repeated with little further effort.

Once the full set of test procedures has been specified the project manager will use the information to calculate a more accurate resource estimate for system and acceptance testing. Hopefully, this will be similar to that produced at the early stages of the project! [1]

During the execution of system and acceptance tests, the project manager still requires information about the testing process in order to monitor progress. This involves checking how many tests have been completed correctly, how many are awaiting resolution of a problem and how many tests are left to be performed. Therefore, when a test has been completed, or has terminated because of an error, a test report should be filled in. This will include the test results from the test, any problems encountered and how they were resolved. The project manager needs to monitor progress this closely so that he or she will be able to predict the project's completion date.

Thus, throughout the project the project manager uses the test plan to estimate and re-estimate the resources required to perform system and acceptance testing. Then, once testing is underway, documentation in the form of test reports is needed in order to monitor progress so that the completion date for the project can be predicted accurately. Without this documentation the job of managing the project could not be accomplished as easily, if at all.

3.3 SUMMARY

Accurate, pertinent information is necessary for the project manager to perform the job of project management effectively. Therefore, the project manager creates and has access to documents such as the test plan and test procedures, which describe the activities and products of a software project. These documents are needed to plan, monitor, control and predict future activities on a project. As the next chapter of this book will show, the information in these

---

[1] Unfortunately, however, this estimate will only be available late in the project.

documents would be much more useful if some aspects of this information were numerical in nature.

SOFTWARE METRICS

AIMS

- To describe what a software metric is.
- To describe two typical software metrics.
- To outline how software metrics can be used on software projects.

4.1 INTRODUCTION

Chapter 3 emphasized the importance of information for the software project manager. This information is used to assess current progress, to guide the project towards successful completion and to predict future performance. Most of this information is informal in nature, and does not have the accuracy which could be attained using numerical measures; such measures would hence be an invaluable aid to the project manager. Some numerical measures of the products and processes that make up the software project do exist; they are called *software metrics*.

4.2 MEASUREMENT AND THE SOFTWARE PROJECT

Measurement and statistical inference are used in many fields to project future performance. In the area of home construction, for instance, the estimating function is based rigorously on statistics collected from past activity. An estimator in the construction trade works with a 'bluebook' or estimators handbook.... For the princely sum of $8.25, you can buy an estimator's bluebook for wood-frame house construction. If such a book were available for software estimating, I hope that you would have the good sense to buy it....

(DeMarco, 1982)

Once something can be measured, you move away from the world of opinion towards the world of fact. Most measures of project progress are informal, and hence open to interpretation, but the careful use of numerical measures can introduce precision and clarity to the process.

Consider the following spectrum of answers which you might hear when asking a project manager how complete the implementation phase on a project is.

1. It is almost complete.
2. It is 90 per cent complete.

3. We have finished the detailed design phase. We have programmed and tested 75 per cent of the estimated code.

4. We have finished the detailed design phase. We have programmed 15 000 lines of code. The original prediction of the project manager who planned the project was that the software would occupy 23 000 lines of code. So far we have discovered that these estimates have been 10 per cent too optimistic. On the basis of this I would estimate that we are about 60 per cent $\left(\dfrac{15\,000}{23\,000*1.1}\right)$ complete.

5. We have finished the detailed design phase. We have programmed 15 000 lines of code. The original prediction of the project manager who planned the project was that the software would occupy 23 000 lines of code. So far we have discovered that these estimates have been 10 per cent too optimistic. The code that we have yet to program is much more complex than the code that has been produced. On the basis of the manager's past performance, and figures from other projects about the influence of program complexity on implementation time I would estimate that we are 40 per cent complete.

The first answer is not very satisfactory. What does *almost complete* mean? The project team could have implemented 95 per cent of its program units yet the 5 per cent of code remaining could be very complex code with tortuous logic and may take very much more than 5 per cent of project resources.

SAQ Why may the second answer be misleading?

SOLUTION Although answer 2 mentions a figure, there is no indication of what this figure means. Does it mean that 90 per cent of the code has been programmed? Does it mean that 90 per cent of the resources of the project have been expended? Perhaps it means that 90 per cent of the intended function of the system has been implemented?

You can see from the answer to the SAQ that providing informal measurement in the shape of numerical data is not necessarily helpful, and may be misleading if the meaning is not explained. It is therefore obviously necessary to be cautious about the use of figures—they can be misleading simply because they lend an air of certainty to information.

Answer 3 is a little better since it does at least give an idea of what the figure means. However, it still does not state what factors have been taken into account when this figure was produced, e.g. has the complexity of the system's logic been allowed for?

The fourth answer is quite an improvement.

SAQ Why is the fourth answer an improvement?

SOLUTION The fourth answer is an improvement since it not only indicates what the figure is measuring and how it has been produced, but it also takes into account data about the estimating expertise of the manager who originally costed the project.

The last answer, number 5, goes a bit further than the fourth answer, and is by far the best of the group. Not only are the quoted figures explained, but the project manager also uses two different sets of historical data to produce a realistic estimate of the state of implementation. These are:

1. the efficiency of the estimating manager;
2. the effect of complexity on implementation.

Being able to measure something numerically is a great advantage. Probably the most cogent expression of the advantages of attaching a number to an idea has been made by Senator Daniel Moynihan:

> There is a rule of sorts in government, or ought to be, that you never do anything about a problem until you learn to measure it. Paul F Lazarsfeld, the great Columbia University professor who developed the art of polling, used to tell his classes that the moment you attach a number to an idea you have learned something. You know more than you knew before. The number seems too large, too small, about right. You are already thinking in a more precise way.   (DeMarco, 1982)

A similar point was made by Lord Kelvin in addressing the Institution of Civil Engineers in 1883:

> I often say that when you can measure what you are speaking about, and express it in numbers, you know something about it; but when you cannot measure it, when you cannot express it in numbers, your knowledge is of a meager and unsatisfactory kind.
>   (DeMarco, 1982)

4.3 SOFTWARE METRICS—A RESEARCHER'S PERSPECTIVE

Software metrics are numerical measures of the products and processes that make up the software project. The system's architecture and a program unit are typical of such products, while system designing and system testing are typical processes.

The following extract contains sections of an interview with Martin Shepherd, a prominent metrics researcher who is Head of the Computer Science Department at Bournemouth University. Martin discusses the role of measurement and metrics on the software project with Darrel Ince, including both current practice and possible future uses.

Darrel: Why are software metrics useful?

Martin: Well, I think if you think about measurement in general, we realize that in fact it's pretty fundamental to most scientific and engineering disciplines. For example a lot of measurements must be taken before we can build a bridge safely. We need to know the width of the span, size of the beams, the load that is required to be supported, and so forth. The last thing you would do is go and get yourself a piece of wood, and lob it down in the direction of the thing that we wish to span, and hope that it'll all be alright. Unfortunately, I think that's a practice that is often adopted by software engineers. So, I think measurement's important, if you like, for prediction purposes. The other area in which I think measurement is very important, possibly more important for the current state of art, is analysis. It may be we have a catastrophe and the bridge collapses, and we need to be able to analyse the reasons for this. What went wrong? What can we learn from it? Unfortunately, the usual understandable human reaction is to try and run away from the problem and put it out of sight, and try and pin the blame on somebody else. And, generally not derive any benefit or learn any possible lessons from mistakes that have been made in the past.

Darrel: So what you're saying Martin is that since measurement plays a major part in the vast majority of engineering disciplines, if the development of software is going to resemble engineering, then we have to have the same sort of discipline of measurement there?

Martin: Yes, that's absolutely right, and the areas that we need to address with measurement are those areas of analysis, to understand the engineering processes, and the products that software projects build, in order to produce predictions to help us in the engineering process itself.

Darrel: Now, what would you say the rule of measurement is on a software project?

Martin: Well, ideally, it would be very extensive. There are two things we must bear in mind. Firstly, there are many stages to a software project, and secondly, there are different people with different perspectives on the software project. For example, we have the software manager, we have the software engineer, and we have the customer. Ideally, we should use measurement to obtain predictions early on concerning the cost of the project. For example, we might try and measure attributes of the specification[1] in order to get some feeling for how much the project is going to cost.

Darrel: This would be during project planning, for example?

Martin: Yes, this would be very early on in the software project; and it would be from a management perspective: there would be a certain cost threshold beyond which the project is not feasible, and the earlier on that this can be determined, obviously the better for all concerned. Another area where measurement could be usefully applied is at the design stage; this might be used to give help to the software engineer to choose a system architecture, for instance, that will maximize reliability.

Darrel: So you might do that when you carry out system design?

Martin: Yes, this would be an integral part of the design process, because we could evaluate different system architectures and produce three or four competing alternatives. The metrics might guide you towards the most effective design. We can also measure design in order to pinpoint potential trouble-spots. If we can identify that certain components[2] of the software system are going to be very difficult to implement, then management could allocate experienced staff to deal with them. We could schedule accordingly if we know that one component is going to be very complex, then extra testing resources could be allocated to that module. Another area where

---

[1] The system specification.
[2] Modules

measurement is important is quality control. Again this is, I think, a management issue. Management may set certain quality control thresholds. For example, it may state that a module must not exceed a certain number of connections to a database.[3] Or we may say the module must never exceed a certain size. This is a mechanism whereby we can try and introduce quality into the software project at the early stages. Traditionally, we use execution-based testing[4] to try and impose quality on the project once a system has been developed and this has not been altogether successful. There are other situations where execution-based testing is either very difficult, or very expensive. I'll give you some examples. Let us take a fly-by-wire system.[5] If there are any software faults in the aeroplane, it would be very expensive if we kept crashing planes during testing; therefore, the more quality that can be introduced into the software, the better. Examining different techniques and methodologies for the development of software are other areas where a project may wish to use software metrics. Management might be interested to know whether technique *A* is more effective than technique *B* and what impact does technique *A* have on reliability, and so on. So those are the questions which must be dealt with by measurement. Finally a very important, and often neglected application is some sort of review process after the project has been developed. It's very important to see what lessons can be learnt from a software development, particularly if it's been a monumental disaster.

Darrel: Perhaps you could give some examples of metrics in action. Are there any British projects that you know of, that have successfully used metrics?

Martin: Well, at the moment, metrics are still very much in a developmental stage. However, I can give one or two examples. A very major project is that of the Inland Revenue[6] and their Telford Development Centre. Here they are computerizing the British income tax system. At the moment, they have just concluded a pilot scheme, which has used measurement to try and predict the cost of new development, and also to monitor productivity. Now the way they've done this is to use a technique known as function point analysis.[7] What they do is look at a specification for a project to see how many files must be accessed, how many screens must be displayed, how many user queries must be satisfied and so on. Different types of tasks are then given different weightings, and this allows us to obtain a score, which is called the function point count. From this they can predict the size of the development. The Inland Revenue have been using this technique, partly because of the early availability of these figures, and also because they're independent of any methodology or language, and they've obtained some quite good results. They've found a correlation of 0.89 with actual effort or person-years required to staff a project. So they are now actually building some software tools to

---

[3] Martin is referring to the number of times a module reads and writes to a database in a design.
[4] System testing and acceptance testing.
[5] A fly-by-wire system is a safety-critical system whereby the flaps of a plane are controlled by a computer rather than the pilot.
[6] The British tax authority.
[7] Details of this technique can be found in Albrecht and Gaffney (1983).

obtain these metrics automatically. The other interesting thing of this project is they're not just using one metric, they're not just using function points; they're also using source lines of code in order to corroborate the results they get from the function point analysis. In particular they found that a few systems didn't fit a general pattern, and that the use of source lines of code would help to identify and explain why this should be the case. So here we have the example of two metrics being more powerful than a single metric.

A second example is that of Lucas Aerospace.[8] Now, here, they're using design metrics to try and identify components of the system which are going to cause maintenance problems. Lucas have experienced a lot of maintenance problems because their customers change their software requirements quite regularly. So what they want to do is use metrics to try and identify those components which are going to be hard to change; the idea is that if metrics can be obtained before the coding is carried out this will allow them to avoid systems that are unmaintainable. To do this, they've used information-flow-based metrics, where they look at the flow of information between the different modules of the system. And those modules that have very high connections, or high counts of flows into or out of them, tend to be those modules that are, in fact, the hardest to maintain. If the designer is armed with this information, then they can rework those parts of the design which are the most problematic, and thus reduce their maintenance problems. This approach is very promising, and in our work with Lucas we have found high correlations between this design metric and maintenance problems.

Darrel: I can think of a large number of things I could measure on a software project: I could measure the number of people that smile at me when I come into the building; I can measure the number of lines of code in a subroutine; and I could measure the number of letters of the alphabet that I find in a specification. There's plenty of things we can measure in a software project. How do you judge whether one of these measures or metrics is better than another one, or whether it's good, or whether it's bad?

Martin: The crucial thing for judging whether a metric is good or not is to have a clear idea of what the purpose of that metric is. Even your example of the number of people who smiled as you enter the building may be significant if you want to get some index of employees' satisfaction, or happiness. It might not be so useful if you're interested in software quality. Similarly, lines of code may be a useful metric if we want to know the amount of paper that we're going to consume to print out a program, but is probably less useful if we want to know something about the reliability of that software. So the first thing is to know what we wish to do with the metric. The second thing that we need to do is to examine the model or the theory on which that metric is based. People don't make measurements randomly. The measurements must enter into some theory or some belief that you have concerning the object or the process which you're measuring. If our goal is to know

---

[8] A British company extensively involved in the aerospace industry.

about reliability, and our measurement is lines of code, then we have some theory that connects lines of code with reliability. Our theory might be that errors are proportional to the number of lines of code. So if we double the size of the software, then we will double the number of errors. We can then examine that model, to see if it actually stands up to scrutiny: whether the model contains contradictions or whether it's consistent with current thinking in software engineering. Very often, a lot of metrics which are currently presented are, in fact, based on very strange or very weak models of software engineering.

Finally, when we're evaluating a metric, if we're satisfied that we understand it's purpose, and we're satisfied with the model or theory which it's based upon, then we need to do some empirical work. We actually need to go out into the field, if you like, and see that the metric performs as we would expect. To do this properly can be very difficult. For a start, we need a large number of data points and this can be costly to collect. And secondly, we often need to collect from a variety of different environments. There is a danger of just one team of researchers reporting results that strongly support their work. If nobody else investigates this, then we must have a few suspicions, or reservations.

Darrel: So you'd actually go out into a software project, look at a metric, and see whether it predicts something which is of use to you.

Martin: Well, that is an important way of doing it. There is the alternative approach, which is to carry out some sort of experiment in controlled laboratory conditions. This approach has the advantage that you can control what's going on much more carefully. It has the disadvantage that you're almost invariably restricted to very small-scale software, and short time-scales. Most of the difficulties in software engineering relate to the very large scales of the enterprise, the large number of people involved, and the long time-spans of the project.

Darrel: One of the most important activities in a software project is design: system design. How would you say we could use metrics in the design process?

Martin: A number of researchers have found that design metrics—measures of system architecture—tend to be strongly associated with many software quality factors. Factors such as: reliability, development effort, ease of maintenance and so on. Therefore, if we can derive measures from a design early on in the life-cycle of the project, then this can give us some useful feedback. Design errors tend to be very costly, so really we want to avoid as many as possible. We wish to get the design as good as possible before it's committed into code. Our work has found that measures based on information flows between modules of a system are very effective at identifying problematic modules. If we can identify rogue or outlier modules— those with very abnormally high metric values—and show these to the engineer who's developed them, this may give him an opportunity to rework that part of the design, or at least to understand why these modules should have such unusual values. So that's an important technique, and it can be very easily integrated into the design process. Increasingly, people are using walk-throughs or inspection techniques[9] at the design stage, and the use of measurement is an important input to design inspections.

Darrel: The study of metrics is still in the early days, can you predict how metrics might be used in the software project of the future?

Martin: I think one important ingredient is that of automation. Most metrics are difficult to obtain and involve very onerous calculations, so some automated support is an imperative. There's a lot of work at the moment in developing software tools and integrated project support environments, and I see it as a natural development that metrics be integrated into these tools. Another facet of automation is that of databases: one very rapidly gets large quantities of metric data which are very hard to maintain or to manage, and the database system which provides browsing and retrieval facilities, plus sophisticated statistical analysis tools and graphical presentation techniques will be a very important aid for anyone who wants to use metrics in a software project.

The other possible area where I think software metrics are going to be used is that of certification. If you purchase a motorbike crash helmet you'll see on the side there's a little BSI kite symbol to say that the crash helmet is of a certain standard. Customers can see whether they are getting a safe helmet. There is an analogy for software; it's certainly quite a seductive idea. If this is to take off, then metrics must be an important part of this process.

Darrel: One of the things you mentioned right at the beginning of our conversation was prediction, and that I guess is a long-term aim. Would you say that it's actually feasible to predict things from metrics?

Martin: Well, it very much depends what you are trying to predict and how far in advance. But I think the general answer at the moment is no. I think prediction is too ambitious. And one of the reasons for this is that the models that we have of software, and software development processes, are very, very naive. At most they contain a couple of variables and it is very optimistic to expect that using such simple models we can obtain accurate predictions. This means that there are various alternative techniques that are available. One of the most promising that we have actually exploited quite effectively, is that of outlier analysis. This is a statistical technique to identify components or measures which are abnormal. We've used outlier to detect abnormal design components and found that these are strongly associated with subsequent problems like: difficulty of development, high incidence of errors and so forth. If we are going to have prediction, I think it's very important to state the accuracy you expect to obtain.

Darrel: So you're saying that eventually we'll be able to do some prediction, but it might even then just be fairly rough prediction?

---

[9] Validation techniques which involve a meeting of technical staff who work through a document or some program code looking for errors.

Martin: Well, I think that's inevitable. It depends again how early in the software project that you are trying to predict, but there are so many variables and factors that are involved that I think the best we can hope for are engineering approximations, given the large number of variables that affect a software project. You see many of them are factors involved with people and are very hard to quantify.

Martin mentions two key roles for measurement on a software project. These are *prediction* and *analysis*. Predicting future progress from metrics can be used for planning and estimating the effect of changes to the project. If a project manager can accurately predict the cost of a project, then it is more likely that the developer will make a profit, and that the customer will receive an appropriate system on time. Analysing metric information can be used for monitoring progress and if a project fails to meet objectives, then measurements taken throughout the project can be used retrospectively to identify what went wrong, and hopefully therefore to avoid such failure in the future.

Traditionally, metrics have been extracted from the later stages of the software project which has inevitably limited their usefulness in predicting the course of a project, both at the planning stage and for monitoring and controlling purposes. However, metrics which are intended to be used early on in the life-cycle are beginning to emerge. Although their use appears to be somewhat experimental at the moment, Martin mentioned two current British projects which are successfully using some.

Of course, there are many numbers which can be attached to a software project; a selection of possible metrics is given below:

- The number of decisions in the detailed design of a program unit.
- The length of a program unit.
- The number of discovered errors in a software system during the first six months of operation.
- The amount of effort expended on a project.
- Time for each stage in a project.
- Number of faults found during a testing activity.
- The number of faults found in the first n months of use.
- The number of modules in the structure chart design of a software system.

However, not all numbers are useful, and it is important to be able to distinguish good metrics from bad ones. Martin mentioned three tests which can be used to determine whether a metric is a good one or not.

SAQ What tests can be applied to determine whether a metric is a good one or not?

SOLUTION The following tests should be applied to any potential metric:

1.   There should be a clear idea of the purpose of the metric.

2.   The model on which the metric is based should be examined for suitability.

3.   The metric should be studied in practice to ensure its applicability.

However, before these tests are applied, it is worth studying the characteristics of the metric itself, since a truly useful software metric must have the following four characteristics.

A software metric must be measurable

It probably seems that we are stating the obvious to say that a metric must be measurable, but it is quite common for opinions, which are not measurable, to be used as metrics. For example, asking a programmer about the complexity of a program unit, and using the answer as if it were an accurate measure is not uncommon. To use such an opinion as a metric would be poor practice since, for example, one programmer's idea of complexity may differ from that of another programmer. Also, there is always a tendency for a programmer to excuse poor performance by stressing how difficult a task was because of its complexity.

A software metric must be independent

A metric is only useful if it is independent of the influence of project staff. Project staff have a direct interest in attaining good metric values, such as delivery of a document within a particular time. If the project team has the ability to change a metric without changing the quality or efficiency of a project then they may do so. For example, a commonly used, but poor software metric is concerned with the date on which a document is due to be delivered. Often, some weight is placed on whether that document is delivered on time or not, such as stating that the project is 43 per cent complete when the system specification is complete. If a project is running late, it is common for the team carrying out the project to bundle up the incomplete system specification and announce that the project is 43 per cent complete on time, even though the document is clearly unfinished, since completing a stage on time will gain management approval.

There are very few independent metrics available to the software project manager. This is connected with what Tom DeMarco has called the 'slightly revised Heisenberg uncertainty principle'.[10]

> You may think that there are no such things as truly independent metrics and, indeed, they are rare. The reason that you seldom encounter independent metrics has to do with
>
> Heisenberg's uncertainty principle (slightly revised)
>
> Measuring any project parameter and attaching evident significance to it will affect the usefulness of that parameter. The key word here is *evident*. If the project members know that you can count the number of smiles on Monday mornings and use that as an indication of project morale, then when they want you to believe that morale is high, they will all start smiling on Monday mornings. If, on the other hand, you keep to yourself the metrics you are using and the significance you attach to them, their usefulness (if any) will not degrade over time.   (De Marco, 1982)

There is always the temptation for staff to behave in the way you expect them to behave.

---

[10] Heisenberg's original uncertainty principle comes from the world of physics and states that an electron cannot be located exactly in terms of both its space and momentum coordinates, or in terms of both its time and energy coordinates.

SAQ A project manager decided to see whether the complexity of a program unit could be used to predict the number of changes required to that program unit during unit testing. He reasoned that if a program unit was complex then a programmer would make a large number of mistakes and this would show up as the number of edits that the programmer applied during implementation. Consequently, the manager arranged for the editor used on the project to be modified so that the number of edits performed on each user file was stored. Is this is an independent metric?

SOLUTION Yes, it is a good independent metric. Even if programming staff knew that this value was being monitored then they would have little chance of reducing it because in reducing the value they might start producing poorly tested program units in which errors had been discovered but not rectified. In fact, if project staff knew about the use of this metric then the poor practice of guessing errors, editing and running a large number of times might be restricted.

A software metric must be accountable

Information about the metric and its uses should be documented. This is not only important for the project manager to be able to understand the significance of metric values, but it is also important for other areas. Metrics can be used for sensitive tasks such as appraising staff performance and monitoring the progress of a project. If a senior manager notifies a project manager that a high rate of errors was found during system testing then that project manager has every right to ask for further details. In particular, he or she would want to know what metrics were used and the process whereby the senior manager concluded that the project was performing below the standards expected. Therefore, when metrics are applied to a system, the following information should be stored: how the metrics were measured, who measured them, when they were measured and, as a source of comparison, equivalent values for other projects.

A software metric must be precise

Metric values must be associated with a precision value. Some software metrics are precise, such as the number of lines of code in a program, assuming that it was defined properly, for example, by omitting comments. However, a large number are imprecise, such as the number of hours worked by programmers in unit testing, which can only be estimated with some degree of tolerance. If metric values are going to be used effectively, then the level of tolerance allowed in the figures must be clearly stated.

SAQ What characteristics should a software metric have if it is to be truly useful?

SOLUTION If it is to be truly useful, a software metric must be measurable, independent, accountable and precise.

4.4   RESULT METRICS AND PREDICTOR METRICS

Software metrics can be classified in two ways, depending on how they are used.

A *result metric* is an observed quantity of a system which is normally measured at the end of a project or at the end of one phase of a project. Common result metrics include the manpower expended on a project, the number of defects discovered during system testing and the number of lines of code in a software system.

A *predictor metric* is a metric which is measured during one phase of a project and which can be used to predict the value of another metric which can be measured during a later part of the project. Examples of such metrics include the estimated number of lines of code in a program unit and the number of functions that a software system is to implement. For example, the estimated number of lines of code for a program unit may be used as a predictor metric for estimating the amount of manpower needed to implement the program unit. The number of functions in a system may be used as a predictor metric for the size of the system being built.

A metric can only be considered as a result metric if it has been predicted earlier in the project by a predictor metric. For example, the amount of manpower needed to implement a program unit can be predicted by the estimated number of lines of code, and is therefore a result metric. On the other hand, the number of functions in a system cannot be predicted by another metric, and therefore cannot be regarded as a result metric, only as a potential predictor metric.

SAQ Is the estimated number of lines of code in a system a result metric or a predictor metric?

SOLUTION This metric may be regarded as either, since it can be predicted by the number of functions in a software system, and is hence a result metric, but it can also be used to predict the amount of manpower needed to implement the system, and is hence a predictor metric.

SAQ Classify each of the following metrics as a predictor metric or a result metric. For each result metric, suggest a predictor metric (not necessarily in the list) which might have been used to predict it.

    (a)   The number of person-hours[11] expended on a project.

    (b)   The number of IF statements in a program unit.

    (c)   The size of the functional specification for a system.

    (d)   The number of defects in a program unit discovered during system testing.

    (e)   The complexity of a system design.

---

[11] This is a measure of the resources used which refers to actual time rather than elapsed time. For example, nine person-hours may refer to one person working nine hours, or three people working three hours each, and so on; person-days, person-months and person-years are also used.

(f)   The amount of effort expended during maintenance.

SOLUTION

(a)   The number of person-hours expended on a project is definitely a result metric since it can be predicted by other metrics measured early in the project's life, such as size of the system. This is one of the main determinants of project cost, therefore it is an important result metric.

(b)   The number of IF statements in a program unit is a potential predictor metric since the more IF statements that a unit contains the more tortuous its logic will be and hence the more effort will be required to test it. It is therefore a potential predictor of result metrics such as the number of discovered errors and the amount of time spent on implementation.

(c)   The size of a functional specification for a project is a potential predictor metric. The size of the functional specification is related to the number of functions in the system, which is related to the size of the system when completed, which is related to the cost of producing a system. Thus, the size of a functional specification is one of a number of metrics that might be used to predict the cost of a project. It is important to point out that this is only a good metric if there is some reasonable consistency in content and style between projects.

(d)   The number of defects discovered during system testing is a result metric, since this could be predicted by, for instance, the complexity of the functions listed in the functional specification.

(e)   The complexity of a system design is a potential predictor metric. A highly complex design is usually associated with a lot of information which the designer must work with. It is well known that human beings have a limit to the amount of information which they can handle efficiently at any one time. Therefore, the probability that the designer will make an error is higher and a high number of errors in the system design indicates that there will be more errors discovered during implementation. Hence, the complexity of the design is a potential predictor of errors in activities such as unit testing and system testing.

(f)   The amount of effort expended during maintenance is a result metric since it can be predicted by, for instance, the complexity of a system. Since this metric is measured during the last stages of a project it is difficult to see where it could be used as a predictor metric, except of course for future projects.

4.5 EXAMPLE METRICS

In this section, we introduce you to two specific metrics and give you some practice in their use. The intention is to give you a flavour of what might be entailed in calculating and using a metric, not to give a detailed review, since this would fill a book on its own. For further information, you are referred to the references cited.

4.5.1 Cyclomatic complexity metrics

During the detailed design phase of a project, the flow of control for each program unit in a software system is determined. The flow is expressed in terms of some detailed design notation such as a program design language. The following example represents the detailed design of a procedure to calculate the average of a series of temperature readings stored in an array:

```
sum := 0; count := 1;
do count < 10
   sum := sum + temperature[count];
   count := count + 1;
od;
average := sum/(count - 1);
```

At the end of the detailed design phase the whole of a system will be expressed in a detailed design notation such as that shown above. This representation of the system is amenable to measurement; a project manager frequently revises the estimates of progress and resources needed which were made initially during the early phases of the project, and by the time detailed designs are available for the program units, there is enough detailed information to be able to make quite accurate estimates. The estimate which a project manager would most like to know about at this stage is how much effort and time might be spent in executing the implementation phase of the project. To obtain this estimate would involve quantifying how complex the software is and how much testing it would require.

SAQ What characteristic of a detailed design would enable the project manager to predict the amount of time spent on unit testing by a programmer?

SOLUTION The number of control structures in the design would enable the project manager to predict the amount of time spent on unit testing by a programmer. The more decision and loop constructs which are contained in a design, the more possible paths through the program unit there are, and hence the greater the amount of testing required.

The relationship between the number of control constructs and the amount of testing required by a program unit was first investigated by a researcher called Thomas McCabe in 1976. In order to understand McCabe's work it is first necessary to digress and describe a simplified way of representing detailed design notations diagrammatically. We shall represent the control structure of a fragment of detailed design by a directed graph. A directed graph consists of a set of nodes[12] and directed lines joining these nodes known as arcs.[13] A node represents the point where a decision is made, or the end of some processing associated with that decision, and the arcs represent the actions that occur in a particular branch of the program unit. For example, the directed graph for the following detailed design fragment is shown in Fig. 4.1:

```
if temperature > limit then alarm(temperature);
else print(temperature);
fi
```

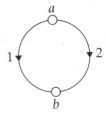

Figure 4.1 An example of a directed graph.

In a directed graph the nodes are labelled with lower-case letters while the arcs are labelled with numbers; the arrow attached to an arc shows the direction of processing. Figure 4.1 shows that the fragment can be represented by two nodes *a* and *b*. Node *a* represents the decision in the **if** statement (temperature > limit) and node *b* represents the point where the processing in the two branches of the **if** statement join up, i.e. at the point represented by **fi**. Assuming that the left-hand arc represents the first branch of the **if** statement and the right-hand arc represents the second branch, then arc 1 represents the processing alarm(temperature) and arc 2 represents the processing print(temperature).

Note that although the program design language shows two conditions, there is only *one* decision point (at *a*) and that the actions associated with the two conditions appear in the graph as two arcs. In general, therefore, *n* conditions in a selection statement result in one deciding point and *n* arcs. Loops are easily depicted, by an arc back from a node at the end of the loop to a condition node at the start, or by an arc from a decision at the end of a loop to the node representing its start, depending on the type of loop.

---

[12] Nodes are also known as vertices.
[13] Arcs are also called edges.

SAQ Draw the directed graph of the following design fragment:

```
do i < 20
    i := i + 1;
    if   valid(data[i]) → sum := sum + data[i])
        invalid(data[i]) → print(message); error := true
    fi
od
s :=s+1
if error → check(monitors)
    not error → average(sum)
fi
```

Describe the directed graph, and relate it to the above fragment.

SOLUTION The graph corresponding to the above fragment is shown in Fig. 4.2. It consists of five nodes and seven arcs. Node *p* represents the decision at the start of the do statement, node *q* represents the decision in the first **if** statement, node *r*

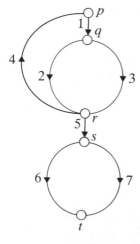

Figure 4.2 The directed graph of the design fragment for the SAQ.

represents the destination of both parts of the processing associated with the `if` statement, and nodes *s* and *t* are associated with the second `if` statement. Arc 1 is associated with the processing `i := i + 1`, arc 2 is associated with the processing `sum := sum + data`, arc 3 is associated with the processing `print(message); error := true`, arc 4 represents the loop back to *p* in order to re-execute the `do` loop, arc 5 represents the transfer of control from the `do` statement to the second `if` statement which includes an assignment statement, and, finally, arcs 6 and 7 represent the two processing actions `check(monitors)` and `average(sum)`.

Directed graphs have been known to mathematicians for some time and have been used in applications such as the design of pipelines, the calculation of currents and voltages in electrical systems and the design of optimal one-way traffic systems in a city. Mathematicians have developed a number of measures of the complexity of a graph in terms of the number of its nodes and arcs. Probably, the most important of these is the *cyclomatic complexity* of a graph which is defined as follows:

$$v = a - n + 2$$

where v = cyclomatic complexity of the graph
a = the number of arcs in the graph
n = the number of nodes in the graph

Using this definition the cyclomatic complexity of the graph shown in Figure 4.2 will be as follows:

$$v = 7 - 5 + 2$$
$$= 4$$

It is therefore possible to calculate the cyclomatic complexity of a program unit by first drawing the corresponding directed graph and then calculating its cyclomatic complexity.

Consider the following design fragment:

```
Total := 0; Index_temp := 1; Count := 0;
do Temp_readings[Index_temp] = -1
  Ignore_reading := false; Index_ignore := 1;
  do Index_ignore > 10
    if Temp_readings[Index_temp] = Ignore[Index_ignore] then
      Ignore_reading := true
    fi
    Index_ignore := Index_ignore + 1
  od
  if not Ignore_reading then
    Total := Total + Temp_readings[Index_temp];
    Count := Count + 1
  fi
  Index_temp := Index_temp + 1;
od
if Index_temp > 1 then Average := Total / Count
fi
```

To calculate the cyclomatic complexity of this program unit, the first thing to do is to draw its corresponding directed graph, and count up the number of arcs and nodes; this is shown in Fig. 4.3. Note that the program design language which precedes the do loop is represented by arc 1. This graph has 7 nodes and 12 arcs. Its cyclomatic complexity is given by substituting these values into the equation above.

$$v = 12 - 7 + 2$$
$$= 7$$

McCabe postulated that the higher the cyclomatic complexity of a directed graph representing a program unit the more difficult the program is to read, comprehend, implement and test.

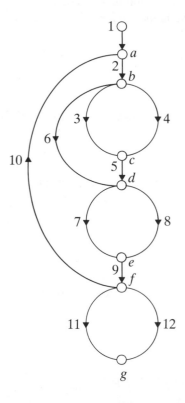

Figure 4.3 The directed graph of the design fragment

SAQ Do you think that this is a reasonable hypothesis? Why?

SOLUTION This is a reasonable hypothesis since if the cyclomatic complexity of a program unit is high then it must contain a high density of loop and decision constructs. This in turn means that the unit is more difficult to read, implement and test because it contains more possible execution paths, each of which needs to be understood, programmed and exercised with test data.

In the paper describing his work (McCabe, 1976) McCabe suggested that a cyclomatic complexity value greater than 10 for a graph representing a program unit was intolerable, and the unit should be redesigned. He related his experiences in applying the measure to a group of programs from a software project that he was not involved with. In the extract that follows FLOW is a software tool that McCabe used to monitor and calculate the cyclomatic complexity of FORTRAN subroutines:

> It has been interesting to note how individual programmer's style relates to the complexity measure. The author has been delighted to find several programmers who never had formal training in structured programming but consistently write code in the 3 to 7 complexity range which is quite well structured. On the other hand FLOW has found several programmers who frequently wrote code in the 40 to 50 complexity range (and who claimed there was no other way to do it). On one occasion the author was given a DEC tape of 24 FORTRAN subroutines that were part of a large real-time graphics system. It was rather disquieting to find, in a system where reliability is critical, subroutines of the following complexity: 16, 17, 24, 24, 32, 34, 41, 54, 56 and 64. After confronting the project members with these results the author was told that the subroutines on the DEC tape were chosen because they were troublesome and indeed a close correlation was found between the ranking of subroutines by complexity and a ranking by reliability (performed by project members). (McCabe, 1976)

Not much empirical research has been carried out on the relationship between graph metrics and the amount of effort spent on implementation. However, this does not invalidate McCabe's work. The idea that graph measures such as cyclomatic complexity have a major influence on the quality of a software product and the amount of work carried out during implementation is now recognized by software engineers.

SAQ Given that we cannot predict accurately the relationship between graph complexity measures and programming effort, how then can McCabe's research be profitably used in a software project?

SOLUTION McCabe's work on cyclomatic complexity can be used in the establishment of quality standards during detailed design. A manager can monitor the cyclomatic complexity of designs. Any design which is greater than an upper limit (McCabe suggests 10) would be rejected and the designer asked to redesign the program unit. This may entail using fewer control structures or partitioning the program unit into two further program units.

If the cyclomatic complexity metric were to be used on a project, then its use and an upper limit to the allowed complexity would be stipulated in the quality plan.

4.5.2 Impact matrices

Impact matrices are used to help determine the amount of resource that a particular system is going to consume during maintenance. A project manager wants to know as early as possible in the development process whether a design is going to be at all troublesome during the rest of the system's life. If this information is made available during system design then the project manager could instruct that the program unit or subsystem be redesigned without the large increase in project expenditure which would ensue if the substandard design were allowed to slip through.

In order to tackle this problem, a technique was devised whereby the quality of a system's design could be quantified. This technique relied on the premise that the better the software design, the more the individual program units in the design were isolated from each other. (In other words, the more loosely coupled the program units, the better.)

SAQ Why should design quality be measured in terms of the relative isolation of a design's program units? *Hint*: Consider the processes involved in software maintenance, and the kind of problems which maintainers may encounter.

SOLUTION During software maintenance staff have to modify the individual program units that make up a system. If a program unit is closely coupled to other program units then they will have to keep a large amount of information in their heads when assessing the effect of a modification and checking that a modification does not affect other program units. Consequently, staff have to expend more effort and may produce more errors.

A change to a program unit often means that another change is needed to another unit which, in turn, leads to a further change to another unit, and so on. The idea of one program unit directly affecting another can be represented by an *impact matrix*. This matrix is a two-dimensional table which shows the probability that a modification to one unit will directly lead to the need for a change to another unit.

The mathematics used to construct an impact matrix is complicated and, for brevity, we do not discuss here how these probabilities are derived; it is their interaction and use which is of primary interest to us. However, the derivation of impact matrices is outlined at the end of the section.

An impact matrix for a small system of five modules is shown in Fig. 4.4. The program units are A, B, C, D and E. The first row shows that if there is a change to A then there is a probability of 0.1 that, as a direct result of the change to A, there will be a change to B, a probability of 0.2 that there will be a change to D, and there will definitely be no change to E. Notice that the leading diagonal of the matrix contains the probability value of 1. This is just common sense, since if there is any change to a program unit it is certain that there is a change to that program unit. Notice also that the matrix is symmetrical about its diagonal: if A affects C, then C affects A. This is a simplification of what one might expect for most software systems, since the probability of a change to A causing a change to C is not necessarily the same vice versa, but we have chosen to make this simplification so that we can present some examples in a reasonable amount of space.

	A	B	C	D	E
A	1.0	0.1	0.1	0.2	0
B	0.1	1.0	0.3	0	0
C	0.1	0.3	1.0	0	0.1
D	0.2	0	0	1.0	0.4
E	0	0	0.1	0.4	1.0

Figure 4.4 An example of an impact matrix.

From this matrix you can gain an idea of the direct effect that a change to one program unit has on another program unit. You can also gain an idea of second-order effects, that is, those changes which occur to a program unit M because a change to another program unit has affected a program unit which affects M. The higher order effects between program units can be more easily seen by showing the information in an impact matrix as a diagram. The impact matrix of Fig. 4.4 is depicted in Fig. 4.5. From the figure it is easy to see, for example, that program unit A can affect C via B as well as directly. The probability of this second-order effect of A on C is calculated thus:

- a change to program unit A has a probability of 0.1 of affecting program unit B;
- a change to program unit B has a probability of 0.3 of affecting program unit C;
- hence a change to program unit A will have a probability of affecting program unit C by means of a second-order effect of $0.1 \times 0.3 = 0.03$.

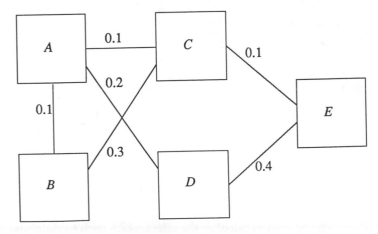

Figure 4.5 A diagrammatic version of an impact matrix.

SAQ There are two ways in which a change in program unit E can affect program unit A as a result of a second-order effect. Calculate the probability for each case.

SOLUTION The two second-order effects of E on A are via D and via C. A change to program unit E has a probability of 0.4 of directly affecting program unit D. A change to program unit D has a probability of 0.2 of directly affecting program unit A. Therefore, a change to program unit E has a probability of $0.4 \times 0.2 = 0.08$ of affecting program unit A as a result of the second-order effect via D. Similarly, the probability of a change via C is $0.1 \times 0.1 = 0.01$.

If two possible second-order effects exist, as in the previous SAQ, the overall probability can be calculated using the following formula.

$$P(XY_2) = P(XY_{21}) + P(XY_{22}) - P(XY_{21}) \times P(XY_{22})$$

where XY_2 represents the event of a change in X causing a second-order effect on Y and XY_{21} and XY_{22} represent the events associated with the two second-order effects. For example, the total second-order effect of E on A is calculated as follows:

$$
\begin{aligned}
P(EA_2) &= P(EA_{2D}) + P(EA_{2C}) - P(EA_{2D}) \times P(EA_{2C}) \\
&= 0.08 + 0.01 - 0.08 \times 0.01 \\
&= 0.09 - 0.0008 \\
&= 0.0892
\end{aligned}
$$

Of course, in general, third, fourth or higher order effects may exist (as they do in the matrix in Fig. 4.4); these effects are particularly likely when considering larger and more complex systems. Higher order effects can be calculated in a similar way to second-order effects.

You can see from Fig. 4.5 that C is affected directly by A and indirectly through B, but that they also interact via D and E (a third-order effect). To calculate the probability of A affecting C via D and E, we take the probability of a change to A causing a change to D (0.2), the probability of a change to D causing a change to E (0.4) and the probability of a change to E causing a change to C (0.1) and multiply them together (0.008).

SAQ Calculate the probability of a change in program unit A affecting program unit D as a result of a third-order effect.

SOLUTION There is a third-order effect of A on D, via C and E. A change to program unit A has a probability of 0.1 of directly affecting program unit C. A change to program unit C has a probability of 0.1 of directly affecting program unit E. A change to program unit E has a probability of 0.4 of directly affecting program unit D. Therefore, a change to program unit A has a probability of $0.1 \times 0.1 \times 0.4 = 0.004$ of affecting program unit D as a result of the third-order effect via C and E.

Mathematical probability theory can be used to calculate the effect which each module has on every other module, not just by first-order effects but also second-order effects, third-order effects, etc. The details are somewhat complicated. The full details can be found in Yau *et al.* (1978). However, once these effect metrics are computed a designer can gain a very good idea of the quality of a design in terms of the ripple effect that occurs when a change is made to a design during software maintenance: that one change gives rise to another set of changes which, in turn, gives rise to other changes, and so on.

Note that, in practice, software tools are used to generate impact matrices and to derive dependency matrices. These tools determine the coupling of program units and calculate the probability values for the impact matrix. Dependency matrices are easily calculated by these tools using matrix algebra.

4.6 SUMMARY

A software metric is a numerical measure of a product or process that is part of a software project. Software metrics are useful to the project manager because they provide clear and precise information about the progress of a project, and are hence useful for monitoring project progress. The two key roles of metrics are prediction and analysis. Metrics measured early in the project can be used to predict the future course of the project while analysing metrics taken at critical points in the software development process can help in monitoring progress.

There are many numbers which can be attached to the software process and its products, but for a metric to be truly useful it should be measurable, independent, accountable and precise. That is: it should be based on facts not opinions; it should not be possible for project team members to alter its value without affecting the quality of the software; details about how and when the metric was measured should be documented; and the level of tolerance allowed when measuring it should be known.

There are two types of metric: predictor metrics and result metrics. Predictor metrics are metrics which can be used to predict the value of other metrics, called result metrics, which are usually measured at the end of a project, or a phase of a project.

We have described two example metrics. McCabe's cyclomatic complexity is a measure of the complexity of the detailed design of a program unit, and can be used to predict the amount of resource necessary to test the unit. Impact matrices are used to quantify the interconnectivity of program units in terms of the effect a change to one has on the other. In particular, they can be used to predict the effort required to maintain a system after it is in operation.

4.7 FURTHER READING

De Marco (1982) is an extremely readable but slightly Utopian book which describes how metrics can be used in an industrial environment. Fenton (1990) stresses the possible basis of metrics in the scientific theory of measurement. It contains a chapter by one of the authors of this book (DCI) which describes the history of metrics and how they can be currently used on industrial projects. Basili and Rombach (1988) is an excellent description of how, by asking the right questions, answers can be obtained which lead to the productive use of metrics on software projects.

BIBLIOGRAPHY

Albrecht, A.J. and Gaffney, J.E. (1983) 'Software function, source lines of code, and development effort prediction: A software science validation', *IEEE Transactions on Software Engineering*, **9**, 6, pp. 639–48.

Basili, V.R. and Rombach, H.D. (1988) 'The TAME project: towards improvement-oriented software environments', *IEEE Transactions on Software Engineering*, **14**, 6, pp. 758–73.

De Marco, T. (1982) *Controlling Software Projects*, Yourdon Press, New York.

Fenton, N.E. (1990) *Software Metrics*, Chapman and Hall, London.

McCabe, T.J. (1976) 'A complexity measure', *IEEE Transactions on Software Engineering*, **2**, 4, pp. 60–5.

Yau, S.S., Collofello, J.S. and MacGregor, T. (1978) 'Ripple effect analysis of software maintenance', *Proceedings COMPSAC 78*, pp. 60–5.

PROJECT PLANNING

AIMS

- To describe the nature of software project planning.
- To outline the contents of the project plan.
- To examine what project planning means to a project manager.
- To outline how a project manager plans a project.

5.1 INTRODUCTION

The initial planning of a software project which is completed as part of the bidding procedure was introduced in Chapter 2. This chapter now explores the planning process in more detail, and looks at the kinds of information which need to be considered during project planning.

The project is initially planned in outline prior to the start of a software project and normally forms part of the proposal for developing the system. At this stage, the important elements of planning are the estimated project cost, the resources required and the project's compatibility with the company's overall business plan. If the developer is given the go-ahead to carry out the project then project planning is considerably expanded during the requirements analysis phase, and the emphasis moves towards more mundane, detailed matters. Obviously, some areas of information which are considered during planning are of interest solely to the developer, while some elements are of interest to both the developer and the customer. For example, how the developer intends to achieve the goals set out by the customer is important for both parties, whereas whether the project is compatible with the developer's business plan is likely to be of only minor interest to the customer. There are also details which, although they may be of interest to the customer, are likely to be kept confidential by the developer. For example, the details of the project's estimated cost and the risk assessment process are unlikely to be shown to the customer since they specify information such as the developer's profit margin!

A software project needs to be planned carefully, and the plan must be documented carefully. A project which is not carefully planned is difficult to manage well, which can lead to problems for the developer and the customer. In order to understand why careful planning is needed, and to identify some of the information requirements that the planning process should address, consider the following questions. These are the kinds of questions which may be asked during the course of a software project and which the project's management should be able to answer:

- This project is concerned with developing a system for administering the movement of ground forces during tactical combat. Who should the analysts talk to at army headquarters about tank movements?

It is important for any software project that clear lines of communication should be established between the developer and the customer, i.e. members of staff on both sides who will be involved in liaison should be identified.

- How far has this project progressed and is it on schedule?

This information could be interesting to the developer's senior management, the project manager, or the customer. The customer is rightly concerned that the system being paid for is delivered on time; the developer's senior management and the project manager are both concerned to avoid litigation and the poor reputation that follows from a late delivery. The method used to decide whether the project is on time must be considered.

- How will the software be validated against the statement of requirements?

SAQ Why is the method of validating the system of significance?

SOLUTION The method to be used for validating the system is of interest to the customer because he or she wants a system which functions as described in the statement of requirements. However, it is also important for the developer. Failure to meet customer requirements, even when a project is on time and within budget, can involve litigation; the consequences of such failure are often more wide-reaching than simply upsetting the company's plan for future projects. There is, therefore, a need to outline how the developer will carry out the activities of validation and verification. This is still an important question even when the customer and the developer work in the same company.

- How many staff will be leaving the graphics project and at what times? There is another project to be staffed which overlaps with the graphics project and it would be helpful to know how many of the staff can be transferred to this project.

In order to carry out activities such as evaluating the feasibility of future projects in terms of manpower availability, the developer's senior management need to know the manpower utilization of the current project.

- What impact will this project have upon the cash flow of the company?

The developer's senior management will be anxious about cash resources in the future. By knowing the net inflows and outflows of cash they can efficiently plan the future activities of the company.

In short, information is needed which details what tasks need to be performed, what resources are needed to perform them, who is to perform them, how long they will take and their relationship to other tasks. All of these questions, and more, should be addressed during project planning, and the information should be documented. The document which contains this information is known as the *project plan*.

Thus, the project plan details information about the project which is vital to managing that project. The project plan is initially devised in outline prior to the start of a software project and is regularly updated during the project.[1] Therefore, project planning takes place before development begins, and throughout system development. During requirements analysis the emphasis in project planning moves away from high-level concerns such as the impact of the project upon the developer's business plan, towards more mundane, detailed matters which are important for the execution of the project.

For example, outline descriptions of tasks are expanded and the skills of the staff who are to carry out the tasks are exactly specified. The emphasis is now on ensuring that the project satisfies its individual objectives of delivery time, cost and adherence to customer requirements rather than meeting the global objectives of the developer and the customer.

5.2 THE PROJECT PLAN

The project plan is one of the key documents on which a project depends (the other key document is the system specification). As already stated, the plan is produced initially in outline and is expanded as development proceeds. The main difference between the contents of an outline project plan and its expanded version is the level of detail recorded. In the discussion which follows, therefore, we shall not distinguish between different versions.

The contents of the project plan should be similar to that shown in Fig. 5.1 in which the principal components of each section are listed underneath the section heading. This document is handed to the potential customer as part of the developer's proposal when bidding for the project, and so areas of information which are not relevant to the customer's viewpoint are not included. Note that there are no sections detailing the project's compatibility with the developer's overall business plan, or details of the cost estimation process. It is worth pointing out that many of the sections of the project plan, at least in outline, will be placed in a project proposal by a project manager bidding for a project.

The contents of the project plan would be as shown in Fig. 5.1 for a large project. Normally, the style of the contents is tailored to particular projects. For example, on a small project the phase plan would often only contain simple bar charts.

The project introduction

This describes in a few paragraphs the job that is to be carried out. It also outlines how the project plan is organized and the intended readership for each section. For example, it should state which sections should be read by the customer's high-level management for an overview of the project. The introduction should also list the assumptions that have been made by the developer in producing the plan.

SAQ Why is it important to list the assumptions made by the developer in producing the plan?

---

[1] It is usually a contractual document.

SOLUTION The project plan determines the course of the project, and if the developer has made assumptions about anything which may affect that plan, then these should be documented for all to see. If they are not documented, then the plan may be invalid and indeed unworkable.

Typical assumptions which you might find in a project plan, are as follows:

1.   The customer should supply test data for system testing in machine-readable form at least four weeks before the beginning of the system testing phase.
2.   The command interpreter will be subcontracted to Language Interface Associates. This company will deliver the interpreter no later than week 47 of the project.
3.   The customer will review all documentation within two weeks of receipt of that documentation.

1. The Project Introduction
- project plan outline
- any assumptions made when the plan was produced
- the project schedule

2. The Project Description
- project products
- acceptance criteria for products
- customer involvement in development tasks

3. The Phase Plan
- project phases and associated tasks
- project milestones and associated dates

4. The Organization Plan
- staff and their responsibilities

5. The Support Requirements Specification
- software development facilities required
- hardware development facilities required

6. The Development Process Specification
- development techniques and standards to be used

7. The Change Control Plan
- methods for handling change during the project

8. The Documentation Plan
- methods of documentation production
- document format

9. Appendices
- test plan
- quality plan
- example development notations

Figure 5.1 The contents of the project plan.

The first and third assumptions give the customer precise information about how actions within his or her control will affect the execution of the software project; they establish that there are some occasions when the customer may be responsible for project slippage. The second assumption documents the reliance which the developer is placing on an outside contractor. External factors can affect the success of a software project and it is therefore wise to document any reliance which is being placed on them. Normally, these assumptions have to be agreed with a customer before the main project is started.

Finally, the introduction should describe an overall schedule for the project. This schedule should list the project's milestones and their associated dates.

SAQ For each assumption listed below, give one good reason why it is important for it to be documented, i.e. what impact could it have on the course of the project?

(a)   The minicomputer which will be supplied by the customer for developmental activities will be the same in every respect as the minicomputer on which the software will be installed (see Appendix A3).

(b)   All liaison with customer staff for the purposes of requirements analysis will be with the same designated person, unless extreme circumstances occur such as staff leaving the customer's employment.

(c)   The customer will use the program design language chosen by the developer for all software which is produced by the customer but is intended to be maintained by the developer.

SOLUTION

(a)   This assumption should be included because different models of the same computer have different performance characteristics depending on which low-level instruction set is used. This assumption is being made so that the developer can be sure that the performance characteristics being measured during system testing will be the same as those being examined during acceptance testing.

(b)   Requirements analysis is a difficult enough task when only one person communicates with the developer. However, when substitutes are sent to meetings to discuss requirements it can be even more difficult. This assumption is made so that the developer gains a consistent view of customer requirements.

(c)   This assumption is documented in the project plan to ensure that a system which is to be produced jointly by the developer and the customer has a consistent notation describing its design. This is important because the estimated cost for the maintenance phase of the project may have been based on this assumption. If a mixture of notations were used then the developer would probably have produced an increased estimate.

The project description

The project description specifies what work is to be carried out, what products will be delivered to the customer and the acceptance criteria used to judge the adequacy of the delivered software. It will also define all the development tasks to be carried out and any customer involvement in those tasks. This should agree with and refer to the system specification since customers may get confused about what is being delivered: the software described in the project description or the software described in the system specification.

The phase plan

This contains the list of the tasks that make up a software project. For each task the phase plan should detail when the task should be carried out, who will perform the task and the sequencing of the tasks relative to other tasks. The phase plan should also include milestones and their associated dates. The phase plan is an important part of the project plan, and therefore will be explained in detail in Chapter 6. It is quite a common practice in the computer industry to include a list of project deliverables in this section and also a list of any non-staff resources such as equipment required for the project.

The organization plan

The organization plan for the project shows how the project should be organized and the responsibilities of each member of staff employed on the project. The major functions of such a plan are to describe the amount of interaction that occurs between people involved in the project, and to establish limits for the responsibilities of each member of the project. The organization plan will normally be structured hierarchically and show the subdivision of the project into groups and the subdivision of groups into project staff within each group.[2] An extract from an organization plan which details the responsibilities of the design group is given below:

DESIGN GROUP

The design group are responsible for:
* The production of the system design document.
* The production of the detailed design document.
* The conduct of all design reviews.
* The implementation of all changes to the system design document after the system design phase has been completed.
* The implementation of all changes to the detailed design document after the detailed design phase has been completed.
* The development of all user documentation specified in Appendix S1 of this document.

The design group will consist of a principal consultant designer and one other designer.

---

[2] While other ways of organizing projects are possible, for example, the matrix organization, the vast majority of software projects are organized as a hierarchy.

SYSTEM DESIGN PHASE

During the system design phase the individual responsibilities of the design group will be:

Principal Consultant Designer

- The production of the overall architecture for the system.
- The production of the program unit specifications for the communications sub-system.
- Chairing all design reviews of the system.
- Defining the overall structure of the user documentation.

Designer A

- The production of the data design for the system.
- The production of the program unit specifications for the command and control subsystem and the retrieval subsystem.
- Attendance at all design reviews which examine these subsystems.
- Attendance at the design review of the query processing subsystem.
- The production of the terminal operator's user guide.

IMPLEMENTATION PHASE

Principal Consultant Designer

- The implementation of any system design and detailed design changes to the software discovered during this phase.
- The review of all user documentation.

Designer A

- The production of the management reports user guide.

By structuring the organization plan in such a way questions about responsibilities can be answered quickly and efficiently.

SAQ Which sections of the project plan should be consulted in order to answer the following questions? If none of the sections so far discussed contain the answer then answer 'none'.

(a)   How many program units are there in a particular subsystem?

(b)   What are the responsibilities of the analysts attached to the project?

(c)   How long will the detailed design of a particular subsystem take?

(d)   Should we assume that the customer will provide a test database for acceptance testing?

(e)   What tasks are carried out in parallel with the integration of the command subsystem?

(f)   What is the cost of designing the retrieval subsystem?

(g)   Is the principal consultant designer responsible for the system design of the retrieval subsystem?

    (h)   What equipment is available during the integration phase?

SOLUTION

    (a)   None.

    (b)   The organization plan.

    (c)   The phase plan.

    (d)   The project introduction.

    (e)   The phase plan.

    (f)   None.

    (g)   The organization plan.

    (h)   None.

The support requirements specification

This section lists all the support facilities required to complete the project. This includes software development facilities, hardware development facilities and support from both the developer's company and the customer's company in terms of services outside the software development team, such as secretarial support.

> SAQ What items of software support should the support requirements specification contain?

> SOLUTION Typically, it would include software tools used during the development process, such as test data generators and program libraries. The support requirements specification should also include a description of the operating system to be used for development.

As well as the software support required, the following should also be listed:

1. The specification of the computer system on which the software is to be developed, together with the dates on which it is to be made available.
2. The amount of computer resource required, and the exact computer configuration to be used.
3. Support required from within the developer's company and the customer's company.
4. If any of the software for a project is subcontracted then the support expected from the subcontractor should be specified.
5. Support requirements from the developer which include the use of staff such as secretaries, filing clerks and hardware engineers.
6. Support requirements from the customer which include the use of staff for liaison during requirements analysis and acceptance testing.

The development process specification

This details the techniques and methods used to develop the software. This is particularly important for the outline project plan since it is often used by the customer during the bidding process to evaluate the professionalism of a company's approach to software development. Such a specification is intended to answer questions such as the following:

- How will the developer ensure that the statement of requirements will be met by the system produced?
- Is the developer using an up-to-date technique for design?
- Is the developer using state-of-the-art software tools?
- How will the developer ensure that the customer will adequately validate the system specification?

In order to answer such questions the development process specification should include a description of the methods, tools and notations used by the developer. Usually, this section will contain references to the software development standards normally employed by the developer, which will be bound as an appendix to the project plan.

The change control plan

The change control plan describes how the developer will organize the inevitable process of change that occurs during a project.

The documentation plan

This plan outlines how project documentation is to be produced and the format of this documentation. It will define how documents are to be published, typed, proofread, edited and to whom documents are to be circulated.

Appendices

The appendices of the specification will include a test plan, a quality plan and example development notation to be used on the project. The test plan, introduced in Chapter 3, describes how the developer will ensure that the software that is to be constructed will match the customer's requirements. It defines test tools, test procedures and the responsibilities of the personnel involved in the testing process. The quality plan describes how the developer will ensure that the software product conforms to the standards which he or she employs, or which are specified by the customer.

5.3 SUMMARY

This section of the book has looked in outline at the main components of the project plan. We have seen that such a plan consists of the project introduction, project description, phase plan, organization plan, support requirements specification, development process specification, change control plan, documentation plan, and a number of appendices including a test plan, quality plan, and example development notations. The overall contents of a project plan is shown in Fig. 5.1. Some items of information considered during project planning are not included in the project plan because this document is handed to the customer, and some areas covered during planning are not relevant to the customer's business.

THE PHASE PLAN

AIMS

- To introduce the idea of a phase plan.
- To describe the contents of the phase plan.
- To demonstrate how PERT networks can be used to store information held in the phase plan.

6.1 INTRODUCTION

Producing a software system involves a large number of tasks, for example, developing the system specification, integration testing a system with a new program unit, preparing the user manual and so on. In order to monitor the progress of a project, to estimate the resources required and to cost a project, the project manager requires information about these tasks, such as the nature of the tasks to be carried out, the specific expertise required for each task, the relationship between tasks, i.e. those that can be carried out in parallel and those which have to be carried out in advance of others, and the resources needed. Therefore, the project manager must identify and examine all the tasks which are necessary to complete the system.

Before looking at the complete process of developing a phase plan, let us consider a project in which the system architecture, as shown in Fig. 6.1, has been identified. We shall look briefly at how you might develop a phase plan which considers the detailed design, implementation and integration testing of this system.

The first step is to identify the tasks which need to be completed. Obviously, the tasks required to complete this project include producing the detailed design for program unit A, producing the code for program unit A, unit testing program unit A, producing the detailed design for program unit B, producing the code for program unit B and so on. In addition, tasks concerned with integration testing for the system must be specified. The exact list of tasks depends on the integration strategy to be adopted. For example, if program units are to be integrated one at a time then the tasks associated with integration testing might include: integrate program unit B with the rest of the system, integrate program unit C with the rest of the system and so on. Therefore, before the complete list of tasks for this project can be produced, the integration strategy must be decided upon. We shall assume that a bottom-up strategy is to be used, i.e. that program unit E will be integrated with program unit B before B is integrated with program unit A.

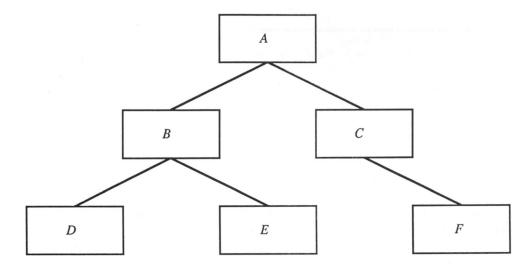

Figure 6.1 A system architecture.

The second step is to identify the sequence in which tasks must be performed. Some tasks are fixed in relation to other tasks. For example, producing the detailed design for a program unit, producing the code for that program unit and unit testing it have to be carried out in a strict sequential order. However, the order in which each program unit is implemented depends on the resources available and the integration strategy adopted.

For example, if six designers were available for the time it took to produce a detailed design for a program unit, then all six program units could be designed in parallel. Similarly, if six programmers were available for the time it took to produce the code for a program unit and to unit test a program unit, then these activities could also be carried out in parallel. However, if only one designer were available, then the detailed designs for the program units could only be produced in strict sequential order.

If only one programmer and one designer were available and a bottom-up integration strategy was adopted then one possible set of tasks for our example, and their sequencing is as follows:

1.   Produce the detailed design for program unit F.
2.   Produce the code for program unit F.
3.   Unit test program unit F.
4.   Produce the detailed design for program unit E.
5.   Produce the code for program unit E.
6.   Unit test program unit E.
7.   Produce the detailed design for program unit D.
8.   Produce the code for program unit D.
9.   Unit test program unit D.
10.   Produce the detailed design for program unit C.
11.   Produce the code for program unit C.
12.   Unit test program unit C.

13. Produce the detailed design for program unit B.
14. Produce the code for program unit B.
15. Unit test program unit B.
16. Integrate program unit F with program unit C.
17. Integrate program units D and E with program unit B.
18. Produce the detailed design for program unit A.
19. Produce the code for program unit A.
20. Unit test program unit A.
21. Integrate program units B and C with program unit A.

The above representation for listing the tasks and for indicating their order of implementation is rather clumsy and difficult to use. There are, of course, better ways to express this information and they will be introduced later on in this section.

As you can see from this fairly small example, simply listing and sequencing the tasks in a project can be a huge task in itself, and for the example here the program units to be implemented had already been identified; just imagine how many tasks would need to be considered if we included those necessary to produce this architecture as well! In order to develop the phase plan for a complete project, the following steps should be taken:

1. Produce a system specification and system design document. From these activities a number of major tasks can be identified.
2. Identify tasks to be carried out. Initially this means identifying large tasks such as 'produce user guide' or 'develop system specification'.
3. Partition each task into subtasks such as 'carry out the design of subsystem A', then partition these subtasks into smaller subsubtasks and so on, until no more sensible partitioning is possible.
4. Establish the relationship between these tasks. This involves identifying considerations such as the order in which tasks should be carried out and which tasks can be carried out in parallel.
5. Estimate the resources required for each task. This involves estimating not only the amount of staff time needed but also the support facilities and, for later phases of the project, the amount of computer time required.
6. Specify the expertise of the staff who carry out the tasks.

SAQ Why should at least outline requirements analysis and system design be performed prior to developing the detailed phase plan?

SOLUTION In order to specify tasks such as 'test subsystem 7' and 'produce the detailed design for program unit B', the project manager will need to know at least an outline architecture for the system. The architecture can only be specified after some degree of requirements analysis and system design have been carried out.

The steps listed above will be used to produce the phase plan for the initial project plan, which is based on an outline design, and will then normally be repeated throughout the project in order to refine it. Obviously, as the project continues, more and more detailed tasks can be identified, and the phase plan can be expanded. Once the phase plan has been completed the project manager should have documentation which answers questions such as the following:

- What is the effect of an outside subcontractor delivering the software late?
- How much manpower is used during system design?
- Which tasks need to be rescheduled because the customer has changed the statement of requirements?

6.2 TASK IDENTIFICATION

A wide variety of tasks connected with software development may be identified for any one project. For example, consider the following list:

- Prepare the system test files.
- Unit test program unit 7A.
- Develop the system design document.
- Design the architecture for the invoice subsystem.
- Decide on the queueing strategy to be used for the report generator subsystem.
- Identify the constraints present in the statement of requirements.

The list above consists of a mixture of large and small tasks, for example, 'develop the system design document' is a major task, while 'unit test program unit 7A' is a smaller task. The smaller tasks normally form a subset of the larger ones, and can be represented in a hierarchic manner. In fact, tasks are usually identified in a hierarchic fashion as well, since it is unlikely that a subtask of a task will be identified before the main task itself is identified.

In order to represent the hierarchic relationship between tasks many software projects employ a tree-like graphical notation known as a *work breakdown structure*. All tasks associated with the project, those concerned with producing the actual software and those which deal with other tasks such as documentation, must be included in this breakdown.

Figure 6.2 shows a typical work breakdown structure for a project which includes an element of hardware development. Note that each node contains the name of the task and the name of the person responsible for the task, and that all nodes apart from the topmost one also contain a unique reference number. Note also that no sequencing is implied by the order in which tasks appear in a work breakdown structure.

At the top level there is a node which represents the task of producing the system; Wilson is the member of staff responsible for this task. At the next level there are a series of nodes which represent the subtasks concerned with producing the system. For example, the task of managing the project on a day-to-day basis is the responsibility of Roberts and has the reference number 4, and the task of software development is shown in box 3. Each node at this level should then be split up into a series of further subtasks. For simplicity's sake, this is only shown for the task represented in box 3, software development, which is split up into requirements analysis, system design, detailed design and implementation.

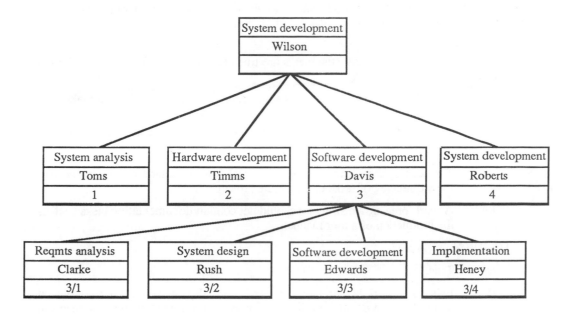

Figure 6.2 A work breakdown structure.

SAQ What tasks might you expect to appear at the next level of the hierarchy from box 3/2?

SOLUTION The next level will contain tasks associated with the design of the system's data structure, and with detailed design tasks. They will be numbered 3/2/1 and 3/2/2.

Each task in a work breakdown structure has to be uniquely numbered. The reason for this is that during project execution the project manager will want to account for each task individually, in order to report on project expenditure and task completion. A good numbering scheme is illustrated in Fig. 6.2 where each task, apart from that at the first level of the work breakdown structure, contains the number of the immediate higher task together with a digit which identifies the task.

Since most developers will only have performed an outline requirements analysis and an outline system design when the initial phase plan is developed, a number of levels of the work breakdown structure may be missing. For example, in Fig. 6.2 the work breakdown structure that lies underneath box 3/2 would not feature detailed design tasks for particular program units since their existence would not yet be specified. However, as the project progresses the lower levels of the work breakdown structure can be filled in.

Normally, after system design has taken place the work breakdown structure should be complete. However, modifications to a proposed system always occur during a project; for example, new program units may be added to a package. Consequently, the work breakdown structure will always need to be modified. It has already been stressed that the project plan is a dynamic document; the work breakdown structure is no exception to this.

SAQ Which of the following statements are true and which are false? If you think a statement is false explain why.

(a)   A work breakdown structure is a hierarchic view of the tasks that make up a software project.

(b)   The work breakdown structure should be complete prior to the start of requirements analysis.

(c)   The developer can examine the work breakdown structure in order to discover the sequencing of tasks in a software project.

(d)   A work breakdown structure should not contain documentation tasks such as the production of a user manual.

SOLUTION

(a)   True.

(b)   False. The work breakdown structure is normally only produced in outline at this stage. The details are filled in during requirements analysis and system design.

(c)   False. The work breakdown structure contains no sequencing information. It should only contain the hierarchic breakdown of tasks.

(d)   False. All tasks should be entered into a work breakdown structure, not just developmental tasks such as system design or implementation. Documentation consumes a major part of a project's resources and a work breakdown structure would be incomplete without it.

6.3 TASK SEQUENCING

Once a work breakdown structure has been completed, the next stage in the production of the phase plan is to describe the temporal relationship of each task to other tasks in the plan. This means considering which tasks have to precede other tasks, which tasks can be carried out in parallel, which tasks can only start after a specific date and which tasks have to be completed by a specific date. The following examples have been taken from real projects:

*   The system design of the command and control subsystem cannot be started until that part of the system specification which specifies it has been completed.
*   The operator interface subsystem needs to be demonstrated to the customer early in the project. This means that all the designers on the project will initially be involved in designing this subsystem and, consequently, the design of all the remaining subsystems has to follow this task.
*   The monitoring subsystem and the reports subsystem can be developed in parallel since they are almost completely isolated from each other.

The ordering of tasks in the software project will be dictated by the following four classes of factors.

1. *Development constraints.* These are inherent in the development process itself. In producing a software system the developer is faced with no choice over the sequencing of particular tasks. For example, the implementation of a module has to be carried out after it has been designed.

2. *Customer constraints.* These are imposed by the customer and are normally contained implicitly in the statement of requirements. For example, a customer may require the developer to deliver a software system in three versions with each version exhibiting increased functionality. This would normally mean that the developer must develop the first version, followed by the enhancements needed to the first version in order to produce the second version and then the enhancements required to produce the third version.

3. *External constraints.* These are imposed by events external to a project. One typical example is the date on which computer equipment for acceptance testing is installed. Obviously, acceptance testing cannot begin until the relevant equipment is installed. Another example is the customer insisting that the system specification be read and accepted before development proceeds. This means that system design can only start when the customer has signed off the system specification.

4. *Resource constraints.* These are caused by a project not having sufficient resources to carry out a number of activities in parallel. For example, consider a software project in which six subsystems are to be designed and only two designers are allocated to the project. If one designer can only process one subsystem at a time then this implies that a maximum of only two subsystems can be designed in parallel at any one time.

SAQ   Classify the following constraints as development constraints, customer constraints, external constraints or resource constraints:

(a)   Because only three designers are allocated to the project, subsystem 5 can only be designed after subsystem 7.

(b)   Since the customer's liaison officer is only available after week 50, acceptance testing can only start after this date.

(c)   Integration testing of program unit Z can only be done after it has been unit tested.

(d)   Integration testing of program unit Z can only be done after program unit F has been unit tested, since F is the only program unit which uses Z.

(e)   Since the Pascal compiler will not have been validated by the supplier until week 78 we cannot start the implementation phase until then.

SOLUTION

(a)   Resource constraint.

(b)   Customer constraint.

(c)   Development constraint.

(d)   Development constraint.

(e)   External constraint.

A convenient graphical notation used to represent the temporal relationship between tasks in a software system has been devised; it is known as a *PERT network*. PERT stands for Project Evaluation Review Technique.

An example of a PERT network is shown in Fig. 6.3. It shows part of the detailed design, implementation and integration testing activities for a subsystem consisting of three program units. Each circle represents the end of an activity. A line joining two circles represents an activity. When a set of activities can be carried out in parallel then their lines all emanate from the same circle. When an activity has to be carried out after a particular activity then the first activity leads into a circle and the next activity emanates from the circle.

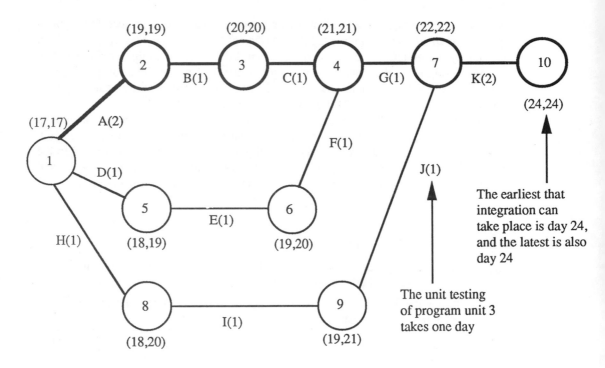

Activities

A – Produce detailed design of program unit 1
B – Produce code for program unit 1
C – Unit test program unit 1
D – Produce detailed design of program unit 2
E – Produce code for program unit 2
F – Unit test program unit 2

G – Integrate program unit 1 with program unit 2
H – Produce detailed design of program unit 3
I – Produce code for program unit 3
J – Unit test program unit 3
K – Integrate program unit 3 with program units 1
     and 2

Figure 6.3 A PERT network.

In Fig. 6.3 the first circle on the left of the figure represents the end of system design for the subsystem. The lines emanating from this circle represent the tasks of producing the detailed designs for the individual program units; these tasks can be carried out in parallel. The individual development of the program units can also be carried out in parallel, as shown. However, for each program unit, the tasks of producing the detailed design, producing the code and unit testing are shown in the PERT network as sequential activities since they cannot be carried out in parallel. After all, a program unit cannot be unit tested at the same time as it is being designed!

Such a network enables the project manager to show graphically each task, together with its relationship to other tasks, the duration of the task, its earliest starting day, its latest starting day, its earliest finishing day and its latest finishing day. It may also be useful to mark the amount of resource to be used by each task on the network.

Since PERT networks are so widely used, there are many software tools[1] available that are able to process them and produce data for the project manager. Given information such as the name of each task, its duration, the amount of resource it requires, the earliest date it can be started and its relationship to other tasks, these tools can produce information such as the following:

- The total resource utilization of the project.
- The tasks and the time spans during which they can be carried out.
- A calendar showing the tasks to be carried out in temporal order.
- For each task, the amount of time that the task can be delayed without affecting the completion date of the project.

Probably the most important piece of information that all PERT tools produce is the *critical path*. This is a series of tasks which lead from the start of the project to its completion. If any of these tasks is delayed, the completion date for the project will also be delayed. In Fig. 6.3 the critical path is displayed in bold.

A PERT chart is often used by project managers to give an overall picture of the software project during its planning stage. However, full value can only be extracted from a PERT tool if the manager uses it to examine what may happen under the various circumstances which may affect the project. For example, the project manager might examine the effect of events which are not under the developer's control. If an analyst assigned to the project leaves for another company during the early stages of the project, and a replacement would be delayed by a few weeks, what overall effect would this have on the project's schedule?

SAQ The main parameters for a PERT network are the duration of each task, the amount of resource it requires, the earliest date it can be started and its relationship to other tasks. Suggest some events outside the project manager's control whose effects can be examined by changing the parameters of a PERT network.

SOLUTION Events which occur outside the developer's company whose effect can be examined using a PERT network include the following:

---

[1] These tools are virtually mandatory since the project plan will change during the lifetime of a project.

- The late delivery of a piece of equipment needed during acceptance testing.

- A subcontractor delivering a software system late.

- The customer taking more time than planned in examining and accepting a project document.

- The customer taking less time than planned in delivering acceptance test data.

Other events which occur internally in the developer's company but which are still outside the project manager's control include the following:

- A programmer or group of programmers being reassigned to a more important project and being replaced by inexperienced staff.

- Key staff leaving for other jobs during the project.

- Staff promised for a project arriving early because their current project was finished early.

The solution to the SAQ above lists many of the more common 'uncontrollable' events that occur in a software project, but while such events might be uncontrollable, many of them can be predicted. It is vitally important for the project manager that their effects be quantified and all external parties be made aware of them. This requires the project manager not only to experiment with a tool such as a PERT network processor but also to list all assumptions about customer and subcontractor behaviour. The importance of listing assumptions in the project plan was mentioned in the last section, and it is worth stressing the point again. The use of a PERT network processor can help to emphasize the significance of particular assumptions and therefore the wisdom of documenting them.

The following important points should be made about a PERT network:

1. Like the work breakdown structure a PERT network will evolve gradually during the course of a project. During the bidding and planning stages of the project it will normally contain high-level tasks such as 'develop the update package'; however, as the project proceeds the level of detail will increase. Normally, the PERT network will be complete at the end of the system design phase when the work breakdown structure will also be complete.
2. There will be an exact correspondence between tasks expressed in the work breakdown structure and activities in the PERT network. This provides continuity for accounting purposes.
3. The PERT network is a dynamic entity. Many managers use it for planning and then consign it to a cupboard. A project is never static for a number of reasons; for example, the customer may not complete tasks on time, subcontractors are often late, staff leave a project and new staff arrive and so on. Consequently, the PERT network has to be kept up to date so that events such as the discovery of a new critical path or an increase in project duration[2] can be identified as early as possible.

---

[2] For example, when a problem such as equipment being delivered late occurs.

After the work breakdown structure and PERT network have been produced the project's milestones and associated dates can be identified. This is the last component of the phase plan.

6.4 SUMMARY

The phase plan is the section of the project plan which details information about the tasks necessary to complete the project. For each task, the phase plan will include its name, its duration, the resources it requires, its earliest starting day, its latest finishing day, and its relationship to other tasks. The project's milestones and associated dates are also listed in the phase plan.

Most software projects employ a work breakdown structure to document the complete set of tasks. This notation clearly shows which tasks are subtasks of other tasks, and also who is responsible for ensuring that each task is carried out.

Sequencing information about tasks can be expressed using a PERT network. This is a graphical device which can show the relationship between tasks, the duration of each task, its earliest starting day, its latest starting day, its earliest finishing day, its latest finishing day, and the resources it requires. The PERT network for a project can be used during the planning stage of the project, but it is also useful during later stages when it can be used to identify potential problems as circumstances change.

Like the rest of the project plan, the phase plan is produced in outline before software development begins and is refined as development progresses. It should be complete by the end of the system design phase, but modifications to it may be precipitated by changes in the project's circumstances.

7

COST ESTIMATION, RISK ASSESSMENT AND THE SOFTWARE PROJECT

AIMS

- To describe how software projects can be assessed for risk.
- To describe a relatively simple costing procedure for software projects.
- To outline some advanced costing techniques.

7.1 INTRODUCTION

It is important that a developer can estimate accurately the resources required to complete a project before the full details of that project are available. For instance, when bidding for a project the organization cannot afford the manpower, and probably would have neither the time nor the facilities, to perform detailed requirements analysis and system design. It is therefore necessary to be able to produce an accurate estimate based only on outline project information. This chapter looks more closely at the two most significant parts of this estimation process.

7.2 THE RISK ASSESSMENT OF PROJECTS

An important task to be carried out in project planning is the identification and documentation of any factors which may result in the software product being delivered late and/or over budget. This is called *risk assessment*. These factors can usually be divided into certain categories, the commonest of which are now described.

7.2.1 Characteristics of the application

There are many characteristics of an application area which determine how risky the software project for the application may be. These include the nature of the application area, the size of the application, the complexity of the application and the similarity of the application to previous projects carried out by the developer.

In general there is a hierarchy of project difficulty. The most difficult projects are those which produce software for real-time applications, such as weapons systems, where there are stringent requirements for response time. The next most difficult projects are those in commercial data processing, for example, applications in insurance and banking. The easiest projects tend to be for numerical applications such as calculating stresses in a bridge during peak loading. In judging an application area for risk the following questions should be asked:

- Is this application required to interface with another application which is regarded as risky? For example, if the project is a commercial data processing project does a significant part of it deal with communications?
- Is this a novel application within a particular application area?
- How experienced is the developer in the application area?
- How large is the application? For example, does it involve a large number of computers and stored databases which are to communicate with each other using non-standard interfaces?

SAQ Consider the following application areas. Which would you expect to be the riskiest in terms of software development?

(a)   A statistics package.

(b)   The controlling software for a commercial airliner.

(c)   An invoicing system for the local bank.

SOLUTION Since it is a real-time system, the controlling software for the commercial airliner would be the riskiest project.

7.2.2 The degree of external involvement in the project

The more a project relies on the actions of external agencies, i.e. agencies which are outside the developer's control, the riskier the project becomes. Typical actions include the installation of communication lines, the provision of existing documentation for a system which is to be modified, the approval of key documents such as the system specification and the provision of test data for system testing and acceptance testing.

SAQ Under what circumstances may it be less risky for the developer to consult an external agency than to avoid doing so?

SOLUTION In cases where the developer may not have the expertise to perform a particular task, contracting out that task is the only feasible way for it to be carried out. Under these circumstances the use of an outside contractor to perform a task is less risky than the developer carrying out the task.

7.2.3 Customer-specific factors

A major problem in developing a software system is the inexperience of the customer, which may result in a number of things. Firstly, the customer may not grasp what it means to produce an engineered product, and consequently insist on requirements changes late in the implementation stage. Even when a developer has a watertight contract which controls such changes, a large amount of effort can be spent by the developer in convincing the customer of this fact.

An inexperienced customer is also unlikely to comprehend large amounts of software documentation easily. This usually results in the developer's staff spending much valuable time in explaining the documentation in minute detail. It also results in delays in acceptance of project documents.

When a customer who is inexperienced in computer applications realizes that inexperience, he or she will often hire a consultancy company to look after his or her interests. Although this marginally improves the situation, it does not lower the risk level of a project significantly. By introducing a third party between the developer and the customer, further delays may be introduced simply due to the extra communication effort required. This solution does not even begin to address the real problem of customer ignorance, since it simply moves the responsibility of explaining documents to the customer from the developer to the consultant.

7.2.4 Developer-specific factors

There are a number of factors which are connected with the developer's staff which contribute to the risk of a software project. A major factor is the inexperience of the staff assigned to the project, and their roles. For instance, a project which has inexperienced analysts and managers is riskier than a project which has inexperienced programmers.

A further staff factor which increases the risk of a project is the continuity of staff on the project. Obviously, if staff are going to leave a project there will be a delay while new staff are hired and then trained. This problem is exacerbated by overreliance on a key member of staff. A project is obviously at risk if a few members of staff are vitally important to its success, since the departure of such staff can turn a smooth-running project into a disaster.

7.2.5 Hardware factors

A factor which is often forgotten when assessing the risk of a project is the hardware upon which a system is to be implemented. There is so much emphasis placed on the problems of software development, that it is easy to forget that there can be serious hardware problems as well.

For instance, although it may seem to be a good idea to have the latest computer model for developing the system, this is not necessarily an advantage. Often this means that little high-level software is available, and that the software that is available contains substantial errors.

Another risk is that the developer uses a computer which is not powerful enough for developmental activities. Although the system which the new application is to be run on is to be upgraded in terms of hardware, the customer may, for economic reasons, delay the purchase of the new hardware until the last possible moment (system or acceptance testing).

An underpowered computer will mean that memory utilization will be low, input/output channels may be congested and machine response will be slow. This has two deleterious effects on a project. Firstly, developmental activities will take a much longer time and secondly, if the project is to deliver real-time software with precise performance requirements, then there is unlikely to be much opportunity to judge early on in the project whether these requirements will be met.

7.2.6 Software factors

An important category of risks are concerned with the software that is to be used on the project. For example, a project which uses a poor software subsystem provided by a customer is riskier than a project which may use off-the-shelf software.

7.2.7 Maintenance factors

If a developer contracts for a project concerned with the maintenance of an existing system in which substantial changes are required, and the developer was not the original producer of the software, then that project is riskier than a new project of comparable size.

Many developers have a checklist for project managers to complete in order to assess the risk of a project. Answers to questions on these checklists are usually associated with numerical values. On completion of the checklist, a project can be given an index of riskiness which can then be compared with other previously completed projects. Such checklists are useful to project management, as they are not only a good indicator of the risk inherent in a project, but also a good check that a project has been planned properly. Example entries from a checklist are given below:

```
STAFF FACTORS

1. List the staff number for each member of staff who will be
carrying out the developmental tasks under each job category. Also
estimate the total number of years' experience each member of staff
has and also the total number of years' experience with this
particular type of application.
      Project manager   :
      Analysts    :
      Designers   :
      Programmers     :
      Others (specify)  :
      Staff number    :
      Total years' experience  :
      Total years' experience with application area :
  .
  .
  .

2. Estimate the project manager availability, experience and
training. Tick the relevant items.
      ( ) The project manager is not yet identified.
      The project manager has been identified and has the following
      experience level:
          ( )   Successful experience in managing a similar
                project.
          ( )   Successful recent experience in managing part of a
                similar project.
          ( )   Formal training.
          ( )   No recent applicable project management training or
                experience.

3. Estimate the senior programmer availability, experience and
training. Tick the relevant items for each senior programmer.
      ( ) Senior programmer not yet identified and recruited.
```

Senior programmer recruited with the following experience level:

( ) Successful experience as a senior programmer on a similar project.

( ) Successful experience as a senior programmer on projects which are different to this one.

( ) Successful experience as a programmer on a similar project.

( ) Successful experience as a programmer on projects which are different to this one.

4. What proportion of the analysts will continue to be on the project during the system design phase?

5. What proportion of the designers will continue to be on the project during the implementation phase? ...

CUSTOMER FACTORS

1. Is this the first time that we have developed software for this customer?

2. Is this the first time that we have developed software for this division of the customer's company?

3. User personnel who work with the project team are considered to be:

( ) Knowledgeable about the computerization of this type of application.

( ) Not knowledgeable about the computerization of this type of application but are knowledgeable about computerization of other categories of application.

( ) Knowledgeable about the application area.

( ) Relatively inexperienced.

4. For each phase of the project and for each member of the customer's staff involved in the project answer the following questions:

What proportion of time has been allocated to project liaison for this person during this phase?

Has the customer agreed that there will be no substitution of the person by other, perhaps less experienced, members of the customer's organization?...

COMPUTER FACTORS

1. What is our experience of developing software on this range of computer?

( ) We have developed software on this particular model.

( ) We have developed software on another model in the same range.

( ) We have not developed software on this range of computer.

2. Is the software to be developed on the computer on which it is to be implemented?

( ) To be developed on the computer on which the software is to be implemented.

```
( )    To be developed on the same model of computer but not on
       the actual computer on which the software is to be
       implemented.
( )    To be developed on a computer which is in the same range
       of computer on which the software is to be developed.
( )    To be developed on a dissimilar computer.
```

```
3. How long has the computer been on the market? Answer this
question for the specific model of computer on which development is
to take place and not the range.
```

```
4. Are there any restrictions on computer use?
       ( )    No restrictions.
       ( )    During certain periods of the working day we cannot use
              the computer.
       ( )    During certain periods of the working day we cannot use
              the computer configuration on which the software will be
              operational. For example, other existing applications
              prevent full operational memory utilization.
```

SAQ Write down questions in the style of the above checklist which investigate the amount of interaction that occurs with external agencies on a project.

SOLUTION A small selection is shown below.

External interactions:

1. How many representatives of the customer are involved in signing off project documents?
2. How many representatives of the customer are involved in requirements analysis?
3. How many representatives of the customer are involved in acceptance testing?
4. How many subcontractors are involved in providing hardware deliverables for the project?
5. How many subcontractors are involved in providing software deliverables for the project?
6. How many external agencies deliver other services, for example, the provision of communication lines by British Telecom?

A risk assessment is vitally important for the vast majority of projects. Without it, a project many run into serious resource difficulties when problems arise. The project manager should use the risk assessment as a basis for increasing the cost estimate of the project if necessary so that later problems can be covered adequately.

7.3 THE COST ESTIMATE

A major task to be performed during project planning is to estimate the cost of the system to be delivered. This section outlines two procedures for cost estimating. The first is based on a pragmatic technique which is used on many non-software projects, and the second takes a mathematical approach.

The cost of a software project can be subdivided into seven categories, as follows:

1.   *Staff costs.* This not only includes the cost of development staff such as programmers and designers, but support staff such as typists and technical writers.

2. *External subcontractor costs.* For example, the costs associated with subcontracting hardware development to an experienced electronics fabrication company.
3. *Computer time costs.* This is a major cost item which includes time not only for developmental activities such as integration testing but also support activities such as running a PERT program or entering and maintaining project documentation.
4. *Data entering costs.* This includes activities such as clerks typing in test data for system testing and acceptance testing and secretaries typing in documentation.
5. *Physical facilities costs.* This normally includes office space and furniture but can also include special facilities such as providing classified storage for a high-security project.
6. *Consumables costs.* Consumables such as printer paper and diskettes will be needed by the project team and an allowance in project cost should be made for them.
7. *Travel and subsistence costs.* Many projects involve developer staff travelling to a customer site in order to carry out requirements analysis, attend progress meetings and take part in acceptance testing; if the project is physically remote from the developer the subsistence costs for this can be substantial.

A relatively simple costing procedure is outlined below; it consists of 12 steps:

1. *Define an outline set of software requirements.* At this stage where a precise estimate of cost is impossible to calculate it is only worth performing a rough requirements analysis.

2. *Produce a rough system design.* From the outline requirements produce a rough system design. For each program unit identified during this process estimate the number of lines of program code.

3. Produce the work breakdown structure for the system that has been designed. Since the system design has only been developed in outline at this stage, the work breakdown structure will again only be in an outline form.

4. *Construct an outline PERT chart.* Define the development tasks and activities to be carried out and then construct an outline PERT chart from the work breakdown structure.

5. *Determine the effort and experience of the staff required for each task.* For developmental tasks many organizations have their own rules of thumb regarding productivity figures. These should be used with a little care. For example, if a manager is told to use the figure that programmers produce 10 lines of program code per person-day then the manager has every right to question the assumptions upon which this figure is based. For example, is it a language-specific figure or is it an average over a large number of projects with a good spread of languages? An allowance should be made if the assumptions upon which the productivity figure are based do not hold for the project being estimated.

6. *Estimate the amount of time spent on non-developmental tasks.* For example meetings with the customer, travel and off-site training of the customer's staff will all take time which needs to be accounted for.

7. *Estimate the development support tasks.* These include computer time, data entry and other clerical support.

8. *Convert the estimates for both developmental and non-developmental tasks into money.* Using the PERT chart generate a month-by-month time bar chart for the project and apportion the costs for each task to the month in which the task is to be carried out. If any task occupies a number of months then the cost should be shared between the months on a proportional basis.

9. *Add a contingency factor to the estimates.* Again each organization applies an upward weighting to estimates, in order to cover factors such as staff illness or leaving. If a contingency factor is applied, it is important that all the factors that were taken into account to produce it are written down. The cost estimate will be validated by senior management and, in order to judge the appropriateness of the contingency factor, they will need to know exactly what was taken into consideration and what was ignored.

10. *Examine all the risk factors that are associated with the project and decide how they impinge on the phases of the project.* For example, if the customer is very inexperienced in the application to be computerized then the cost of requirements analysis for the project should be increased. The amount that risk factors impinge on the cost of a project can only be estimated by past experience with other projects. There is no hard and fast rule available.

11. *Check the estimates.* There are four checks which can and should be carried out:

    (a) Check that the proportion of resource expended on each phase of the project matches the proportion of resources expended on similar completed projects. For example, if the project produces real-time avionics software and requires half as much resource on requirements analysis as that expended on design and previous real-time avionics projects required twice as much resource then your figures are probably very wrong.

    (b) Check that the estimates for similar parts of the system are the same. For example, if you have two packages which have roughly the same number of program units of the same complexity, and the resource expended on their design is the same, then your figures are probably correct.

    (c) Check the resource estimate of parts of your system with similar parts of other completed systems.

    (d) Check that differences between well-understood and simple parts of the system and complex parts are reflected in the estimates.

12. *Add a profit figure to the cost estimate.* Once you are convinced that the cost figures are correct then the profit should be added to the estimate. This, of course, will be a figure specific to the company developing the software, and would normally reflect factors such as its current business plan, the current financial policy of its directors and the long-term potential of the business.

The estimating process detailed above starts with an outline requirements analysis and rough system design for a system. This gives an estimate of the number and type of program units and leads to a size estimate in terms of the number of source statements. A measure of programmer productivity is calculated from previous projects and amended by considering factors such as the complexity of the system to be built. From this productivity factor development costs are calculated and added to non-developmental costs to give the overall cost estimate for the project.

This is a very attractive but simple view of the estimating process. It seems to work well on small- to medium-sized projects. However, it tends to break down when estimating large projects. The costs of large complex projects have often exceeded the estimates obtained using the above procedure by as much as a factor of 2 to 3. This has led to the practice of software developers using the above technique but then adjusting the estimate by a factor of between 2 or 3. Currently, this coarse approach is acceptable to customers. Inefficiencies in software production have meant that in the past there was a backlog in producing software, and customers were less worried about paying a high price for a software system than they would be for other engineered products where production is efficient.

However, as we improve the software production process over the next few years, and reduce this backlog, then the resulting increase in competition between software producers will mean that there will be a definite market edge for the developer who can accurately estimate project cost. The problem with the cost estimating technique described above is that it relies on assumptions which do not hold for large projects.

SAQ What assumptions have been made in the above costing procedure which are appropriate for small- to medium-sized software projects but which do not apply to large projects?

SOLUTION There are two assumptions:

1.   Productivity in terms of source statements per person-year is constant and can be set by management.

2.   Output of a software project in terms of source statements is directly proportional to effort and person-months.

Productivity is not constant and it cannot be dictated by management. There are a host of other factors upon which productivity depends. For example, system complexity and the naivety of the user are two major factors which reduce productivity. While such factors can be identified during the planning stage, it can be very difficult to estimate exactly their effect on the cost estimate. Productivity is therefore influenced by properties of the system and customer which are out of the control of project management.

Project output is not directly proportional to the effort and person-months put into a software project. As projects become larger and larger the amount of communication between staff increases dramatically. Consequently, more and more time in a project will be spent in vital, but non-developmental activities, such as senior programmers communicating with designers and designers communicating with analysts. In a small- to medium-sized project the increase in this overhead can be small; hence, the assumption that increasing the number of staff proportionately increases the amount of code produced will approximately hold. However, in large projects the communicational overhead rises almost to the point where gains in adding staff to a project are marginal, as Brooks (1975) explains:

> The second fallacious thought mode is expressed in the very unit of effort used in estimating and scheduling: the man-month. Cost does indeed vary as the product of the number of men and the number of months, progress does not. Hence the man-month as a unit for measuring the size of a job is a dangerous and deceptive myth. It implies that men and months are interchangeable.
>
> Men and months are interchangeable commodities only when a task can be partitioned among many workers with no communication among them. This is true of reaping wheat or picking cotton; it is not even approximately true of systems programming.
>
> When a task cannot be partitioned because of sequential constraints the application of more effort has no effect on the schedule. The bearing of a child takes nine months, no matter how many women are assigned. Many software tasks have this characteristic because of the sequential nature of debugging.
>
> In tasks that can be partitioned but which require communication among the subtasks, the effort of communication must be added to the amount of work to be done. Therefore, the best that can be done is somewhat poorer than an even trade of men for months.
>
> (Brooks, 1975)

In an attempt to provide better estimates of project cost a number of researchers and developers have attempted to derive mathematical models. One typical model is described below. It is based on research carried out into project planning for hardware projects where it has been shown (Norden, 1977) that the resource devoted to each phase can be described by the following equation:

$$y = 2kate^{-at^2}$$

where

y	=	the number of staff currently working on a project at time t
k	=	the total number of person-months in the phase
a	=	$1/2t^2_{peak}$ is a factor which indicates how short a phase is
t	=	the number of months from the start of the phase
t_{peak}	=	the month in which the number of staff allocated to the phase peaks, i.e. it is the month when the maximum number of staff is working on the project

The graph of this function is plotted in Fig. 7.1. The bar marks the point at which the operational software is delivered to the customer, i.e. at the end of successful acceptance testing. The area under this curve represents the number of person-months used in a phase up to month t. This is given by the following expression:

$$k(1 - e^{-at^2})$$

Researchers have found that these equations for phases in a hardware project also provide accuracy when applied to the whole of a software project.

Figure 7.1 shows a gradual smooth descent to the point during maintenance where no staff or a fraction of one person is allocated to a project. The major difference between the mathematical curve shown here and what actually happens lies in its behaviour after delivery; an idea of how real behaviour may vary is given in Fig. 7.2. Instead of the gradual smooth descent of Fig. 7.1, Fig. 7.2 shows a discontinuity just after the software is delivered to the customer. This represents the fact that the project manager felt a sense of relief at completing the project, and allocated a low number of staff to handle any errors, hence the resource used suddenly dropped.

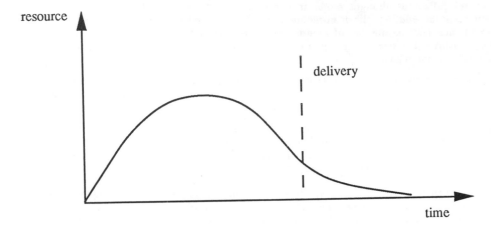

Figure 7.1 A curve of resource against time.

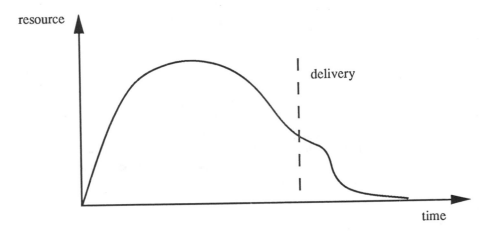

Figure 7.2 An actual curve of resource against time.

For real projects, the level of resource required, and hence the behaviour of the curve after the point of delivery, really depends on the nature of the application and on the contractual agreement between the developer and the customer.

SAQ Why does the behaviour of the curve shown in Fig. 7.2 depend on the nature of the application?

SOLUTION If the application is a well-understood one such as a payroll system then the level of manpower needed would probably be constant and small during the maintenance period since there should be few remaining errors. Normally, only members of the original project team would be used to rectify errors.

If the application were a risky one then after an initial period of constant or slightly decreasing resource usage, it is likely that there would be a gradual buildup of staff. This is because there would be an initial period when the customer was becoming familiar with the software, and few errors were detected followed by an increased use and hence detection of more errors. This buildup in staff would be necessary to supply the effort required to remove errors, however in a more risky application the volume of errors would be larger.

The manpower utilization after delivery also depends on contractual factors. For example, the customer for an application requiring a high level of reliability, such as a controller for a power station, might include penalty clauses in the contract for errors detected and the time taken to detect them. Given such a situation a developer may feel that a larger number of staff who are familiar with the software may have to be kept on the project full-time in order to respond to errors.

However, apart from these fluctuations which occur after software delivery, the model outlined above provides a relatively good estimate of manpower utilization during a software project. The study of such models is still in its early days and there are still not enough results from empirical validation to be fully confident about their utility. Therefore, it is advisable to use them as a check against the manpower estimates obtained from more conventional techniques.

A good way to carry out this process is to start by producing an estimate using the pragmatic planning technique outlined above. From this estimate the peak month for staffing and the number of staff allocated to that month can be obtained. The life-cycle curve can then be drawn and the number of staff allocated to each phase up to delivery can be determined and compared with the number calculated using the pragmatic technique. A discussion of the use of life-cycle curves such as the one described in this section is contained in Aron (1983).

It is important to point out that an area which has a major effect on resources is the staff learning curve. Staff who are allocated to a project often take some time to learn what the project is about and what software is to be produced. From the cost viewpoint it is often cheaper to restrict the number of staff on a project below the estimated peak loading.

7.4 SUMMARY

When planning a project, the project manager must assess the level of risk it involves and the amount of resources it requires so that an estimated budget can be produced. Risk assessment is the identification and documentation of any factors which may result in the project running late or over budget. Six factors which contribute to a project's level of risk are: the characteristics of the application itself, such as its size and complexity; reliance on people and organizations outside the project manager's control; an inexperienced customer; problems with the developer's staff or resources; hardware difficulties; and whether or not the project is concerned with maintenance of existing systems. Many developers have a standard form listing these factors which the project manager must complete after the initial planning stage.

Estimating the cost of the project is also important, but there is no foolproof method for obtaining such an estimate. Certain factors which must be taken into account are staff costs, external subcontractor costs, computer time costs, data entering costs, physical facilities costs, consumables costs and travel and subsistence costs.

A relatively simple costing procedure was introduced in Sec. 7.2, but it is only of value when estimating for small projects since the assumptions made do not apply for large ones. Research into the use of mathematical models in this area is proving to be encouraging, but it is still in its early days. A combination of mathematical and pragmatic methods is probably the best that we can do at the moment.

BIBLIOGRAPHY

Aron, J.D. (1983) *The Program Development Process*, Addison-Wesley, Reading, MA.

Brooks, F.P. (1975) *The Mythical Man-Month*, Addison-Wesley, Reading, MA.

Norden, P.V. (1977) 'Project life cycle modelling: background and application of the life cycle curves', in *Software Phenomenology*: Working papers of the Software Life Cycle Management Workshop, Fort Belvoir, VA., HQ US Army Computer Systems Command.

MANAGING A PROJECT IN PRACTICE

AIMS

- To describe in outline how a project is managed in practice.
- To show by referring to an interview some of the main functions of the project in action.

8.1 INTRODUCTION

This and the following four chapters describe the actual execution of a software project and how the project manager keeps track of the products generated and the activities used to generate the products. To this end, we concentrate on the project manager's responsibilities during the life of one complete project.

In order to be certain that the project is completed successfully, the project manager has to ensure that the project plan is adhered to if at all possible; any deviations must be noted and justified to high-level management and any consequent delays concerning major milestones should be corrected where possible. For example, a project manager may discover that because the customer has been late in commenting on a project document then part of the detailed design of a system cannot be completed on time according to the project plan. However, if re-scheduling it with the detailed design of another part of the system avoids any delay in the delivery of the detailed design document, then this should be done. This rescheduling should be noted, justified and communicated to the project manager's immediate manager.

To help structure the discussion, we shall divide the project manager's responsibilities into five areas. These are subcontract management, software system engineering, software production, quality assurance and configuration management.

Subcontract management is the process whereby subcontractors for software are selected, monitored and controlled. The term *software system engineering* is used to describe the process of performing requirements analysis and system design. *Software production* covers the detailed design and implementation of a software system. *Quality assurance* is the term used to describe those activities which ensure that a contractually acceptable product is delivered by a project; this will be described in more detail later in this book. *Configuration management* describes those activities which ensure orderly control of the products generated in the software project and also ensure an effective mechanism for incorporating change into a system. Configuration management covers methods for reporting changes, evaluating their impact and for notifying project personnel of their effect.

The relationship between these five areas of responsibility and the phases of the software development process is summarized in Fig. 8.1.

	Subcontract management	Software system engineering	Software production	Quality assurance	Configuration management
Requirements analysis	• identify areas to be subcontracted. • receive and evaluate bids.	• produce the system specification. • conduct the system specification review. • analyse existing computer facilities. • define the system's interfaces.		• attend the system specification review. • produce outline test plans using verification requirements.	• expand configuration management practices from project plan.
System design	• clarify requirements for subcontracted software. • monitor the development of subcontracted software.	• produce the system design document. • conduct the system design review.		• attend the system design review. • expand outline test plans.	• control versions of documentation produced.
Detailed design	• perform acceptance tests on subcontracted software. • document experience with subcontractors.	• co-ordinate changes to system specification and system design document. • liaise with software production staff.	• produce the detailed design document. • conduct detailed design reviews.	• produce test procedures. • perform acceptance testing on subcontracted software. • monitor testing activities.	• control versions of code and documentation produced.
Implementation		• apply any modifications to the system specification and the system design document. • produce the operating instructions manual and the user guide.	• produce code for the system. • unit test the program units. • perform integration testing. • perform program walk-throughs. • perform unit development folder audits.		

Figure 8.1 Responsibilities and their relationship to development phases.

The remainder of this chapter returns to Tim Hadden, the project manager we met in Chapter 2, who discusses his role on one complete project from beginning to end. The subsequent four chapters step through the phases of software development introduced in Chapter 1, examining the activities associated with each area of responsibility during the phases. Finally, we consider how project management is affected by using different approaches to development.

As with any activity, the more people involved and the more products expected at the end, the more organization is needed to ensure that the project is successful. Therefore, the bigger the project, the more important the project management. While reading this unit, you may feel that some points which are raised are exaggerated. However, it may be that the issues relate to projects much larger than those in your experience. If you find this happening, it may help you to see the relevance if you stop and remember that we are considering a large project team, consisting of many people who may be spread over many geographical sites.

8.2 PRACTICAL PROJECT MANAGEMENT

This section presents a second interview with Tim Hadden, the project manager at EDS Scicon. This time, Tim discusses his role on one complete project. This project concerned developing the controlling software for an emergency escape gangway for a vessel stationed in an off-shore oil field, as shown in Fig. 8.2.

Figure 8.2 BP Petroleum Development's escape gangway for North Sea rescue operations, fitted on the energy support vessel Iolair, is controlled by a sophisticated computer system developed by EDS Scicon.

This interview is intended to give you an idea of the kinds of practical steps and practical problems which a project manager must deal with over the life of a whole project. That is, it highlights some of the experiences which a project manager is likely to have when trying to put a project plan into action. While you read it, try to note the different circumstances and problems which Tim encounters during the life of the project.

Helen: Could you give us a good example of the type of project that you are involved in the planning for?

Tim: The best example is a project that we completed in 1988. This was the provision of a control system for an emergency gangway for a vessel used by BP[1] in the Forties field, the vessel is on-station at all times to provide support to the engineering services and it carries out diving operations. But its prime reason for being there is in case of an off-shore emergency; it's a major firefighting vessel. In the early eighties BP were committed to a programme to provide this vessel with an emergency escape gangway which in conditions up to force nine could swing out, land on the platform, and stay on the platform under computer control, so that people could literally walk across a bridge onto the emergency vessel. We were contracted to provide the electronic control system, based on two microcomputers. At any one time one computer was actually controlling the gangway and the other was following it through monitoring all the input, so that if the first machine broke down the second would take over automatically.

This involved us in a very wide range of activities, it involved us in actually repackaging the microcomputers, designing and building an interface board which made it compatible with the rest of the equipment, writing the control software itself, and also writing some modelling software to represent the gangway and the sort of environment it would expect to meet out in the North Sea, so it was quite a diverse project.

The first activity is always to understand the problem and draw up a plan. On this particular project it was decided that the duties that I would perform in fact included the preparation of the detailed plan myself, basically because I was the person that had the systems background to take the overall view. Now, in drawing up the plan it is important to be able to understand what is required in each area; therefore, you rely very heavily on the technical expertise of individuals. On the hardware side we were involved in subcontracting the cutting of metal, making the printed circuit boards, so one had to interact with outside subcontractors as well as our own drawing office and production facilities on-site.

Helen: Is this plan produced before you've actually got the contract?

Tim: An outline plan and an outline breakdown[2] are always produced before the work is won. However, the first job of any project manager and his project leader is to produce a detailed plan which tells him how much the job is going to take. It's not always the case that it corresponds with the price or the time-scale that the job has been won at, and that is often the first problem that faces a project manager.

Helen: But you would have been involved in the original plan?

Tim: In an ideal world, yes. In this particular case for various reasons the answer was no. However, we produced a plan, and decided that this was a high-risk project, so

---

[1] British Petroleum who administer this field in the North Sea.
[2] A work breakdown structure.

having produced the plan we very carefully analysed the plan and the risks associated with it.

Helen: Are these risks of running over time or over budget?

Tim: Risks of things not happening when they should. Yes, certainly risks of parts of the work taking longer than they should; if they take longer then they cost more. But risks associated with using subcontractors; you at least can take some action against people who are working directly for you, you have much less control over subcontractors. At the end of the day your ultimate sanction is to put them out of business, but if he goes out of business you don't get what you need, and therefore it's against the interests of the project to do so.

Helen: But you had to go to subcontractors, because you needed the technical backup?

Tim: Yes, we don't have the facilities for cutting or bending metal or making metal boxes, we don't have the facilities to actually make a printed circuit board. We can design them, we can do the layout, we can do all the artwork that is necessary to produce a printed circuit board, but we don't have facilities for etching copper and producing multilayer boards. And that is a specialization which is under a great deal of pressure, which means that there is a very high risk that you won't meet that date. The ways that you can ensure that you do meet the date are by paying a premium to get your work higher on the priority list, and so you can buy contingency in that way. Sometimes you can go to two subcontractors and get each of them to make some. Various risks like that can be accommodated in that way but ultimately, as I say, you have very little sanction against a subcontractor to make him get the work done on time, so that constitutes a major risk.

Helen: So once you have got your detailed plan where do you go from there?

Tim: A project leader is assigned. The project leader must be involved in getting not only the work plan, but the quality plan together and that must be discussed and agreed. You have to ensure that you have the facilities in terms of space, the computer—the date of arrival of the computer is very relevant when you are drawing up your plan. You need to sort out the logistics of what is going where and where the actions need to take place, so it's identifying the milestone activities and dealing with the ones that are urgent. Once you have that, it is important to go and discuss it with the client, so that the client is aware of what you intend to do, when you intend to do it, what his part is, and if there are problems with him being able to provide what is necessary at a given time. Then those must be discussed and resolved and solutions found.

           It's then important to brief the team so that the people working on the project understand what the project is, what it means to the company, in terms of both money, prestige and follow-on work, how important their role is, how long they are going to be on the project and what new skills they are going to learn as a result of it.

Helen: Might this also involve them going to see the vessel in question?

Tim: Indeed on that particular project we did take the opportunity when the vessel was in dry dock in Hamburg to take the whole team of 10 people to see it. We visited the vessel in dry dock and spent time walking around it, this also helped in that not only were they seeing the vessel and the installation, but they also saw the environment that they would be working in, because the first time we would be driving the real system was off-shore. The gangway had already been installed before we had any software or hardware to drive it. So each member of the project in turn had the opportunity to go off-shore during the installation and work up the equipment.

Helen: So how much time was spent here developing the software before the project team went up there?

Tim: The year was effectively split into four three-month slices, the first three months were spent writing and agreeing the specification for the requirements of the gangway system. The second three-month period was spent in implementing that design—both in hardware and software. We had a period of approximately three months on-shore integrating and testing that equipment and then we spent three months off-shore testing, commissioning and finally accepting and handing over the system to the client.

Helen: So, before those three months spent off-shore was that the simulation software that was used to test the system?[3]

Tim: Yes, indeed. Some of the simulation was derived from the motion sensors that were on board the vessel. We had a tape recorder which actually recorded the motions of the vessel and we played that back into the computer so at any time we could simulate calm conditions, medium conditions and rough conditions. We also had this extensive model of the gangway and the hydraulic system.

Helen: Did you find any major problems when you went off-shore?

Tim: Certainly not with the models, the models were very, very accurate indeed. We did have one or two little problems of logic where things happened in the wrong sequence and we had one or two little pieces of equipment where things happened that we weren't expecting.

Helen: The real test is did you walk across the gangway in a force nine?

Tim: Not in a gale force nine. It wasn't until the gangway was accepted that we were able to walk across the gangway, there was a safety requirement that it had to be proven. We certainly proved it in trials on a gale force nine, and I was standing on the open platform on the oil rig where the gangway was landed, taking a video film of the thing landing, so I had to put faith that it would land and stay put. Yes, I did, I was the fifth person to walk across the gangway when it had been landed, it was a very, very satisfying experience.

Helen: Was it difficult drawing up a test plan for that kind of software?

---

[3] System testing.

Tim: Yes indeed, on that particular project in fact I took a more active role in the integration than would normally be expected from a project manager. It was important that somebody who had been through a major systems integration[4] was drawing up the plan. It was also fairly important that somebody from a fairly senior level within the company was with the team off-shore, so that they had support, if there were any problems and if there were any conflicts between our main contractor and ourselves, that the individual team members weren't taking the flak, that they had a level of protection. So I was the main representative of our company off-shore and BP had a trials manager designated, and when it came down to discussing points of conjecture we would go away and do that behind closed doors.

Helen: So you actually spent time off-shore?

Tim: Yes, I think I spent a total of seven weeks out of the three months off-shore.

Helen: That's a long time?

Tim: Yes it is, it's also a fascinating experience.

Helen: Indeed. It sounds a very smooth project development, were there in fact any crises which occurred?

Tim: There were a number of crises, some of them were major indeed. The first of those was that we were supposed to be using some existing software from a previous control system and the plan that had been drawn up was that we would simply port this across. When it came to the event of specifying the requirements in detail, in fact there was not a very good match at all, so we had to completely reimplement the software from scratch.

Helen: So instead of being able to take a piece of software already tested and finished you had to reimplement it?

Tim: Absolutely. And when we looked at the programme we had a period of six weeks in which to do it. And the only way we did it in six weeks was because the teams worked late nights, weekends, shifts and to their credit they produced the goods on time. It cost the company in terms of extra payments, but that was totally irrelevant considering the problem that we had, and it's one of the reasons why, when looking at the finances, the project manager will always have some budget contingency to meet such a crisis.

Helen: Did this happen early on in the project?

Tim: We were four and a half months into the project. We had tried re-using the software, and it was only by actually re-using it that we realized that it was inadequate for the purposes. It didn't meet its specification, the documentation that was supplied to us was incomplete, inconsistent and all in all it was a major headache, which nobody could have foreseen at the time we started.

---

[4] This is not the integration of modules in the software system but the integration of software subsystems with the hardware.

Helen: But did you see it relatively early on in the project?

Tim: We saw it halfway through the phase in which we were supposed to be doing the software development. The software development phase was a three-month phase so we spent the first six weeks seeing what we could do about the software, and the second six weeks putting together the software which would really work.

Helen: So in that situation you weren't actually involved in reallocating staff but you had to make sure that the staff you had could cope?

Tim: Yes, indeed. And in those situations staff morale is really to the fore: you have to ensure that when people are working shifts, they all have vehicles or some form of transport available to them, if not you have to organize lifts—simple things like that become major issues. And if you remember that it's not just the individuals who are directly in front of you but the families and friends that are around them who are affected, you stand a much better chance of being able to maintain the morale and maintain the effort.

Helen: Were there any other crises that you had to deal with?

Tim: We had the situation where we were expecting some goods out by sea, and the weather blew up and the ship was unable to replenish us, so we stopped for a while. We also had a hydraulic problem with the gangway, which caused it to block itself up in the safe position, which is fully elevated. Now the idea is that under normal circumstances you can recover from that fairly quickly. In the event of a hydraulic failure you can't recover it quickly, because you can't recover it until you get hydraulic power back on. The problem that had arisen was that there had been a fault on a one inch hydraulic pipe which had burst. Fortunately, the facilities are there on board in a 15 hour period. Starting at midday, they fabricated a new pipe, they tested it for soundness using X-ray techniques, they refitted it, we got the system up and running and managed to recover the gangway and got to bed at three in the morning.

Helen: It didn't seize because of your software?

Tim: No, indeed, not on that occasion. We did have a couple of software bugs that left it forlorn and in the air, but we soon overcame these.

Helen: It sounds like you had a lot of problems to overcome which were totally extraneous, in fact, to your own work.

Tim: Yes. The problems that were associated with our software were fixed on a day-to-day basis. I think in total 35 software fixes during our three month period off-shore, and that is not a very high number for a system of that sort. None of them were major problems, and all of them were fixed within 48 hours of arising. So we were very lucky, we had a good design and a good basis to start on. When drawing up the plan we did a detailed risk analysis and, having done that, we planned contingency in the programme to accommodate that risk. Now in the event, of course, it wasn't those areas we had the problems with, it was always in the unexpected areas. But the contingency was such that we could use it in the problem areas. So the important thing is to always have contingency for the level of risk you foresee, rather than the specific risks that you foresee.

Helen: So, with hindsight on that particular project, is there anything that you feel you would have done differently?

Tim: I think that the main thing that we would have done differently was at the beginning, we should have done a much more detailed analysis of the software product that we were supposed to be taking on board. That would have saved us an awful lot of aggravation at a critical time in the project.

The other thing we should have done is we should have tied down the specification much earlier. One of the problems that we had was that although we spent three months deciding on the specification, unfortunately, one of the prime users of the system who had experience on previous shore trials was not a party to drawing up the specification. So we went through a whole series of changes when we were in development. It's something that you can often accommodate in terms of prices and it's something you can often accommodate in terms of time-scale. Its biggest effect is on the motivation of the staff, and so we would certainly ensure that we did have a rigorous specification and it would be tied down right at the beginning.

Helen: Is there a continuation project in terms of maintenance that you're involved with?

Tim: Yes, indeed. We provide maintenance support to BP. This is normally in the form of providing training to new staff going off-shore—the system is operated by BP personnel—and also supplying advice and information on problems. Again, to the credit of the team, we have only had two minor software bugs to fix in the time since it was commissioned, and also in that time we have helped sort out a number of system problems which turned out to lie in areas outside the equipment that we supplied.

Helen: So this far on you are still involved in that project and will, I assume, be until the system is decommissioned.

Tim: I would assume so, it's an important system: it is there to save life. It is operated under rigorous safety constraints, and we assume that the client will want on-going backup until the system is decommissioned.

Tim mentioned explicitly producing a project plan, identifying milestones and assessing the level of risk involved in the project. These areas were discussed in Chapter 2.

SAQ List six occurrences or activities with which Tim Hadden was involved during the project he described, but which were not, strictly speaking, part of the software development process.

SOLUTION Tim mentioned at least eight occurrences which were not part of software development, but which affected the project's execution:

1. Employing a subcontractor to cut metal and make circuit boards.

2. Ensuring that staff members' travel arrangements were adequate when working overtime.

3. Taking the project team to see the vessel for which the gangway was designed when it was in dry dock so that they were able to gain a wider view of the system they were developing.

4. Making sure that the people working on the project understood what the project was, what it meant to the company in terms of money, prestige and future contracts, and how important their role was.

5. Ensuring that there was space available for the hardware when it arrived.

6. Coping with a hydraulic failure which was unconnected with the software, but which had to be rectified before the software could correct the situation.

7. Being delayed because goods from the shore could not be sent to the off-shore vessel due to bad weather.

8. The unavailability of a prime user of the system when the system specification was produced which led to many changes to the system specification being required.

SAQ Tim stated that after performing a detailed risk analysis, he concluded that the project was a high-risk project. What was the main factor which contributed to the high-risk nature of this project?

SOLUTION The need to use subcontractors for cutting metal and making printed circuit boards.

An important point that cannot be overstressed, and one which emerged from the interview, was the functions of monitoring, controlling, representing and planning which were exercised by Tim. For example, during the monitoring of the project Tim discovered that software which was intended to be re-used was inadequate for its purpose. This meant that Tim had to exercise control and redirect his staff to produce some new software.

The functions of planning, monitoring and control are intimately related. During the planning stage a project manager will organize his project so that he can adequately monitor the progress of the project, for example, by setting milestones: major events which have to be notified to the project manager. He or she will also have at their disposal reports on tasks completed, and the date on which they were completed. From these milestones, reports and informal discussions with staff, a project manager is able to discover whether the project is on course, i.e. it meets the time and resource targets specified in the project plan.

Once a project deviates from a project plan the manager will have to exercise control. For anything but the simplest project this deviation will occur, so it is worth pausing here to look at some of the options that the project manager has when exercising control. In examining these options we shall assume a common scenario: that a project manager has discovered that a design is more complex than was first thought, and that not only has the design phase taken more time than thought but the implementation (programming) phase is also predicted to take more time. Some of the options are:

- *Add more resource to the project.* Move more programmers to the implementation phase. This might be an option for a project which has a handsome profit associated with it and where the project manager and her or his manager feel that some of that profit can be sacrificed for extra staff.
- *Extend the duration of the project.* This is only an option if the project manager feels that the customer would be happy with late delivery as against some of the options presented below.
- *Skimp on one task and hope that another task will pick up the errors.* An example of this is integration testing. The project manager may have decided to integrate a small number of modules at a time, say three, but because of lateness directs the project staff to integrate ten at a time, hoping that system testing will pick up the errors which would normally have been picked up by thorough integration testing.
- *Reduce the functionality of the system.* This is sometimes an option when the software customer is very keen on delivery time. The project manager will find out what the important functions of the system are, and then deliver a version with only these functions implemented. He or she might plan to produce a later version which contains all the functions. This option is quite a useful one. The important functions of a system are often embedded in as little as 50 per cent of the program code, with the remaining functions being facilities that the customer would quite like, but which are not vitally important.

The important point about exercising control is that the project manager must be aware of the tradeoffs between time and resource. Some of the options above attempt to keep a project on time while one option involves slipping a project. In selecting an option the customer's wishes are, of course, paramount.

It is important to point out that if everything is fixed, i.e. there is no room to manoeuvre with respect to time and budget, then the project must be very low risk and the project manager's activities will be purely monitoring.

9

EXECUTING THE REQUIREMENTS ANALYSIS PHASE

AIMS

- To describe the activities that have to be carried out during requirements analysis.
- To examine how requirements are validated.

9.1 INTRODUCTION

Software requirements analysis consists of a series of tasks which are carried out by processing the customer's statement of requirements. The main aim of requirements analysis is to produce a system specification which sets out, in an unambiguous way, what is required of the system being developed.

9.2 SUBCONTRACT MANAGEMENT

Staff responsible for subcontract management should be identified during this phase. Towards the end of requirements analysis it should be clear how much of the system is to be subcontracted. Normally, the need for subcontracted software is identified during initial planning when an outline system specification and an outline system design document are produced. However, it is only towards the end of requirements analysis that the exact nature of the software can be confirmed.

During requirements analysis, the staff responsible for subcontract management produce tender documents, evaluate bids from subcontractors and develop a monitoring plan whereby the developer can check on the progress of the subcontracted software.

SAQ In what way does the role of staff involved in subcontract management differ from that of staff involved in other project activities?

SOLUTION The staff involved in subcontract management behave like a customer since they are, in effect, the customer for an externally developed software system.

Evaluating a subcontractor is difficult and can be a time-consuming process—a full examination of a company's software competence can last a few weeks. This process can be shortened, however, by asking a number of pertinent questions about the subcontractor when the request for a proposal is first issued. For example:

128

1.   Can you trace functions, expressed in your system specification, to the program code that implements the functions, and vice versa?
2.   What proportion of your validation effort is spent on testing?
3.   When do you derive the system tests and acceptance tests?
4.   What are your risk assessment procedures, and how are the results from these procedures used on your projects?
5.   What products are generated during the unit testing process?
6.   What baselines[1] do you have and what configuration management practices do you use?

Each of these questions is discussed in more detail below. On a small project the project manager would be the member of staff who would answer these questions. On larger projects the staff he managed would be involved in the process, with the manager checking that the question-posing process was carried out properly.

Can you trace functions, expressed in your system specification, to the program code that implements the functions, and vice versa?

The ability to identify the program units which implement a given function is known as *forward traceability*; the ability to identify all the functions which use a particular program unit is known as *reverse traceability*. There are two reasons why forward traceability is important:

1.   It guards against coincidental correctness during system testing. Coincidental correctness, where the right result is given by a system test, but the wrong program units are executed, is a common error. If the developer has a means of tracing functions to program units, however, the execution of a system test can be monitored to ensure that the correct program units are executed.
2.   It helps in validation. A common error in development is to miss out parts of the design.[2] By checking the functions of the system against the program units which have been programmed, the developer is easily able to spot any which are missing.

Reverse traceability is also an important asset for system testing. As an example of this, consider a developer who has just carried out a large number of system tests, the last of which failed. One response to such a failure is to discover the error, rerun the test that failed, and carry on system testing from that point. However, there is no guarantee that no further errors have been introduced by the changes implemented. A better approach would be to trace all the functions which use the affected program unit(s) and to rerun the tests which correspond to those functions.

Forward and reverse traceability are clearly important. However, ploughing through thick documentation in order to answer relevant questions is a very inefficient use of time. Therefore, a simple matrix notation is usually used to represent the relationship between functions and program units in which the rows represent functions and the columns represent program units.

---

[1] The term 'baseline' is used to describe a snapshot of the system at a point in its development. For example, the system specification can be used as a baseline since it describes the emerging system at the end of requirements analysis.

[2] Yes, that is right!

An example of this is shown in Fig. 9.1 for a very simple system containing four program units A, B, C and D and three functions F1, F2 and F3. A cross in the table indicates that the function in the row containing the cross is implemented by the program unit in the column containing the cross. In Fig. 9.1, therefore, when function F1 is executed the program units A and C are executed. Representing the information like this clearly makes it easier to read.

	A	B	C	D
F1	X		X	
F2		X		X
F3			X	

Figure 9.1 Matrix notation used to represent forward and reverse traceability.

What proportion of your validation effort is spent on testing?

Testing is a vital and necessary part of the software project. However, it suffers from one major disadvantage: it can only occur late in a software project, when a large proportion of project resources have been expended. Errors committed during requirements analysis, which remain undetected until system testing, can cause major budget and time overruns, and have caused software projects to be cancelled.

Reviews, which were first introduced in Chapter 1, are an exceptionally effective front-end validation activity which can be used to detect errors early in the development process. The amount of resources which a software developer devotes to the reviewing activity relative to the testing activity is a good gauge of the developer's competence. A 50/50 split would seem to indicate competence and an 80/20 split, or worse, is a cause for concern.

SAQ Is it better for a larger proportion of effort to be expended towards testing or towards conducting reviews?

SOLUTION It is better if more effort goes into conducting reviews than into testing. The more time spent on activities such as reviews which occur in the early stages of a software project, the more likely it is that any errors in the system specification and system design document will be identified before implementation begins. Hence, fewer corrections to these documents should be necessary during the later stages of the project.

When do you derive the system tests and acceptance tests?

A common answer to this question is: just before system testing and acceptance testing is due to begin. However, a prudent developer will develop these tests, in outline, during requirements analysis, and refine them during system design. Taking this approach leads to the production of a clearer system specification and the ability to predict resources for these activities at an early stage in the project.

What are your risk assessment procedures, and how are the results from these procedures used on your projects?

The risk assessment process was discussed in Chapter 7. A good subcontractor should have a risk assessment procedure as part of the project's planning standards; this procedure may not be sophisticated and might just last half a day; but it is essential in order to carry out forward planning.

Many large companies have detailed checklists which consist of over 50 such questions. The most sophisticated of these have a marking system, in which the answer to a question is given as a numerical value. At the end of the assessment the marks are totalled to produce a figure which gives the overall level of risk for the project.

What products are generated during the unit testing process?

Unit testing is usually carried out by the programmer who developed the unit, and this can lead to problems. In general, the management of unit testing need not be as tight as it is for system, acceptance and integration testing, because it is an informal process. However, the products of unit testing should be carefully collected together as some form of documentation, normally known as the unit test folder or programmer's notebook.[3]

Such documentation should include the code of the tested unit, the design of the tested unit, the location of the test data, the location of the files containing the test outcomes, an assessment of the thoroughness of the test data in terms of percentage of statements executed or percentage of branches executed, and detailed reasons why a particular set of data was used.

Only the very best developers include all these items. However, the minimum to expect is the first four items. The probability of needing to retest a program unit is very high, for example, during maintenance or during system testing when an error has been found. If unit tests need to be rebuilt from scratch each time they are used, a large amount of resources will be wasted.

What baselines do you have and what configuration management practices do you use?

Software development is dynamic, and the way in which a developer copes with change is a good indication of their maturity. This is illustrated by their configuration management practices, or lack thereof.

A software developer should define a number of baselines for each major product of the development process such as the system design document or the system specification. Once a product has been baselined, any change has to be carefully considered by both the company's quality assurance department and the development team, usually by means of a change control board. Up to the point of baselining, a change can occur freely.

A very poor software developer will have no configuration management system. A poor one will only have a system for administering change to program code. The competent software developer will place all important products under configuration management.

Change is a major force in a software project. Any changes made to the statement of requirements after the system specification has been agreed by the customer will require the

---

[3] This kind of documentation is explained in Chapter 13.

development team to rewrite existing documents. The later in the project that changes occur, the more costly the changes are.

SAQ Why is a developer who only has a system for administering change to program code to be regarded as a poor one?

SOLUTION If rigorous change procedures are only applied to program code then major documents such as the system specification will be ignored. Consequently, the functional specification and design documentation will be out of step with the program code, and this could lead to difficulties later on in the project during maintenance, or when further changes are requested.

9.3 SOFTWARE SYSTEM ENGINEERING

During this phase those staff responsible for software system engineering prepare the system specification; these people are usually known as *systems analysts*. Preparing the system specification involves a large amount of interaction with the customer during which the statement of requirements is expanded and checked for ambiguity, completeness and correctness. The major activities conducted during this phase are discussed below.

9.3.1 Analysis of existing computer facilities

During the initial planning stage the developer will have produced an outline system design document and will have a good idea of the hardware capabilities necessary to implement the system so that it conforms to the customer's set of non-functional requirements.

If the statement of requirements does not specify particular hardware but leaves the choice to the software developer then this choice will be made late in the system design phase when the non-functional requirements have been established and an estimate of the system's size can be calculated.

If the customer includes a hardware specification in the statement of requirements then it is during requirements analysis that a full analysis of existing computer capabilities and resources should be carried out.

SAQ Why might the customer include a hardware specification in the statement of requirements?

SOLUTION There are two reasons why the customer might include a hardware specification in the statement of requirements. Firstly, the system to be developed may be destined for an existing computer system which already runs a number of applications. Secondly, the customer may already have a particular computer in mind which he or she believes to be the best one for the application.

If the new system is to be run on hardware already owned by the customer which is currently running other software, a full analysis of the computer capabilities and resources available should be conducted to ensure that they are sufficient for the system under development. This analysis should address a number of questions, the answers to which should be carefully documented. If the new system is to be run on hardware already owned by the customer which is not currently running other software, then the analysis involves asking questions such as:

1. What free memory is available during the working day of the computer?
2. What input and output devices are available and what is their utilization during the normal working day?
3. What file devices are available and what is the file utilization of the current computer system?

What free memory is available during the working day of the computer?

In a computer system which currently runs a number of systems the amount of free memory available will vary during the day. It is necessary for the system designer to know how memory utilization varies under the computer's current workload in order to produce a design which fits into the available memory. This information can be discovered either by measuring the size of current systems from their program code or by observing memory utilization. The feasibility of using the latter option depends on the facilities offered by the current support software; many operating systems do offer this facility, but some do not.

If it is discovered that not enough memory is available, then the customer will have to modify the goals for the current project, or invest in different or additional hardware.

What input and output devices are available and what is their utilization during the normal working day?

SAQ Why is it important to ask the above question when analysing current computer facilities?

SOLUTION The more input and output that occurs in a software system the more the system's response time degrades. Therefore, knowing the current amount of input and output traffic together with the capacity of the input and output channels, the system designer will be able to define a system design which satisfies the non-functional requirements of the system to be developed. This information should therefore be written into the system specification.

What file devices are available and what is the file utilization of the current computer system?

It is necessary to know whether there is enough storage capacity for the new system and also whether the increased file access will have a detrimental effect on response time for both existing software systems, and the one currently being developed. This information should include estimates of the amount of file traffic currently passing through the computer system, maximum and minimum values of traffic and the amount of file storage used.

9.3.2 Interface definition

All computer systems communicate with their environments via devices such as VDUs, line printers, actuators, communication lines and wireless links. Some of these communications are exclusively between machines, such as the software system sending a signal to a satellite instructing it to change course. Others are between a machine, the computer, and a human being, the operator.

The form which this communication takes will have been considered during the initial planning stage of the project, and standards governing the interfaces will have been laid down. The information about a function which is documented in the system specification during requirements analysis should include details of its interface needs, if any.

The specification of the technical interfaces, i.e. machine to machine, are necessary to ensure that both the desired response time can be achieved, and the machines involved are able to talk to each other!

The consideration of human–computer interfaces has become more and more necessary in recent years. These issues are important because it has been found that systems which are built without considering the needs of the actual user are often used infrequently or not at all. The standards laid down in the project plan, and the initial study which will have been performed during the initial planning stage, will be pursued during requirements analysis. Discussion with potential users of the system to ascertain their requirements for screen and report formats should begin as early as possible. It may be desirable to perform user trials using different screen designs, for example, to determine the most appropriate interface.

At the end of the requirements analysis phase a system specification review should take place between the customer and the developer, the purpose of which is to validate the system specification. Before this, an internal review should take place, the purpose of which is to ensure that few unresolved problems arise during the subsequent meeting with the customer, i.e. to ensure that the meeting with the customer is as much of a formality as possible.

The internal review should consist of the project manager, the staff involved in requirements analysis, a quality assurance representative and a senior member of staff unconnected with the project who, ideally, has considerable experience of requirements analysis and the application area.

Some of the more important questions that the review should answer are as follows:

1. Are all requirements stated clearly in the system specification?
2. Is the system specification complete?
3. Are there any implementation directives or design directives in the system specification?
4. Have we eliminated all computer jargon from the system specification?
5. Do the top-level functions of the system specification match those stated in the customer's statement of requirements?
6. Is each high-level function in the system specification decomposed to other, suitably small functions?
7. How can the requirements be validated?
8. Is it feasible to implement each requirement?

The reasoning behind asking the first four questions should be fairly clear from the desirable properties of the system specification which we listed earlier in Chapter 1. For example, the purpose of the system specification is to state *unambiguously* what the system is intended to do. Therefore, asking whether all requirements are stated clearly is an obvious thing to do. Also, since the system specification of large systems can occupy hundreds of pages of text, it is not surprising that such specifications are often incomplete, and therefore this should be checked.

SAQ Examine the functional and non-functional requirements shown below and identify one instance of lack of clarity for each one.

(a)   The human–computer interface to the monitoring system should be user friendly.

(b)   The function of the DISP command is to display on the originating VDU the lowest voltage reading for that day.

(c)   The system should incorporate comprehensive error checking.

(d)   When a reactor overload occurs then the operator console should display a warning message REACTOR OVERLOAD together with the current temperature and pressure in red.

SOLUTION

(a)   This is a platitude. It does not really say what should be provided. It may mean that help facilities should be provided, or that long and short versions of commands be implemented. The requirements should be stated explicitly.

(b)   The problem with this requirement is that the lowest actual reading for the day might be an invalid reading due to a malfunction in the reading apparatus. It is currently unclear how such a situation should be handled. For example, should the lowest *valid* reading be displayed? If so, what constitutes a valid reading?

(c)   This requirement is at too high a level. While all systems should include error processing, such processing should be specified in much more detail.

(d)   This requirement is not very clear. Does it mean that the REACTOR OVERLOAD message and the current temperature and pressure are all displayed in red?

The other questions listed above are discussed in the following text.

Do the top-level functions of the system specification match those stated in the customer's statement of requirements?

The process of matching requirements in the system specification to the customer's statement of requirements will usually detect incompleteness. The customer's statement of requirements will normally contain fairly high-level expressions of system functions such as the following.

The system should allow the enquiry clerk to interrogate stock levels in the warehouse.

It should be possible to identify such functions in the system specification. Obviously, they will be stated more clearly, and will be expressed in more detail, but they should be clearly recognizable.

If any high-level functions occur in the system specification but do not appear in the customer's statement of requirements then the review should check that there is documentation signed by the customer which either accepts or suggests the inclusion of the new function in the system specification.

Is each high-level function in the system specification decomposed to other, suitably small functions?

The system specification can be thought of as a series of trees with high-level functions at the root of the tree and smaller, low-level functions at the bottom level of the tree, as shown in Fig. 9.2. Functions such as the following will be at the root of the tree:

> The system should allow the plant operator to interrogate the temperature and pressure database in order to discover reactor performance.

Functions such as the following will be at the bottom:

> The purpose of the TEMP_AVERAGE command is to display the average temperature of one of the plant reactors over a particular time. The operator will type the keyword associated with this command followed by the start of the period to be examined, the end of the period to be examined and the reactor name. The period's start and end times are expressed in terms of the 24-hour clock. The effect of the command is to display the average temperature of the specified reactor during the period specified by the start time and the end time.

The participants of the review should check that each high-level function has been completely decomposed into functions which can be implemented easily. Furthermore, each low-level function should be checked to ensure that all error conditions have been specified. For example, the function above should be associated with errors which are displayed when the 24-hour clock format is violated or when an operator types in the name of a non-existing reactor.

How can the requirements be validated?

The reason for involving quality assurance staff in the internal system specification review is that such staff will be intimately involved in system testing and acceptance testing which includes specifying the system tests and acceptance tests. In order to help them specify these tests, quality assurance staff will need to ensure that requirements expressed in the system specification can be validated. Checking the requirements for this property is also a good way of ensuring that the system specification is clear and consistent.

For each requirement the reviewers should ask:

*   Can we specify the steps necessary to carry out the system tests and acceptance tests for this requirement?
*   What software and hardware configurations should be specified for the system and acceptance tests for this requirement? For example, a function in a critical real-time system may require a particular version of the host operating system.
*   What evidence should be presented to the customer later on to demonstrate that this requirement has passed its acceptance test? To answer this question, the review team

will need to be sure that the required outputs are defined and that facilities are available to test non-functional requirements such as response time.

Is it feasible to implement each requirement?

Normally this question is addressed during the initial planning phase. However, during the requirements analysis phase the customer's statement of requirements is expanded, and it may become clear that it is not possible to implement some requirements as requested.

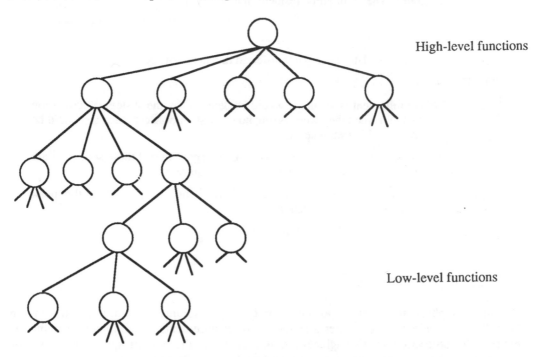

High-level functions

Low-level functions

Figure 9.2 A functional hierarchy.

Also, it is fairly common for the customer to propose new requirements during the requirements analysis period. Often these seem quite innocuous at first, but might prove to be a problem later on. There is therefore a need for each requirement to be examined very closely to see whether it is feasible or not. For example, if the customer requires a comprehensive system with very fast response times, it might be infeasible to provide all the required functionality *and* the fast response time. If a system occupies a large amount of store, thus causing too many demands upon the underlying operating system, response time may be reduced. Another situation in which requirements may turn out to be infeasible is if the proposed system contains an intelligent subsystem. If the customer is unaware of the limits to current achievements in this field, the request may be beyond the bounds of current technology.

SAQ   Examine the system specification extracts shown below. Point out one deficiency in each extract which would be identified by a review team asking the questions listed above.

(a)   The software should be constructed so that it can be maintained easily.

(b)   The query processing functions will be implemented as a series of concurrent programs. They will all be resident in memory.

(c)   The response to the UPDATE_COMMAND should be at most two seconds, even during the peak processing load of the system.

(d)   The salesman data should be transferred in batches of six records.

SOLUTION

(a)   This requirement is vague. It would be detected by the system specification review team when they were asking how a system or acceptance test could be constructed which validates it.

(b)   This requirement is expressed in computer jargon. In fact these sentences are more of an implementation directive than a requirement.

(c)   This requirement is incomplete as it does not specify what the peak processing load of the system is.

(d)   This is another implementation directive.

9.4 QUALITY ASSURANCE

During this phase the staff responsible for quality assurance will monitor the system specification against the customer's statement of requirements, in conjunction with staff engaged in software system engineering. For instance, the system specification review mentioned above will involve the member of staff responsible for quality assurance on the project.

The staff will also produce outlines of the system test plan and the acceptance test plan and will check these plans against the customer's statement of requirements. All documentation produced by development staff will be checked by quality assurance staff to ensure that it meets the standard laid down in the project plan and in the contract between the developer and the customer.

A major activity that has to be carried out at this stage is the extraction of the verification requirements. This activity has already been touched upon in the previous section. During the system specification review, the requirements are checked to ensure that they can be validated. After this, the software functions that will be validated during system testing and acceptance testing are identified. These functions are known as *verification requirements* and represent the visible part of the system to be developed. This process is carried out by quality assurance staff, in conjunction with the customer. The main property of a validation requirement is that it must be easy to validate.

The difference between a requirement that can be validated and one that cannot is shown by examining the following requirements:

12.3 The response to the DISPLAY_TEMP command should be adequate even at peak processing times.

12.3 The response to the DISPLAY_TEMP command should never be more than 2 seconds, even during the peak processing time between 1400 hours and 1600 hours when a maximum of 50 terminal operators will be answering the queries specified in Subsections 4.3 to 4.5 of this document.

SAQ Which of the above requirements is more easily validated and why?

SOLUTION The second requirement is more easily validated than the first because the first requirement is too vague. It does not specify what *adequate* means nor when the peak period occurs. The second requirement is much clearer. It tells the quality assurance staff when the critical time to run the system and acceptance tests is in order to measure response times to the DISPLAY_TIME command, and the exact response time that is required.

The list of functions to be tested should include not only single functions but also collections of related functions. For example, suppose that the system specification contains the following paragraphs:

7.2 The function of the DEPOSIT_PART command is to place in the parts database the name of a part that has been notified to the wholesaler as being a new line.

7.3 The function of the WRITE_DATABASE command is to print on the remote line-printer the names of parts stored in the parts database.

A good test of these functions is to exercise the first function by typing in the DEPOSIT_PART command with a part name and then exercise the second function by typing the WRITE_DATABASE command and examining the printout from the remote printer.

After the process of extracting verification requirements has been carried out the developer has a good idea of the tests that should be executed during system and acceptance testing.

There are two reasons why the developer should be bothering about verification requirements at this stage of the software project. Firstly, deriving the verification requirements helps ensure that the requirements analysis process has been completed thoroughly. Secondly, the verification requirements give the manager a good indication of the amount of resource needed for system testing and acceptance testing.

A point which must be borne in mind and which is described in detail later in the book is that quality assurance activities are concerned with two facets of a project: that the documents and code that are produced are correct and the process used to create the documents has been carried out correctly.

9.5 CONFIGURATION MANAGEMENT

During this phase the configuration management practices to be used in the project, and outlined in the project plan, may be expanded. Usually these will match the standard normally employed by the developer. However, if there are any deviations from these standards then they will be specified during this phase. For example, the customer may require a special type of report format which makes it easier to check on the status of all the items in the project.

Change is a fact of life in any software project; it can occur for many reasons. For example, the customer may modify the statement of requirements, changes in the system's environment may necessitate changes in the system itself, or misinterpretations of the customer's requirements may not be identified until late in the project. Actually changing a software system or its documentation is very easy; interactive editors are now commonplace. However, the effect of change can be disastrous, and it is vitally important that the changes made to a system are carefully controlled. The following account of change and its effect was given by a software developer we met when preparing this book:

> I was working on a project for providing software for a radar installation. We had reached the architectural design[4] stage and had defined each module and program unit in the system. We had done everything correctly and had documented the response times that were predicted from the programs units. One program unit was called by over 40 other program units. The program unit response was very quick as it interfaced with a piece of hardware directly so that the units that called it did not have to be incredibly efficient. Consequently, the detailed designers were given the brief to save storage space rather than aim for fast response time. Unfortunately, the hardware being used in the project was innovative and was being modified fairly constantly during the project. What happened was that the hardware response fell a little and affected the critical unit. Now this modification to the hardware occurred before we started detailed design but nobody told the detailed designers.

> Therefore, they went ahead designing program units on the assumption that the program unit being called had a more rapid response time. We only discovered the mistake late during integration testing when we ran a few non-functional tests and discovered that our non-functional requirements were not being met. It took us a long time to track down the problem. In the end we had to redesign 45 units and, since coding had started on some of them, we had to recode over 20 units. We were beset by these sort of problems and ended up delivering six months late and 15 per cent over budget.

The problem here was that the effect of a change forced on the software project was not evaluated properly nor communicated to the whole of the project team. It is vital that configuration management practices are carefully laid down at this stage of the project, so that this kind of mistake does not happen.

Other configuration management activities conducted during requirements analysis are monitoring changes, measuring the impact of change on the evolving system and approving or rejecting changes. The documents which are governed by configuration control will be the emerging system specification and the preliminary versions of the system tests and acceptance tests.

---

[4] System design.

SAQ Why should the developer be bothering about verification requirements during requirements analysis rather than waiting until later on in the project?

SOLUTION There are two reasons why the developer should be bothering about verification requirements at this stage of the software project. Firstly, deriving the verification requirements helps ensure that the requirements analysis process has been completed thoroughly. Secondly, the verification requirements give the manager a good indication of the amount of resource needed for system and acceptance testing.

9.6 SUMMARY

During requirements analysis, the activities associated with each of the responsibilities are as follows:

- Staff responsible for subcontract management will produce tender documents, evaluate bids from subcontractors and develop a monitoring plan whereby the developer can check on the progress of the subcontracted software.
- Staff responsible for software system engineering will prepare the system specification. This involves expanding the functions listed in the customer's statement of requirements, analysing any existing computer facilities, specifying the system's interface to agents outside the remit of the current system, and conducting the system specification review.
- Staff responsible for quality assurance will monitor the system specification against the customer's statement of requirements, in conjunction with staff engaged in software system engineering. They will also identify verification requirements so as to produce outline system and acceptance test plans. All project documentation will be checked by quality assurance staff to ensure that it meets the standards laid down in the project plan and in the contract between the developer and the customer.
- Staff responsible for configuration management will expand the configuration management practices which were outlined in the project plan. They will also monitor any changes to the customer's statement of requirements, measure the impact of change on the evolving system and approve or reject changes.

10

EXECUTING THE SYSTEM DESIGN PHASE

AIMS

- To describe how the system design phase is executed in terms of the activity categories described in Chapter 8.
- To describe the questions to be asked when a computer is selected for a software project.
- To describe the questions to be asked when software is selected for a software project.
- To describe the components of a system design review.
- To describe how the verification requirments are expanded during system design.

10.1 INTRODUCTION

System design[1] consists of establishing a system architecture and a data architecture which satisfy the requirements established during the requirements analysis phase. The main aim of the system design phase is to produce a system design document which specifies the function of each program unit in the system architecture, and the structure of the data which the program units are to process.

10.2 SUBCONTRACT MANAGEMENT

At this stage of the software project those sections of the system specification referring to externally developed software will have been handed over to subcontractors. Staff responsible for subcontract management will normally be involved in the process of requirements analysis with these subcontractors. As this phase proceeds there will be greater involvement in monitoring the subcontractors' software development processes by means of techniques such as reviews. The developer behaves like a customer for the subcontracted sections of software, although he or she is more knowledgeable about software systems than one might usually expect of the average customer. Hence, staff will be involved in clarifying requirements, accepting documents, and of course, in asking for changes!

---

[1] Sometimes known as architectural design or critical design.

10.3 SOFTWARE SYSTEM ENGINEERING

Those staff responsible for software system engineering will develop the system design document of the system from the functional requirements and non-functional requirements derived during requirements analysis. The major activities conducted during this phase are discussed below.

10.3.1 Computer selection studies

If the choice of hardware and support software is left to the developer, then this activity takes place towards the end of the system design phase. We discussed the process involved in checking the suitability of existing hardware in Sec. 9.2; this section considers the situation where the customer has left the selection of support software and hardware to the developer. Obviously the choice of a computer is critical in satisfying non-functional requirements, but the underlying operating system and the language compilers used also have a significant effect.

SAQ In a project where the customer does not specify the hardware or support software why is their selection left until late in the system design phase?

SOLUTION At the end of the requirements analysis phase non-functional requirements such as response time and the amount of input and output traffic are established. Such requirements must be known before a hardware and software base can be selected. The system design phase must be nearly complete because an estimate of the system's size is also needed.

The analysis of available computer systems and support software should address a number of questions, the answers to which should be carefully documented. The following questions relate to choosing the hardware, and are discussed below. This is not an exhaustive list; it is intended merely to indicate the kinds of questions to be asked. It is important to point out that these questions will be asked by technical staff on a project and that the project manager will be monitoring the process.

1. Is the storage capacity of the computer adequate for the application?

2. Is the processor powerful enough?

3. Is the input and output capacity big enough?

4. Can the computer system expand to meet possible growth requirements?

5. Does the computer system support the software required by the application?

6. Is the delivery time and availability of the computer system compatible with the project plan?

Is the storage capacity of the computer adequate for the application?

Storage capacity has a major effect on non-functional requirements such as response time. A system which occupies a great deal of memory is totally infeasible if the computer selected is a simple micro. If the computer to be selected has paging facilities then there will be a lot of paging traffic.[2] This often leads to a massive decrease in the response time of the software.

Is the processor powerful enough?

This is particularly important in numerical applications where there may be much more processor activity for calculations than file traffic. If the processor is not powerful enough then this will lead to a poor response time.

Is the input and output capacity big enough?

This is important in commercial data processing applications where there may be a large amount of traffic to and from peripherals and file devices. If the capacity is not high enough then traffic will be held up and the response of the system will be low.

Can the computer system expand to meet possible growth requirements?

If a system is successful then it is sure to grow. Software systems always reflect the world in which they are placed, and this world is often expanding. For example, the growth in business of an insurance company may mean that the data processed by a system will increase, leading to the need for more input and output devices and file storage hardware; the merger of two companies often means that new functions will have to be added to one company's system, leading to an increase in software size and a consequent need for more memory.

Does the computer system support the software required by the application?

The application may require specialized languages for activities such as real-time processing. It is important that compilers for such languages are readily available which have been tried and tested for some time in the field. For example, standards exist for certain languages, and some compilers have been validated against these standards while others have not. Systems for defence applications are soon to come under strict guidelines for development, and it will therefore be important for such applications that acceptable languages and systems are available.

Is the delivery time and availability of the computer system compatible with the project plan?

This is an obvious point. There will be a finite time between ordering a computer and the computer being delivered to the customer or the developer. This time must be taken into account. If the delivery time is incompatible with activities such as integration testing then other computers should be considered.

The delivery time problem is usually worse with large mainframe systems than small micro-based systems. One problem bound up with this question is that of newly developed hardware systems. A computer vendor may promise that a newly developed computer system can be delivered at a certain time, but there is no guarantee either that the computer will be delivered on time or that complete documentation and error-free software will accompany it.

---

[2] Paging involves the passage of data to and from the file storage devices of the computer.

There are many instances in the history of software projects of developers being attracted by very powerful new computers at much cheaper prices only to find that when they are delivered the software contained so many errors that development was made considerably more difficult.

The choice of supporting software is also a critical one which has to be made during the system design phase. The following questions relate to choosing this software, and are discussed below:

1.   What operating system should be used for this application?

2.   What programming language should be used for this application?

3.   Is there enough support software for the programming language chosen?

What operating system should be used for this application?

The choice of operating system will be determined by the nature of the application, for example, a concurrent system must be run in an environment which supports concurrency, the delivery time for the software and the non-functional requirements of the system such as response time and memory size. One important characteristic of the operating system which affects the response time of application programs is the tradeoffs made by its developer.

SAQ What kind of tradeoffs do you think the developer of an operating system might have made?

SOLUTION The developer of an operating system must decide whether to give priority to the provision of sophisticated development tools, or to ensuring swift execution of application programs. Some operating systems provide a very rich development environment for the software developer. They contain sophisticated software tools which enable productivity gains to be made during the development process. However, such operating systems are prone to being inefficient. A program being executed in such an environment will run considerably slower than in a less developer-oriented operating system.

The spectrum of choice will be bounded at one end by extremely simple operating systems which provide minimum facilities for the developer but which offer extremely efficient execution of programs, and at the other end by inefficient operating systems which offer a rich set of development tools. For some applications, for example, embedded real-time systems, there will be no operating system to choose.

What programming language should be used for this application?

It is clearly important to match the programming language with the application so that the concepts required by the application can be expressed using the language. In some cases, this may mean that the best course of action is to produce a language which is specifically designed for an application area. However, in most situations, one of the popular high-level programming languages such as Pascal, Ada, PROLOG or Modula-2 will suffice.

Apart from being suitable for the application area, the language should also have a formally defined syntax and well-defined semantics. This may seem to be an obvious requirement, but the older languages such as COBOL and FORTRAN do not have such a well-defined basis. This definition is important so that the programmer can be sure that the intention of the program does not become distorted by an untrue translation when it is compiled. This point also relates to portability since a standardized language is more likely to be portable between a number of machines, although standardization does not guarantee portability.

The issue of portability may be important because the developer perceives that an application has potential for a large number of sales. If this is so then an agreement must be reached between the developer and the original customer. For example, in return for the developer having the right to sell the system to other customers, the system may be developed at low cost to the original customer who may also be paid a percentage of any further sales.

Another reason why portability is important is when a system is expected to have a long life and outlast a number of generations of computers. It is in the developer's interest to produce software that can be ported from one computer to a dissimilar computer as quickly as possible.

Having chosen the language, the choice of which implementation of that language should be used is equally important. For example, there is little point in expending effort to ensure that the language chosen is a standardized one if the compiler and supporting software have not been validated against the language's standard! The subject of standardized languages and validated compilers will be returned to in Chapter 17.

Is there enough support software for the programming language chosen?

A factor which is important in choosing a programming language is the amount of support software that is available for a particular implementation of the language. It used to be thought that tools such as dynamic debuggers, which display variable values during the execution of a program, formatters, which display the structure of a program, and cross-reference utilities, which point out the usage of variables in a program, were essential. However, this admits that complexity has been allowed to permeate through to the implementation phase, and the whole aim of software engineering is to manage the complexity inherent in an application so that it is under control by the time that implementation is attempted.

Nowadays, tools such as static analysers which check the syntax of program code without executing it are more relevant. The efficacy of these tools depends on having a well-defined language, as discussed above, and so they are not, as yet, widely used.

Of course, the choice of hardware, software support and language implementation are intimately related, and cannot be considered as independent. In practice, therefore, the decision process will not be divided as cleanly as is implied by the above discussion; it is more likely that there will be much interweaving between the concerns.

10.3.2 Devising scenarios

Apart from producing the system design document, project staff responsible for software system engineering will devise scenarios which include the major events which the system will encounter during its operation. These scenarios can be used to check that appropriate program units and data structures have been specified in the system design document. The developer can examine each sentence of the event and check that there is a module in the system design which implements the functions in that sentence. If, when stepping through one of these scenarios, it is not possible to find a program unit to process a particular function, then the system design document is obviously incomplete.

One such scenario in which relevant program units have been identified is given below. It describes what happens in a patient monitoring system when a pulse monitor indicates that a patient's heart has stopped beating:

> When the patient's heartbeat stops the pulse monitor will be grounded for a time greater than five times the pulse duration time. When this occurs the program unit MONITORPULSE will call the program unit ALARM. MONITORPULSE will pass the pulse monitor number to ALARM which will then look up the bed location in the patient database. ALARM will then call the program unit PULSEDANGER and BELL. The program unit ALARM will pass the bed number to PULSEDANGER which will then display it in red on the main monitoring console. When BELL is activated the audible alarm on the main monitoring console will be activated.

It is worth pointing out that the technique of devising scenarios can be used during the requirements analysis phase. It is particularly useful when identifying hazards in safety-critical systems.

10.3.3 Documenting forward traceability and reverse traceability

The concepts of forward traceability and reverse traceability were introduced in Sec. 9.1; forward traceability refers to the ability to identify which program units are executed when a particular function is performed and reverse traceability refers to the ability to identify which functions are performed when a particular program unit is executed. Documenting these relationships is performed during the system design phase.

As already mentioned, software is subject to much change during its lifetime; sometimes change is necessary because of errors, sometimes the customer requests changes, and sometimes it is necessary because of change in the outside world. Whenever a change is made to a program unit there is a chance that the change will affect other functions which are implemented by the program unit, and therefore the functions affected must be retested. Documenting the relationship between functions and program units enables development staff to identify quickly functions which need to be retested after a change has been made.

This information can also be used to ensure that system tests and acceptance tests have indeed exercised the program units which they were expected to test, and that the correct result was not given because of coincidental correctness. A prudent tester will usually insert code into each program unit which prints out a message saying that the unit was entered. The printout can then be checked against the expected pattern of program unit usage.

A popular way of documenting the relationship between functions and program units was introduced in Fig. 9.1. This is by constructing a matrix whose rows represent software functions and whose columns represent program units.

10.3.4 Preparing the interface control document

The interface requirements defined during requirements analysis are fleshed out with detail during the system design phase. For machine–machine interfaces, the information in the interface control document includes specifications of data format, data content, data rates and data protocols. The data format describes the way in which the data is represented; for example, it would describe the length of a message in bits sent from an external source. The data content describes what the data is; for example, an employee number or a monitor temperature. The data rate specifies how quickly data arrives at the system. The data protocol is used to describe the conventions used in transmitting data to the system; for example, how the start or the end of a message is indicated.

SAQ Why should the data rate be specified in the interface control document?

SOLUTION The data rate should be specified in the interface control document because this rate has a major effect on the response of a system. Most system specifications include constraints on the response time. In order to calculate whether a proposed architecture meets such a requirement the designer needs to know such rates.

The requirements for human–computer interfaces should be arrived at by discussion with the users of the system, and may involve producing prototype interfaces which are tested in user trials. If this question is addressed early enough then trials should be complete by the end of the system design phase and the screen and report formats should be finalized.

10.3.5 Carrying out the system design review

A major task for staff responsible for software system engineering is the organization and execution of the system design review which validates the products of the phase. At such a meeting the system design document, the interface control document, changes to the system specification, project plan and test plan are reviewed in a similar way to the review of the system specification as described in Sec. 9.2.

Again, a good number of participants for such a review is four. These should include the system designer (chief designer if there is a design team), project manager, a member of staff from quality assurance and a designer external to the project who is familiar with the application area.

SAQ Suggest some of the questions which you think might be asked during a system design review.

SOLUTION Basically, the system design review should ensure that the system design document provides sufficient information for the detailed design team to perform detailed design without having to refer back to the system design team. Typical questions that are addressed in a system design review as follows:

1. Are all the performance requirements described at a sufficient level for detailed design?

2. Are all the memory and file requirements specified at a sufficient level for detailed design?

3. Are all functional requirements implemented in the system design, and are the relationships between requirements and program units documented?

4. Are all interfaces fully specified?

5. Is any part of the design overcomplex?

6. Is an adequate explanation for the design presented in the system design?

7.   Is the environment of the system described adequately?

8.   Are the software tools required to support testing specified exactly?

9.   Are the critical dependencies in the system identified?

10.   Have all the entities and attributes identified during requirements analysis been mapped onto suitable data structures?

11.   Are the requirements met by the system?

The first two questions in the answer above are simply checking that the system design document is suitable to be handed over to the detailed design team. For example, individual algorithms for each program unit are developed during detailed design, and in order to select a suitable algorithm the detailed designer needs to know what restrictions, if any, should be placed on its efficiency in terms of both speed and size. The third question above simply checks the completeness of the system design document. The remaining questions are discussed below.

Are all interfaces fully specified?

At this stage in the software project user interface requirements should have been completed, and all screens used to display information or to prompt users for data will have been defined. The review team should check that all these screens are complete and that all the events that occur in the system, and which require screens, are mapped onto already defined screens. Also, interfaces to hardware and other software systems should be detailed.

Is any part of the design overcomplex?

The system design review team should examine the system design to identify any areas which are complex, and which are therefore likely to cause problems during either implementation or maintenance. Various kinds of evidence may be considered in order to identify these areas, including the values obtained from suitable software metrics, the use of global variables and the number of parameters passed between program units. Any program units which are considered to be too complex should be redesigned while those which are involved in many functions and will hence be executed a large number of times should be identified so that fast and efficient algorithms can be devised for them during detailed design.

Is an adequate explanation for the design presented in the system design?

A design should not be presented without some degree of explanation. For example, a part of a design may be overcomplex but this may be necessary in order to satisfy non-functional requirements such as response time. In order for the review team to carry out their job properly the rationale behind the design should be presented. This rationale should explain why the design is favourable, in terms of timing, size and maintainability concerns. Design is largely a matter of choice, and therefore part of this justification may include descriptions of the major design alternatives which were considered, and the reasons for rejecting them.

Is the environment of the system described adequately?

The computer selection studies and analysis of existing facilities will be complete by the time this review takes place. Therefore, the hardware and support software to be used on the project will have been chosen. This environment into which the system is to be placed should be fully described in the system design document, and the review team should check this description against the system's requirements. For instance, the memory allocation, processor speed and input/output channel capacity of the intended hardware system should be specified, and performance figures for the operating system should be described.

Are the software tools required to support testing specified exactly?

Many software projects require software tools to support the development process, some of which were mentioned in Sec. 9.2. Other, specialized pieces of software may also be needed to test the system. For example, simulators may be needed to mimic a hardware device, test data generators may be needed to produce data for volume testing during system testing and acceptance testing, and test harnesses may be needed to test individual program units. If these tools are to be developed from scratch then they should have been completely specified at this stage. A series of mini system specification reviews and mini system design reviews, one for each tool, should be carried out.

This question is of particular interest to the member of staff responsible for quality assurance, since testing is a major quality activity.

Are the critical dependencies in the system identified?

The review team should ask whether the documentation produced up to the end of system design has adequately documented all critical dependencies within the project. These dependencies fall into three categories: issues relating to the system's environment, issues relating to the timely completion of activities, and issues relating to the correctness of final program code.

- Issues relating to the system's environment would include the critical dependence of non-functional requirements on database access, input and output channels, or the operating system. These concerns should be documented so that if, for some reason, the environment needs to be altered, or elements of the system are changed, then the effect of the change on the overall project can be assessed easily. For example, suppose the customer asks for extra functions to be added to the system. The developer could gain very quickly an idea of whether the request was feasible by looking through the list of critical dependencies and by studying the demands of the new functions on the system's environment.

- Activities on the critical path for the project should be identified, since the completion of the overall project depends on their completion. These activities should be documented because they must be monitored carefully during the remaining phases of the project.

- If a system depends heavily on the correct execution of a single program unit, or a small number of program units, then this fact should also be documented. It may be that the project manager would want to specify particular development practices for such critical program units, and their existence should be highlighted. For example, many software systems contain a relatively small number of program units which are used very frequently. Typically, these program units manipulate data structures, for example adding an element to a queue or removing an element from a queue. If made aware of these program units at the end of system design, then the project manager may insist upon rigorous verification by means of mathematics being performed on the relevant detailed designs.

Have all the entities and attributes identified during requirements analysis been mapped onto suitable data structures?

During system design all the entities and attributes identified during requirements analysis should have been expressed in terms of databases, files, records and fields. In addition, the relationships between entities and the use of those relationships should be reflected in the links between the corresponding data structures. For example, in a file-based employee records system, an employee record containing personal information about an employee such as his or her name, address, telephone number and so on, should be linked to a salary record containing information about the same employee's salary history. Also, the files should be organized so that retrieving and updating salary records via an employee record is efficient.

> SAQ List five activities which are part of the responsibility of the software system engineering staff during the system design phase.
>
> SOLUTION Staff responsible for software system engineering will perform computer selection studies, devise scenarios, document the relationships between functions and program units, prepare the interface control document and be involved with the system design review during the system design phase.

Are the requirements met by the system?

This is the most important question of all. It involves the designer explaining to the review team how each function in the system specification is implemented in the design, and how the design will satisfy constraints such as response time.

10.4 QUALITY ASSURANCE

During this phase staff involved in quality assurance will be monitoring the evolving system design document against the customer's statement of requirements, and checking all system design documentation for compliance with project standards and with the contract for the project; one member of the quality assurance staff will attend the system design review.

They will also be involved in expanding the outline system tests and acceptance tests which were prepared during the previous phase. These tests will be applied to both internally and externally developed, i.e. subcontracted, software.

For example, outline tests like the following will be expanded:

Test set 1237

These tests should check that commands which write data to a full track database will not be executed and that suitable error messages will be displayed.

The above test might be refined to produce two further ones such as the following:

Test 1237.1

This test should check that when the track database is full the DEPOSIT_TRACK program unit will not be executed and that the error: DEPOSIT_TRACK_DATABASE_FULL will be displayed on the originating VDU.

Test   1237.2

This test should check that when the track database is full the DEPOSIT_ID command will not be executed and that the error: DEPOSIT_ID_DATABASE_FULL will be displayed on the originating VDU.

If special software is required to perform system and acceptance testing, then quality assurance staff will be involved in specifying it.

SAQ What kind of special testing software may be required?

SOLUTION Simulators may be needed to mimic a hardware device, test data generators may be needed to produce test data, and test harnesses may be needed to test individual program units.

10.5 CONFIGURATION MANAGEMENT

The work of staff responsible for configuration management increases dramatically during this phase because more and more documents will be produced by staff responsible for software system engineering and they will all need to be controlled and checked against the project's documentation standards. Changes to the customer's statement of requirements and the system specification must also be monitored.

SAQ Which of the following statements are true and which are false? If you think a statement is false then explain why.

(a)   Part of the responsibilities of quality assurance staff during the system design phase is the expansion of system and acceptance tests.

(b)   Staff associated with the configuration management function will have no tasks to perform during the system design phase.

(c)   Staff responsible for software production develop the system design document.

(d)   The project manager and the system designer are the only people to attend the system design review.

SOLUTION

(a)   True.

(b)   False. The documentation being produced during the system design phase and any changes to the system specification must be controlled.

(c)   False. Staff responsible for software system engineering develop the system design document.

(d)   False. The project manager, the system designer, a member of the quality assurance staff and a designer outside the project team attend the system design review.

10.6 SUMMARY

During the system design phase, the activities associated with each of the responsibilities are as follows:

- Staff responsible for subcontract management will be involved in requirements analysis for the subcontracted pieces of software, and in system specification reviews. They will be monitoring carefully the production of the software.
- Staff responsible for software system engineering will prepare the system design document, perform computer selection studies, devise scenarios incorporating the major events which the system will encounter during its operation, document the relationship between functions and program units, detail the system's interface to agents outside the remit of the current system and conduct the system design review.
- Staff responsible for quality assurance will monitor the system design document against the customer's statement of requirements, expand the outline system and acceptance test plans and identify any special software required to test the system. All system design documentation will be checked to ensure that it meets the standards laid down in the project plan and in the contract between the developer and the customer.
- Staff responsible for configuration management will monitor any changes to the customer's statement of requirements and the system specification, and control the numerous documents being produced by other project staff.

11

EXECUTING THE DETAILED DESIGN PHASE

AIMS

- To describe the developmental processes which occur during detailed design.
- To describe the components of a detailed design review.

11.1 INTRODUCTION

During the detailed design phase[1] algorithms for each of the program units specified in the system design document are produced and documented in the detailed design document .

11.2 SUBCONTRACT MANAGEMENT

The staff responsible for subcontract management will continue to monitor the development of the subcontracted software during this phase, although the amount of effort expended on requirements analysis may have dwindled to nothing, since the subcontracted software should be nearing completion by this stage. Many projects schedule the handover of subcontracted software to this phase and, in this case, the staff responsible for subcontract management, together with quality assurance staff, will be involved in acceptance testing of the software.

SAQ Why do many projects plan for the handover of subcontracted software during the detailed design phase of the main software system?

SOLUTION The development of subcontracted software is often regarded as a risky process. If handover is scheduled for the implementation phase or early in system testing, then the developer runs the risk of delaying the main software project while errors in the subcontracted software are rectified. If the software is handed over during detailed design then at least the developer has some time to recover, if necessary.

---

[1] It is important to point out again that often a developer misses out on the detailed design phase, preferring to move to programming immediately.

154

11.3 SOFTWARE SYSTEM ENGINEERING

Staff responsible for software system engineering coordinate any changes to the system specification and system design document which are discovered during this phase. They also liaise with staff responsible for software production in generating the detailed design document for the system.

11.4 QUALITY ASSURANCE

During this phase staff responsible for quality assurance continue to monitor project documentation against the standards laid down in the project plan. In addition, they prepare the detailed plans for system testing, acceptance testing and for test procedures which describe the step-by-step instructions for carrying out the system tests and acceptance tests.

If subcontracted software is delivered during this phase, then they will also be concerned with performing acceptance tests for the software.

11.5 SOFTWARE PRODUCTION

Software production begins during detailed design. Implementation of parts of the system may start during this phase and staff responsible for software production will specify guidelines for the thoroughness of unit testing that is required on the project.

SAQ Why might the implementation of parts of a system start during detailed design?

SOLUTION There are two possible reasons for this. Firstly, it is extremely difficult to allocate staff exactly when they are needed on a project. Because other projects finish early or finish late there will be a gradual buildup of programmers. Normally this buildup peaks during the start of the implementation phase but it does mean that some programmers are attached to the project during detailed design. Rather than keeping such staff idle a project manager may start the implementation of a part of a system which has been fully designed.

Secondly, in real-time systems it is common practice to develop a prototype system in order to check that non-functional time requirements will be met, and this is often done early during detailed design. Once the prototype has been developed, it may either be used as a basis for producing the final system, or, having learnt all that is possible, the developer might simply discard it.

11.5.1 Carrying out detailed design reviews

There are two types of review associated with detailed design. They are major detailed design reviews that occur at the end of the phase and internal detailed design reviews which occur throughout the phase.

The major reason for holding internal reviews is to ensure both that the development team keeps an overall view of the system being developed and that interfaces between parts of the developed system are correct. Development during detailed design is fragmented with large numbers of program units being designed so it is easy for staff to be wholly concerned with their part of the system and to lose sight of the overall aim of the project. Internal detailed design reviews enable such staff to gain an idea of the structure and philosophy of other parts of the system and to share experiences, new techniques and new tools.

It is a good idea for all the project staff to be invited to internal detailed design reviews. Not only does it give an opportunity for everybody to become familiar with the part of the system being reviewed, but it is also useful for dealing with issues that affect the whole of the development team and for maintaining *esprit de corps*.

An internal detailed design review should not normally last more than a couple of hours. During this review, the staff member who produced the detailed design under scrutiny should describe the function of the program unit and the overall rationale behind the design, as well as covering the details. Issues that should be covered include any special problems encountered, any new techniques used and why the particular design structure described was adopted. An internal detailed design review should not become a group design activity. Although issues which require changes to the detailed design will be raised, these should be noted and addressed outside the review.

The major detailed design review is similar to the system design review and the system specification review. It is usually divided into a series of smaller detailed design reviews each of which deals with only a part of the system; for anything but a small project the amount of documentation to be reviewed will be very large and can be dealt with only incrementally. Four or five staff members will usually attend a detailed design review. They are the project manager, a member of staff responsible for quality assurance, the system designer and a staff member who has worked on a similar project, but is totally unconnected with the project. Normally the detailed designer of the part of the system being reviewed will also attend.

The main function of the major detailed design review is to check that elements of the system are specified in enough detail for implementation to begin.

SAQ List some of the questions which you think should be addressed by a detailed design review. It may help you to refer back to those listed for the system design review.

SOLUTION There are, of course, many questions that could be posed at a detailed design review, some of which are more detailed versions of those asked at a system design review. A selection of questions that should be asked is as follows:

1. Are all the performance requirements described at a sufficient level for implementation?

2. Have all the hardware interfaces been designed?

3. Have all the interfaces with the operating system been designed?

4. Has all the support software been designed and has any of this software which is needed in the early stages of implementation been implemented?

5.   Has the processing of each program unit in the system design document been designed fully using a notation such as a program design language?

6.   Have all interfaces between program units been defined?

7.   Have all inputs and outputs to each program unit been defined together with a description of their formats and the range of values?

8.   Have the database and data files been defined?

11.5.2 Carrying out simulation and modelling

Simulation and modelling of the system's intended environment is often used for testing in situations where testing software would otherwise be infeasible. For example, testing the logic of software for controlling a nuclear reactor system during an emergency is not feasible using the real thing! A rather less catastrophic example was given in Chapter 8. The software for controlling the emergency gangway was tested using a simulation of the motion of the emergency vehicle and a model of the gangway itself.

It is also sometimes desirable to use simulation and modelling techniques for the software system itself in order to ensure that the final system satisfies its constraints. In systems where there are demanding real-time constraints the development team will spend a large amount of time during system design estimating response time. Unfortunately, the calculation of response time is an extremely difficult process and in some cases the figures derived can only be rough estimates. Therefore, if the system to be implemented is a critical real-time one and the development team suspect that it only just satisfies its non-functional requirements then the process of modelling will usually take place.

Modelling consists of implementing and monitoring the performance of critical program units. If they do not match up to the required performance figures specified during system design then the algorithms are modified and redesigned. When modelling takes place the staff involved in the process should document all the performance figures together with the various design solutions that were selected for the experiment. Finally, they should document their reasons for selecting a particular design.

Simulation is often used when memory constraints are particularly important. Simulation consists of taking a partially built system and adding dummy program units which match the predicted size of the program units that they replace. This partial system can then be executed to ensure that it does not exceed its memory allocation.

11.5.3 Completion of software to support testing

The support software required to test the final system is specified during the system design phase. Such software may include specialized hardware simulators, test harnesses, test data generators and formatters. If the software is developed by the development team then the detailed design of these tools should be approved and implementation started. If these tools are to be used during subsequent phases, it is important that such tools are completed and fully validated as soon as possible.

11.6 CONFIGURATION MANAGEMENT

The responsibilities of staff involved in configuration management remain the same as those outlined for the system design phase. The only difference lies in the increase in the volume of work carried out. At this stage in the project, the products of a number of phases will have been completed: the system specification, the system design document, the detailed design document, test plans and test procedures. There will be changes in many of these documents and these may rebound on earlier phases. Consequently, there are many changes to many documents which have to be controlled.

11.7 SUMMARY

During the detailed design phase, the activities associated with each of the responsibilities are as follows:

- Staff responsible for subcontract management may be involved in performing acceptance tests for the subcontracted software, since many projects schedule its handover for the detailed design phase in case there are any problems which could otherwise delay the final system.
- Staff responsible for software system engineering coordinate any changes required to the system specification and system design document, and liaise with the staff responsible for software production.
- Staff responsible for quality assurance monitor production of the detailed design document, ensuring that it meets the standards laid down in the project plan and in the contract between the developer and the customer. They also prepare the detailed system test plans and acceptance test plans, and take part in acceptance testing for any subcontracted software to be delivered.
- Staff responsible for software production produce the detailed design document and any items for simulation and modelling, and attend detailed design reviews.
- Staff responsible for configuration management monitor any changes to the project documentation.

EXECUTING THE IMPLEMENTATION PHASE

AIMS

- To describe the processes involved in executing the implementation phase.
- To describe the contents of the unit development folder.
- To outline the conduct of a program walk-through.

12.1 INTRODUCTION

The implementation phase is concerned with the production of executable code for the program units specified during the detailed design phase. This involves writing code, unit testing and integration testing for the system.

12.2 SUBCONTRACT MANAGEMENT

The responsibilities of subcontract management continue with little difference from that outlined for the previous phase. If the subcontracted software was not delivered during the detailed design phase, then it will be scheduled for handover during implementation. In this case the staff involved in subcontract management, together with quality assurance staff, will carry out acceptance testing on this software in conjunction with staff from the subcontractor.

One task remains after subcontracted software has been accepted, and that is to record the history of the project's involvement with the subcontractor. This is a vitally important document which tends to be overlooked on many software projects. If the developer is to make substantial use of subcontractors in the future, then it is very useful to have a record of the performance of various subcontractors, based on finished projects.

SAQ What sort of information should be included in the history of a project's involvement with a subcontractor?

SOLUTION At least the following three items of information should be included:

1. An overall appraisal of a subcontractor's competence from the point of view of the developer's staff.

2. Information about whether there was good communication between the subcontractor and the developer.

3. Details of the performance of the subcontractor in terms of delivery time and the number of errors discovered during acceptance testing of the subcontracted software.

12.3 SOFTWARE SYSTEM ENGINEERING

Before this phase starts all the main documents for the project will have been completed and reviewed. Any changes to the system specification and the system design document will be implemented by staff responsible for software system engineering.

12.3.1 Preparing the operating instructions manual

The *operating instructions manual* is a major product of this phase. It describes the procedures used to load, start, operate, restart and halt a system. Therefore, it is aimed at any person involved with the day-to-day operation of the system, who has some technical background. It is important to point out that manuals usually instruct users how to use a system normally; the better manuals deal with exceptions or errors separately. An excerpt from a typical operating instructions manual is given below:

3.4 Restarting the system after an error state 13

The system will halt with the message: 'Error13 Halt' when an error state 13 occurs. When it does occur the operator on the main console should put the error log file online, put the restart file online and execute the restart program. When this program is executed it will ask the operator for the drive number for these files. This will normally be the rp0131 drive although if the system was in the monitoring state when the error occurred then this will be the rp112 drive. The program will then ask the operator whether the diagnostic program should be run. Normally, this program is run unless there has been another error 13 condition occurring in that same day. The operator should consult the written day log to ascertain whether this is so.

Obviously, the information contained in this extract means little to someone who is not familiar with the system to which it refers. For example, what is the rp112 drive? However, this excerpt does show you the kind of information which would be included in an operating instructions manual.

In a separate section, the operating instructions manual also includes a description of how each function of the system is exercised. Each function which is visible to the external user is documented, and the effect of that function is briefly described in terms of the program units that form the system architecture, which is contained in the system design document. An excerpt describing the function of system monitoring is shown below:

13.4 System monitoring

The function of system monitoring is activated by the operator of the main plant console typing the SYS_MONITOR command. The command is typed first, followed by one of the keywords FULL or SHORT. If the keyword FULL is typed then a full report is produced showing each reactor together with its average temperature over the last minute, the last 10 minutes, the last 60 minutes and the last 24 hours. This function is supported by the module READ_MONITOR_DATA which reads the contents of the monitor file. If the keyword SHORT is typed then the average temperature of each reactor over the last 10 minutes is displayed. This is implemented by the module READ_SHORT_TERM which reads information held in the short-term monitor file.

12.3.2 Preparing the user guide

The *user guide* is extracted from the operating instructions manual and is intended to be read by users of the system who have no technical background. It will contain essentially the same information as the operating instructions manual but without the details of operation, i.e. it will concentrate on explaining how the user can make the system perform the required functions.

SAQ Examine the extract from the operating instructions manual shown above and write the corresponding entry for it in the user guide.

SOLUTION The extract is shown below:

System   monitoring

In order to carry out system monitoring the operator of the main plant console should type the SYS_MONITOR command. If a full listing is required then it should be followed, after one space, by the word FULL. If a short listing is required then it should be followed, after one space, by the word SHORT. A full listing will produce the average temperature for the last minute, the last 10 minutes, the last 60 minutes and the last 24 hours for each reactor. A short listing will produce the average temperature for each reactor for the last 10 minutes.

SAQ Are members of the developer's staff likely to make use of either the operating instructions manual or the user guide, after they have been produced and verified?

SOLUTION The members of staff concerned with maintenance of the system are likely to make great use of the operating instructions manual. This document is vitally important during software maintenance because it enables a specific error to be rapidly tracked to the program unit which may be responsible for the error. Users of the system will report errors in terms of what happened when they exercised functions, rather than in technical terms such as the name of the module executed. Since the operating instructions manual matches functions to program units, it is ideal for tracing the error.

Members of the developer's staff are less likely to make use of the user guide.

12.4 QUALITY ASSURANCE

The workload associated with this responsibility increases steeply during this phase. Staff monitor and check the test activities that occur during unit testing and also check that the integration test procedures they have written are adhered to. If any subcontracted software is to be delivered during this phase quality assurance staff will be involved in its acceptance testing.

Depending on company or project policy, integration testing of the main software system may be performed by the quality assurance staff.

SAQ What would be involved in monitoring and checking the test activities that occur during unit testing?

SOLUTION Quality assurance staff would check that individual programmers have adequately tested a program unit. For example, they would check that test data which represented extremal values was used and that the test data and test results were recorded according to project standards.

12.5 SOFTWARE PRODUCTION

During this phase staff implement the software designed in previous phases. Depending on company or project policy, the staff responsible for software production may carry out integration testing as well. If not then this will be carried out by staff responsible for quality assurance.

12.5.1 Carrying out the program walk-through

A *program walk-through* is a peer group review process which consists of a number of colleagues examining a program unit produced by one of them and checking the code according to a checklist of questions; a program walk-through will usually be conducted before unit testing is performed. These reviews are usually less formal than the system specification review and the system design review mentioned earlier. A typical checklist excerpt is as follows:

1. Are all the constants defined?
2. Are the calculated values stored after they have been calculated?
3. Are all input parameters to the program unit used in the program unit?
4. Are all output parameters to the program unit given a value in the program unit?
5. Are all variables used in a 'while' loop or 'repeat' loop given values which will terminate the loop?
6. Do the 'case' statements process all the possible values of the case variables?
7. Are all array subscripts assigned only values which are within the array bounds?
8. If another program unit is called and has output parameters are the actual variables which are substituted for these parameters used?
9. Is the complexity of the control structure too high?

12.5.2 Preparing the unit development folder

One of the most important documents associated with the implementation process is the *unit development folder* occasionally called the *programmer's notebook*. This is a record of the progress of a program unit through implementation and is maintained by the programmer who is responsible for implementing it.

The unit development folder contains the final program code of the program unit, the final detailed design of the program unit, a description of the tests that were carried out and their results, all documentation generated during the development and testing of the unit, results of program walk-throughs, and any changes which were necessary to the detailed design during implementation together with an explanation of those changes. Sometimes a detailed explanation of decisions regarding implementation strategies which were made in order to satisfy non-functional requirements such as response time will also be included; this is especially important for critical program units within the system.

The final program code and the detailed design are used by staff responsible for maintaining the system. Obviously, if errors are detected then the staff must have access to the program code being executed. If a change to the program code is required for any reason then it is vitally important that the effect of this on the whole unit can be evaluated; this can be easily ascertained from the detailed design.

A record of the tests that were carried out on the program unit is important for quality assurance purposes. Many of them would be extremal value tests which checked whether the program correctly processed highly unlikely values. These kinds of test are necessary in case the designer has overlooked a situation which may cause the system to crash once in operation.

For each unit test there should be a test data file, a results file, an explanation of what the test should achieve, a file containing the steps necessary to run the test and the coverage of the test. The test data file contains the input data which was used during the test, and the results file contains the output data which was generated during the test. These will be reused if any subsequent changes are required to the unit, to evaluate whether the change has affected the functionality of the unit. The explanation of what the test achieves usually includes the location of the test data file and the results file. The coverage of the test would be expressed in terms of the percentage of the program's structural units such as branches that were executed.

The unit development folder should also contain any documentation which was generated during the development and testing of the program unit. Typical documentation includes letters from the programmer to the detailed designer querying the design, replies from the detailed designer and any notes made by the programmer.

Finally, the result of any program walk-throughs that took place on the unit should be included in the folder. This includes information about problems which were identified, the action taken, and the date when the action was taken.

A *unit development folder audit* is another kind of review. It is normally carried out by the programmer involved in producing a unit and a member of staff responsible for the quality assurance of the project. The major issues involved in this audit are adherence to project standards and adequacy of testing. Normally in a major project there is not time to carry out audits on every program unit. Normal practice would be for a sample, say 20 per cent of each programmer's work to be monitored. The following is a transcript of part of such an audit. It takes place between John, who is a programmer responsible for implementing a series of program units for monitoring a chemical plant, and Geoffrey, who is a member of an independent quality assurance team.

Geoffrey: OK, let's have a look at the unit development folder for procedure unit monitor valves. That's the one that had its detailed design changed a number of times, wasn't it?

John: Yes, in fact it was changed halfway through my programming it. I virtually had to start again. It was so frustrating!

Geoffrey: Well, blame the customer. He paid for those requirements changes dearly. Right, let's see; do you have detailed design version 3.1?

John: Yes.

Geoffrey: That looks like the right one. The version header is 3.1.

Because the detailed design had changed a number of times Geoffrey checks that the right version of the detailed design has been coded and that an earlier one has not been used. He checks this by looking at a part of the detailed design in the unit development folder known as the version header. This gives the version of the detailed design used. He checks this against an up-to-date listing of the version numbers of detailed designs.

Geoffrey: Right, let's look at the program code. Why did you use that kind of call to the filing system? It isn't the one specified in the detailed design.

John: Yes, you're right. It's faster than the one specified. I checked it with the system designer and he gave the OK. I think I have the memo here. Yes, here it is.

Geoffrey: Fine.

Geoffrey has noticed a discrepancy between the detailed design and the program code. However, there was a good reason for this and documentary evidence is provided to back this up. Every change from the detailed design has to be explicitly documented in a unit development folder.

Geoffrey: Does the project standard insist that you document all error conditions as comments before the body of a procedure?

John: Yes, I think so.

Geoffrey: Then you've missed the malfunctioning inlet valve condition.

John: You're right.

Geoffrey: You should fix it before the unit gets integrated. Let's have a look at the tests. Test 23 didn't seem to have a very high coverage. What was it—3 per cent branch coverage?

John: Yes.

Geoffrey: This seems very low. Why was this?

John: Well, that test checked what would happen if all the valves were malfunctioning. Therefore, under normal circumstances, what actually happens is that the procedure is exited almost immediately.

Geoffrey: Mmmm. Let's have a look.

Geoffrey checks this by looking at the program code.

Geoffrey: Yes, you're right. Did any of your tests check the condition that only one inlet valve was online?

John: Yes, test 33 checked the condition when one inlet valve was online and test 35 checked the condition when one inlet valve was online and one outlet valve was online.

Geoffrey: Fine.

The review continued with Geoffrey examining more tests to see that extreme values were examined and checking that project standards were adhered to.

12.6 CONFIGURATION MANAGEMENT

This activity continues in the way detailed in the previous section. However, the emphasis changes to include the control of versions of software. On a large project, the number of products to be controlled can be enormous.

12.7 SUMMARY

During implementation, the activities associated with each of the responsibilities are as follows:

- Usually, most subcontracted software will have been delivered and tested by this stage. If there is still some outstanding then staff responsible for subcontract management will be involved in acceptance testing the subcontracted software.
- Staff responsible for software system engineering will be responsible for making any changes necessary to the system specification and system design document. They will also produce the operating instructions manual and the user guide.
- Staff responsible for quality assurance will be monitoring unit and integration testing to ensure that project standards are adhered to. As part of this process, they will also be involved in unit development folder audits.
- Staff responsible for software production organize program walk-throughs and unit development folder audits, and ensure that implementation proceeds as planned.
- Staff responsible for configuration management are still involved in controlling changes to documentation, but they must also be concerned with program code during implementation. Their workload therefore increases dramatically.

13

WHAT IS QUALITY ASSURANCE?

AIMS

- To outline the nature of software quality assurance.
- To look briefly at some quality factors.

The term *quality assurance* was introduced earlier in this book, but its definition bears repeating here since we shall examine the subject in more depth in this unit. Quality assurance is the term used to describe those activities which ensure that a contractually acceptable product is delivered by a project. In other words, a quality piece of software is one which, above all else, meets the customer's requirements. Quality assurance includes many of the good practices which we have already described, such as holding reviews, producing a project plan and documenting activities. It is important to point out that quality assurance is as much concerned with the processes used to create a software system as the system itself.

The production of almost any piece of software requires a certain amount of communication between people, from the smallest program to the largest system. For example, imagine how much communication would be involved when a company's entire finance department and board of directors have to communicate their ideas to a software developer's project team consisting of maybe 15, 20 or even more people. Not only is there communication between the customer's staff and the developer's, but there is a great deal of communication needed within the developer's organization between members of the project team. Obviously, if you are talking about a high-quality product, then it is imperative that this communication is effective, otherwise the developer could end up producing a product which the customer does not want, or different members of the project team could end up producing incompatible program units! One of the aims of quality assurance, therefore, is to ensure that this communication is effective, i.e. to ensure that the developer, in particular the developer's project team, has understood correctly the customer's requirements.

High-quality software is characterized by many other attributes which are not directly related to the customer's requirements. We begin by looking at the following:

- efficiency,
- reliability,
- testability,
- maintainability,
- usability.

Efficiency refers to the behaviour of a system in relation to the resources of the computer system on which it executes. Most often the efficiency of a system is described in terms of its execution speed and storage use. If a system executes as fast as was specified but consumes twice as much storage as was expected, maybe in order to achieve the performance requirement, it is likely to incur the customer's displeasure.

The term *reliability* relates to the number of errors in a piece of software, and hence is a measure of the number of times a software system fails to perform correctly. One might expect a system containing 10 errors to meet a customer's requirements more frequently than one containing 100. (However, this might not be the case; just one of the 10 may be more serious than all of the 100.)

SAQ Write down what you think is meant by the terms *testability*, *maintainability* and *usability*?

SOLUTION Testability refers to the ease with which a software system can be tested. For example, if a system contains program units with a large amount of tortuous logic then it will be difficult to test; if it is difficult to test its design or implementation may be poor and it may be less likely to meet customer requirements.

Maintainability refers to the ease with which a system can be changed once it is in operation. For example, it should be straightforward to replace a function in a system if its system design exhibits loose coupling and high cohesion.

Usability is the ease with which the system can be used; if a system is easy to use, if it has a consistent and clear model of how it should be used, then it is less likely to be misused. This characteristic has much to do with the human–computer interface which is a topic in itself. It is not just a matter of aesthetics or taste since misuse could result in financial loss, environmental damage, or loss of life.

Another important characteristic for increasingly many systems is the degree to which they account for safety. This is discussed fully in Chapter 17.

Software quality is difficult to define, since the characteristics of quality contain a large subjective element, and often depend on the application being considered. Certain characteristics may be demanded by the customer (e.g. usability) while others may be of more interest to the developer (e.g. maintainability), and, in some circumstances, the attainment of quality characteristics may be incompatible. For instance, if a system is to run on a small microcomputer, then it may be more important to make efficient use of memory than to ensure that the system can be maintained by non-specialist programmers.

There are a number of techniques available to a software developer which help the process of quality assurance, for example validation and verification activities such as prototyping, mathematical verification, testing and reviews. Whatever techniques are to be used, it is important that a plan is drawn up at the beginning of the project which details the techniques to use and when to use them. This plan should then be expanded during the project as and when necessary so as to keep it up to date. In particular, the plan should contain details of how the customer will be able to test that the system meets its requirements. In order to support this, the developer must have in place the mechanisms for supporting the planned quality assurance techniques, such as staff, documentation, project support tools and so on.

Quality assurance, therefore, extends beyond the immediate project and has an impact on the whole of a developer company. Ideally, the company will have a strategy for quality assurance and procedures for ensuring quality in its software products. Indeed, in most large organizations there are individuals who specialize in quality assurance. Other than formulating quality assurance policy and practices, these people have two roles: a policing role to ensure that appropriate quality assurance practices are being used correctly; and an advisory role to help project teams when plans go astray, or when special circumstances arise.

Activities associated with quality assurance can be split into three categories. The first category includes the validation and verification activities mentioned above. The second category contains those activities which *check* that validation and verification activities have been carried out correctly. (For example, checking that adequate test files have been produced for system testing.) The third category of activity contains those concerned with *planning* for quality assurance; activities such as system testing and integration testing can consume a large amount of project resource and, just like developmental activities such as requirements analysis and design, they should be adequately planned and estimated.

In the next chapter of this book, we look at quality planning and the quality system. Then we look in some detail at the most widely known and most commonly used validation technique, testing, and follow it with a description of another approach which takes a very different view. Although independent software standards are in their early days, there is some important work in this area, and Chapter 17 examines the area of standards for software development, concentrating particularly on safety critical systems. Finally, we include a case study which shows how quality assurance might be put into practice.

Throughout this part of the book, we use extracts from project documents to illustrate common practice. You are encouraged to study these carefully, not so much to learn the contents of a particular extract, as to learn how concepts may be realized. We quote freely from both established and emerging standards because of their importance in this area.

PLANNING FOR QUALITY

AIMS

- To describe what is meant by the term 'quality system'.
- To examine the contents of the quality plan.
- To identify some questions that should be asked of a quality plan.

14.1 INTRODUCTION

High-quality software is not produced by accident, it has to be planned from the start of the project, and the characteristics of quality must be built into the product. It is no good producing a system, discovering major errors at the testing stage and then trying to correct them to produce a quality product; quality cannot be added as an extra ingredient at the end of a project. Indeed, a developer should have a policy for quality and a strategy for meeting that policy. In this section we look at how developers should approach software quality assurance for all projects and how it should be planned for particular projects.

14.2 THE QUALITY SYSTEM

The software development process introduced in Chapter 1 showed verification and validation as having an impact at all stages of the development process. Quality assurance, which encompasses verification and validation, can cover all aspects of the company's operation from the way it presents itself to the customer, to the programming standards employed on its projects, and from the content and style of its contracts to the conduct of its reviews. Thus, inside a developer's organization quality assurance serves as a management tool, while in relation to a customer contract it serves to build confidence in the developer.

We now quote the internationally standardized[1] definitions of four terms which are fundamental to any discussion of quality assurance:

Quality The totality of features and characteristics of a product or service that bear on its ability to satisfy stated or implied needs.

Quality policy The overall quality intentions and direction of an organization as regards quality, as formally expressed by top management.

---

[1] The quotations in this part of the book are, in the main, taken from British or European standards.

Quality management That aspect of overall management function that determines and implements quality policy.

Quality system The organizational structure, responsibilities, procedures, processes and resources for implementing quality management.

(BS 4778/ISO 8402)

Though explicitly defined in an international standard, the first three of these terms are unsurprisingly vague; the last—quality system—is less so and is the starting point for planning the quality assurance activities for a project. In the context of software development, the general guidelines in the quality system address issues immediately related to the execution of all software projects; the elements of the quality system which are to be used on a specific software project are documented in that project's quality plan. Again, to quote from the relevant standards on management's responsibility for quality policy and on the nature of the quality system:

The supplier's management shall define and document its policy and objectives for, and commitment to, quality. The supplier shall ensure that this policy is understood, implemented and maintained at all levels in the organization.

(BS 5750/ISO 9001)

The supplier should establish and maintain a documented quality system. The quality system should be an integrated process throughout the entire life cycle, thus ensuring that quality is being built-in as a development progresses, rather than being discovered at the end of the process. Problem prevention should be emphasized rather than depending on correction after occurrence.

(BSI DPC 89/97932)

The quality system of the developer's organization is the embodiment of the company's quality policy; it expresses the ideal circumstances. Elements of this system can then be taken and tailored to suit particular projects depending on their application domain and other project-specific factors. This is similar to what happens in other production industries, such as the car industry. For example, when new car factories are set up, car manufacturers do not have to design everything from scratch, because they already know what elements are needed in the new factories. They do, however, have to tailor the machinery by retooling to fit the characteristics of the cars being produced. The system for building cars is not set up for every single car, or even for every different model, since the basic elements and guidelines are already known. In this sense, it is a general system. Software cannot be produced in quite the same way, but the project manager for a new software project will be able to use the company's quality system as a basis for the quality plan, adding or modifying elements of it to suit the particular application.

The quality system specifies the organizational structure, responsibilities, procedures, processes and resources needed to produce a quality product. It includes directives for ensuring correct implementation of configuration management practices, documentation practices, review practices and testing conventions. The quality system of the organization will be documented in a *quality manual*. This should lay down clear guidelines for the following:

- Identifying the developer's and the customer's responsibilities, regarding the attainment of quality.
- The reviews to be conducted, and their format.
- The format of the quality plan for any particular project.

Internal quality system audits should be undertaken. These verify whether the quality system is being adhered to and whether it is an effective system; corrective action can be taken when appropriate. As part of the quality system, procedures for corrective action should be well documented to cover circumstances in which the system which is being or has been produced does not meet the customer's requirements.

Although a quality system covers all aspects of the company's business, it should not be too much of a straitjacket. It need only contain enough information to state clearly how a quality product is developed. However, it must orient development towards correctness, and not towards the detection of faults.

In particular, the quality system covers: presystem development activities such as the bidding process, the format and content of the project plan; contractual matters such as the content of a contract and the style and purpose of contract reviews; and the format and content of documents used during development.

For example, the quality system might address the following points relating to the configuration management practices of the company:

1. How is a change to the software system to be achieved, i.e. who can authorize a change, who else must be notified and what documentation must be completed?
2. How is a change to be appraised, and by whom?
3. How is an approved change to be communicated to the quality assurance staff?
4. How are changes to program code to be reflected in changes to the detailed design document, the system design document and the system specification?
5. What action, if any, must be taken to inform the customer?

SAQ What issues might be addressed by the quality system for project reviews ?

SOLUTION The issues relating to project reviews which a quality system might address include the following:

1.   What reviews should be conducted, and when?

2.   Who should attend each type of review?

3.   A checklist of topics to be investigated or questions to be asked (see Chapters 9–12).

4.   What preparation for the review is required from each attendee?

5.   How is the review minuted?

6.   Who moderates the review, i.e. who acts as referee?

7.   How are changes which have been identified during a review carried out?

8.   The format and content of the documentation input to and output from a review.

The staff organization and the use of automated tools during development might also be specified in the quality system. For example, the use of a particular static analyser with a certain programming language might be specified.

14.3 THE QUALITY PLAN

The *quality plan* is that part of the project plan which details how the developer intends to ensure that the software is a product whose quality meets those standards defined by the quality policy.

Just as it is important to produce an overall plan of the project early on, it is necessary to produce a plan detailing the quality procedures and techniques to be used. The major aim of the quality plan is to be able to demonstrate (to the customer, if necessary) how the developer will ensure that the requirements for a software system are met. The first major quality assurance task is to determine the quality assurance activities that will be carried out during the execution of the project. This means that, for each phase, the quality plan must define explicitly how quality assurance activities (such as design reviews and system testing) are to be executed.

A quality plan is developed for each software project which the developer undertakes; it is based on the company's quality system, and will be agreed between the developer and the customer. Not all the elements of a developer's quality system may be included in every quality plan the developer produces. For example, if the system is for a commercial data processing application, then quality assurance techniques which are relevant only to real-time systems would not be included in the plan.

The following is an extract from a draft of an emerging British and international standard on software quality assurance, describing the contents of a quality plan:

The quality plan should specify or reference the following items

(a)   quality objectives, expressed in measurable terms whenever possible;

(b)   identification of types of test, verification and validation activities to be carried out on product specifications, plans and test specifications together with the methods and tools to be employed;

(c)   defined entry and exit criteria for each development phase;

(d)   detailed planning of test verification and validation activities to be carried out, including schedules, resources and approval authorities;

(e)   specific responsibilities for quality activities such as

—inspections, reviews and tests,

—configuration management and change control,

—defect control and corrective action.

(BSI DPC 89/97932)

The first thing to notice about this extract is the reference to quality objectives, expressed in *measurable terms*. The importance of introducing measurement into software project management was discussed in Chapter 4, and in particular, the notion of software metrics was introduced there; this extract emphasizes the importance of metrics.

The planning and execution of testing activities also feature highly in this extract. The results of testing are the most visible evidence that a software system conforms to the customer's requirements, or that it does not conform! Planning effectively for testing activities is, therefore, a major activity in software quality assurance. Any special software tools or resources for testing must be identified as early as possible so that suitable arrangements can be made for obtaining or producing them. This information would be contained in a special section of the quality plan, known as the test plan, which is described in more detail in Chapter 15.

Notice also that particular attention is paid to the definition of project phases. Since project milestones will usually be based around the project's phases and their products, this is a significant aspect of the project's successful completion. Often, the plan itself will be divided into project phases, specifying the quality activities associated with each phase.

Finally, observe how point (e) requires that specific responsibilities be detailed. This is common practice in other engineering disciplines; a potentially problematic area (such as configuration control) is always treated more seriously if it is seen to be part of your own direct responsibilities, rather than someone else's or indeed nobody's.

The quality plan tells the customer exactly how the developer will ensure that the delivered software meets its requirements. It is, therefore, important that the plan can be understood by the customer and it needs to be compiled in a manner which makes the contents definitive, providing the maximum clarity and avoiding unnecessary jargon.

The quality plan is extracted from a company *quality manual*, sometimes referred to as the *quality system*. The project manager, when planning a project, examines the application and decides which elements of the quality system will be included in the quality plan. If the project is an easy one then the project manager may not include all the elements; however, if it is tough, then the project manager may extract all the elements of the quality manual and even supplement them with extra quality controls. An extract from a typical quality manual is given below, detailing the format of the system specification:

System specification format

The system specification will consist of a series of sections.

The first section will contain the functional requirements for the system. These will be expressed in natural language. Major functions will be written as paragraphs with subfunctions expressed as subparagraphs, etc. The paragraphs will be numbered for identification in later phases of the project. Major paragraphs will be numbered with a single integer, subparagraphs will be numbered with two integers separated by a period, etc.

When a functional requirement is associated with a non-functional requirement, such as response time, the non-functional requirement will be referred to at the end of the paragraph describing the functional requirement by the words:

Applicable non-functional requirement(s)

This extract shows that the developer is taking care to relate subfunctions to functions so that validation is conducted more easily. The importance of being able to relate a requirement to products of the later stages of the project can also be indicated by using a specific phrase, for example:

Numbered for identification later in project.

Providing a cross-linking mechanism between functional requirements and non-functional requirements is an effective aid to validating non-functional requirements. It ensures that adequate documentation will be made available to quality assurance staff carrying out system testing and acceptance testing.

SAQ Why does relating subfunctions to functions ensure that validation is conducted more easily?

SOLUTION   Validation can be conducted more easily because when the system specification is validated, groups of functions which are related to each other are textually close to each other in the document. Thus, for example, a function which refers to access to a database would be close to the various subfunctions which detail the different accesses that are required. This means that when a customer and developer meet to examine the system specification they will not have to search through many pages of text in order to identify related functions. This, in turn, is likely to result in fewer errors being made, with a net result of improved quality.

SAQ Why is it important to be able to relate a requirement to products of the later stages of the project?

SOLUTION There are two common reasons why development staff want to relate a requirement to products of the later stages of the project:

1.   If the customer asks for a requirements change, then the developer can easily discover the sections of the relevant design documentation and program code that implement that requirement and which would need to be changed.

2.   When carrying out an estimate of response time the developer may want to relate a requirement to the program units that implement that requirement.

A second extract from a quality manual is shown below, specifying the conduct of reviews to be carried out during requirements analysis:

Reviews Associated with Requirements Analysis

Two types of reviews will be held during this phase. The first will be internal project reviews....

Internal system specification reviews

The function of these reviews is to check sections of the system specification for clarity, correctness, lack of vagueness, lack of ambiguity, etc. These reviews will be held for each subsystem. The reviews will usually last two hours and will consist of the following personnel:

•   The analyst involved in producing the subsystem specification.

•   A representative from the quality assurance department.

•   An analyst not connected with the project who has experience of the type of system under development.

- The project manager.

Each meeting will be minuted and outstanding issues noted as actions. The developer will make available to the customer, on request, the minutes or the action points.

Outstanding issues will normally be resolved in time for any subsequent meeting. Any issues which are not resolved at the end of two meetings are noted in the project's outstanding issues file. The developer will make this file available to the customer on request.

The format of the review and associated documentation is as follows....

SAQ Suggest what should be the second type of review associated with requirements analysis. Then, following the style of the extract above, describe what personnel should be involved in this second type of review and what is the purpose of the review.

SOLUTION The second type of review is a review of the system specification with the customer. The following extract describes who should be involved and its purpose.

System specification review

The second type of review is the system specification review. The purpose of this kind of review is to allow the customer's representatives to check the system specification for adherence to their requirements. These reviews are normally of two hours duration. The arrangements for outstanding issues will be the same as those for internal requirements reviews. The participants in the system specification review will vary for each project since we find the number and identity of the customer representatives will vary. The developer representatives for the review will be the following:

- The analyst involved in producing the part of the system specification under review.

- The chief analyst for the project.

- The project manager.

The timing of the reviews and details of customer representatives can be found in the project plan (pages 102–107). The format of the review and associated documentation is as follows....

SAQ Assume that the notation you were using for specification was a formal one. What sort of checks would you include in that part of the quality plan which details how an *internal* system specification review would be carried out?

SOLUTION One obvious check would be to see that operations do not violate the data type invariant. A second would be checking that the data type invariant is correct and represents constraints on data established by reading the statement of requirements or interviewing the customer. A third would be to check that the operations on the data are correct.

A major part of the quality plan should also deal with the identification of the verification requirements and the derivation of system tests and acceptance tests from them. This is discussed in detail in the next section. The quality plan should also specify how the integration tests, system tests and acceptance tests are developed and documented. In the majority of projects these are all developed during the later stages of requirements analysis and system design.

The quality plan must describe how the verification requirements are to be expressed, how they are to be reviewed internally, and the mechanisms to be used for gaining the customer's acceptance of these requirements. The first point is usually achieved by just a straightforward reference to the requirements in the system specification; it is quite common for them to be reviewed at the system specification review. Usually the customer will *sign-off* the requirements, i.e. formally accept, by signing a document, that these are reasonable and sufficient requirements to test during acceptance testing, within a specified time of receiving them.

The quality plan should also detail how the integration tests are to be specified and approved by the customer. An extract from a quality system describing this is shown below:

Procedures for integration tests

Towards the end of system design the developer will construct a series of integration tests which check that newly implemented units interface correctly with the system being built up. Each test specification will contain the following information:

1. The name of the test. This will consist of the first six letters of the subsystem in which the unit to be integrated is contained. This is followed by a six-digit number which uniquely identifies the test.

2. The name of the program unit(s) to be integrated and the number of the subsystem version with which it is (they are) to be integrated.

3. The location of the file containing the test data for the test.

4. The location of the file containing the expected outcome of the test.

5. The location of the file containing the actual outcome of the test.

6. The location of the file containing the correct subsystem with which integration is to be made.

7. The location of the file(s) containing the units to be integrated.

8. The purpose of the test, described in English text. This will contain details of which parts of the interface between the unit and the system are tested and the reasons why values of the test data were chosen.

9. Any subsidiary non-functional requirements which the test is meant to validate in a preliminary way.

SAQ Should the customer be asked to review the integration tests produced by the developer?

SOLUTION No, the customer should not be asked to review the integration tests produced by the developer since this is a technical document. The customer will not normally be involved in development activities such as integration testing, although documents such as the acceptance tests and the system specification will be of interest since they relate directly to the system's requirements. The customer will, however, be interested in the section of the quality plan dealing with integration testing which shows how the developer is to specify and organize the integration tests.

The quality plan must specify the format of the test procedures, how the developer will validate these procedures and how the final version of the system tests are checked and agreed with the customer. The kind of information which might be specified for acceptance test procedures is similar to that described for integration tests, such as the name of the test and the location of relevant files. In addition, the following may be included.

Acceptance test procedures

5. Step-by-step instructions for the execution of the test must be given. These instructions usually tell the person performing the test to load programs, make available test files and execute programs. If suites of tests are to be used, then command files which automatically load test programs or provide test data should be given.

6. Detailed instructions for the person performing the test to check whether the test has been carried out correctly shall be supplied. If the output from the test is small, give instructions on how to examine the output from a VDU, from a printer, or in a file. If large amounts of data are to be output as a result of a test, then programs which compare the output with the predicted outcome shall be used and instructions supplied.

7. If possible, timings shall be carried out using facilities in a system's environment (e.g. the operating system). Instructions on how to carry out timings on a particular system must be given.

8. For each execution of the system a checklist that has to be initialled by the person performing the test when each execution leads to a correct acceptance test.

In contractual terms, a vitally important section of this part of the quality plan concerns the means whereby the acceptance tests are to be agreed by the customer. This is important because the acceptance tests are usually legally binding on the customer—by agreeing to the results of the acceptance tests, the customer acknowledges the system's 'fitness for purpose'. Once the acceptance tests have been agreed to they cannot be changed unless with the consent of both customer and developer. The quality plan should indicate the means whereby the test procedures are reviewed by the customer and the developer and how they are signed-off.

A further element of the quality plan might be concerned with software metrics. As discussed in Chapter 4, it is important to be able to measure certain characteristics of software. This is particularly useful in the context of quality assurance, since it allows the standard of quality for a software system to be stated explicitly. Minimum acceptable values for specific metrics can be specified in the quality plan.

14.4 ASSESSING THE QUALITY PLAN

As we have already stressed, the quality plan must be understandable by the customer, since the customer must be able to ascertain whether the developer is going to employ procedures which will produce software that meets the requirements. Since the quality plan is based on the developer's quality system, it is likely that any major flaws in a quality plan are inherited from the quality system. The maintenance and modification of the developer's quality system is an internal matter which should be dealt with by the developer's own quality assurance staff.

However, the quality of a quality plan should be assessed by the customer, and it is important that this can be done effectively.

This section suggests some questions which a customer could and should ask about a quality plan for a project about to start. These should help the customer in assessing the developer's attitude towards quality assurance.

Does the plan define clearly the methods to be employed for achieving the desired quality requirements? Is the application of these methods explicitly defined?

This question covers the overall intention of the quality plan. Validation and verification activities as well as developmental activities should all be referred to in the quality plan. For example, applying this question to the conduct of system specification reviews means the customer asking questions such as:

- Is the expertise and experience of the staff involved in the review adequate for the proper execution of the reviews?
- Are enough reviews scheduled to cover adequately the whole of the system specification?
- How are disagreements between the customer and the developer resolved during system specification reviews?
- How are records of the system specification review kept?
- How will the system specification reviews be structured?
- What are the responsibilities of the participants in the review?

Is there a requirement for the customer to agree to the plan?

In the project documentation there must be a statement about the customer accepting the quality plan. This statement must include details of when the plan must be accepted and who actually accepts it from the customer's staff. This information may be contained in either the project plan or the quality plan. The quality plan should be accepted by the customer very early in the software project.

SAQ Why should the quality plan be accepted by the customer early in the software project?

SOLUTION The quality plan should be accepted by the customer early in the software project because it determines the conduct of many of the activities carried out in a project. This includes early activities such as requirements analysis. Ideally, the plan should be agreed to by the customer before even this activity commences.

Has the relationship of the plan to related quality and other plans (e.g. project and hardware plans, customer and subcontractor quality plans) been identified?

The quality plan is intimately related to many other documents in the software project. Firstly, it bears a close relationship to the project plan; it is physically part of it.[2] The customer should ensure that the quality assurance activities are correctly and adequately dovetailed into the developmental activities of the project. For example, the developer may show the amount of staff resources expended on quality assurance as a bar chart in the quality plan, and the amount of staff resources expended on developmental activities as a bar chart in the project plan. If there is a serious discrepancy between the proportion of the two during a vital activity such as design then the customer should ask some hard questions about the level of quality assurance support provided by the developer.

The quality plan is also closely related to hardware plans. In a project where there is a hardware element the quality assurance plans for hardware and software must complement each other. For example, the customer should check that the acceptance tests for software which is to run on a particular hardware unit produced by the developer follow the acceptance tests for the hardware; they cannot be carried out in parallel.

The quality plan is also closely connected to the quality assurance plans of any subcontractor who is to produce software for a project. The quality plans of the subcontractor should ensure at least the same standard of quality as those produced by the developer. The developer's quality plan normally includes appendices which detail subcontractor quality plans.

What are the procedures for authorization, issue and review of the quality plan?

Normally, the quality plan states the job title of the person or people to authorize the plan, rather than their names. For example, the quality plan may state that there is a representative from the customer known as the 'customer quality assurance representative' and that there is a representative from the developer known as the 'overall project manager' and that both these people should sign and authorize the quality plan.

The substance of a quality plan usually remains unchanged during the duration of a software project. However changes do occur sometimes. For example, a change in the software's requirements may result in some parts of the proposed system being more stringently tested than the majority of the system. This new stringent testing would have to be specified and included in the quality plan. Any changes to the quality plan must be evaluated and approved, and the original plan should detail how such changes are evaluated, who evaluates them, and who is to be empowered to approve them. The quality plan should also detail how versions of the plan are to be issued, to whom they are issued and whether they should be issued with each change.

---

[2] Although it is normally separately bound.

Have the individual and collective responsibilities of members of the project team been clearly defined?

One person, or one group of people, should be identified as being responsible for ensuring that the practices described in the quality plan are carried out correctly. In small projects the quality plan will usually reference one individual by job title.

In large projects a number of staff will have the responsibility of carrying out quality assurance activities. The quality plan should precisely state what each of these members of staff should do. Often during the period when the quality plan is being developed, specific names cannot be placed to each of the quality assurance staff. In this case it is allowable to identify staff by a code word or letter and to specify the experience and background necessary for each member of the quality assurance team.

Even if names can be given it is often a good idea to write down the individual's experience. This will then give the developer a good idea of how well the tasks to be carried out have been allocated to individuals.

Are the necessary human resources and skills available, not only to create the software but also to execute the quality requirements defined in the plan?

The quality plan should specify for all the quality assurance activities the amount of resource to be expended on each activity; not only from the developer but also from the customer. This can then be compared with the following two criteria:

1. The customer's expectation of how much resource the developer will use. If this does not match what is specified in the quality plan then the customer should question the developer's expertise.
2. The total resource that the developer specifies in the quality plan for carrying out the quality assurance activities. If this matches the cumulative total of the resources needed for individual quality assurance activities then the customer should be satisfied.

Does the plan identify specific quality assurance activities at all phases of the project?

A major weakness of many quality plans is that they tend to concentrate on later stages of the software project. They describe in inordinate detail the testing strategies involved during implementation and acceptance testing but skimp on the validation of requirements. The plan should identify all the reviews and activities, such as prototyping and simulation, that occur during requirements analysis and system design, and should describe them in as much detail as later activities such as unit testing and integration testing.

Are quality assurance audit activities specified?

It is vitally important that the developer states exactly how the activities specified in the project plan and the quality plan are to be checked. This means that for every activity the quality plan should specify the level of auditing that is to occur and how discrepancies between the actual execution of project tasks and the standards for the project are identified and rectified.

SAQ Suggest two criteria for auditing the quality assurance activities.

SOLUTION

- The frequency of audits (e.g. weekly, fortnightly).

- The proportion of system and other documents to be audited.

Does the plan identify the codes of practice and other standards to be used by the project team?

It is a matter of taste as to whether codes of practice and project standards are written into the project plan or into the quality plan. What is important is that for all developmental activities these are written down in detail. They range from codes of practice which govern activities such as unit and integration testing to design and programming standards. Typical examples of the former include directives about levels of testing and the selection of test data; examples of the latter include directives about the complexity of the loop structures in program units and the use of identifier names.

SAQ Which of the following should be specified in codes of practice or standards? If any of them should not be specified then give the reason for this.

(a)   The maximum size in lines of program units to be coded.

(b)   The minimum branch coverage to be achieved by unit test data.

(c)   The names of external hardware units which are expected to have a high risk of being delivered late.

(d)   The maximum number of calls to other program units from one program unit.

(e)   The skills of the requirements analysts who are to produce the system specification.

SOLUTION Items (a), (b) and (d) are normally specified in codes of practice and standards. The first would normally be in the programming standards, (b) would normally be in the code of practice for unit testing and (d) would normally be contained in the design standards. Item (c) is totally unrelated to either codes of practice or standards and properly belongs in the project plan. Similarly (e) belongs in the quality plan but in neither a code of practice nor a standard.

Does the plan identify the stages during the project at which the project documents will be reviewed?

The quality plan should specify when reviews occur. This includes the major project reviews and other less formal internal reviews.

The quality plan should describe how unit testing, integration testing, system testing and acceptance testing are to be carried out. In particular it should identify the test procedure documentation to be given to testers. This will be contained in the test plan, which is described in Sec. 15.2.

Does the plan specify the criteria by which the customer's requirements will be considered to have been satisfied?

There are a number of criteria by which a developed system will be accepted. These should be specified in the quality plan. This question does not refer to the individual test criteria by which each acceptance test is deemed to have failed or passed. It refers to the various techniques used to convince the customer that a software system has passed a test. These include:

- Examination of VDU output.
- Examination of the state of a database.
- Comparing the output of the system against test outcomes provided by the customer.
- Comparing the output of the developed system against the output from a similar program.

Are the arrangements for ensuring the adequacy of any proprietary or support software to be used by the project team specified in the plan?

It is important that the quality plan describes how the developer ensures that the software to be used for developing the main system will be of the equivalent quality to the developed software.

For software developed in-house (but maybe by another project team) this is usually achieved by applying the same quality control mechanisms as used in developing the software which has been contracted for. This means that the same requirements specification, design and programming methods should be used as for the developed software and also the same configuration management and testing strategies should be used. There should be an explicit statement in the quality plan which says that the same quality standards are applied to the proprietary software and support software as are applied to the developed software. Any deviation should be specified and reasons given for the deviation.

14.5 SUMMARY

Producing a quality piece of software cannot be achieved using ad hoc methods. The techniques to be used during a project to ensure the quality of its product must be carefully planned and documented as early in the project as possible. The document which contains this information is called the quality plan. Each project within an organization should have its own quality plan, but the organization as a whole should have a quality system on which the individual plans are based. The company's quality system should be documented in a quality manual.

It is important that the customer is able to understand and assess the quality plan, since this is the document which convinces the customer that the developer can produce a quality software system which meets the requirements.

BIBLIOGRAPHY

(BSI DPC 89/97932) Guidelines for the Application of BS 5750: Part 1 to Software.

(BS 5750/ISO 9001) Part 1: 1987/ISO 9001 – 1987, Quality Systems Part 1. Specification for design/development production, installation and servicing.

(BS 4778/ISO 8402) Part 1: 1987/ISO 8402 – 1986, Quality Vocabulary Part 1. International Terms.

15

ENSURING QUALITY IN THE TESTING PROCESS

AIMS

- To outline the relationship between software quality assurance and testing.
- To describe the relationship between verification requirements, system tests, acceptance tests and test procedures.

15.1 INTRODUCTION

Testing is an important validation activity, since it provides tangible evidence that the software performs as it should; testing must therefore be planned and executed carefully. In this section, we look more carefully at issues relating to the testing activity, concentrating on the contents of the test plan and the derivation of the system tests and acceptance tests.

15.2 THE TEST PLAN

When dealing with large systems, and with many programmers, the testing strategy to be adopted must be formally documented both for the members of the project team so that they are aware of the approach to testing which they must take, and for the members of the customer's staff who must be sure that the testing being performed is adequate.

The testing strategy to be used is decided upon early on in a project. Exactly what is tested, how it is tested and what evidence must be supplied to show that testing has been performed satisfactorily must be considered as early as possible so that adequate provisions for resourcing and conducting the testing can be made.

The test plan is that part of the quality plan which relates directly to the testing activity. It includes details of the project's testing strategy, and the test procedures. So far, we have mentioned unit testing, integration testing, system testing and acceptance testing. Each kind of testing has a different objective, and therefore each requires a different testing strategy and documentation technique. The approach which the project takes to each form of testing has to be laid down.

Since the test plan must cover all forms of testing, it will contain information relevant to unit testing, integration testing, system testing and acceptance testing; indeed, the test plan may be divided into sections, each of which covers one of these forms of testing.

The following lists the information which you would expect to find in a good test plan when it is fully developed. Some test plans may not contain all of this information, and others may include other, application-specific details; for example, special testing facilities may be required for software controlling a railway system. Note that some items will need to be repeated for each kind of test, while others will appear only once:

- The objectives of each kind of test.
- The criteria determining when a particular testing phase is complete, e.g. when integration testing is complete.
- The test schedule.
- Individual responsibilities.
- Resources required:
    Support software including testing tools,
    Hardware configuration,
    The amount of computer time,
    Personnel.
- Testing strategy including procedures for:
    Stress testing the software,
    Identifying, generating and documenting test cases,
    Tracking progress,
    Reporting and correcting detected errors,
    Regression testing.
- Documentation produced.
- Test procedures.

The objective of a test

Before considering the objectives of the different forms of testing, let us consider the purpose of testing itself.

SAQ What does the process of testing aim to achieve?

SOLUTION You may feel that testing is concerned with demonstrating the correctness of a piece of software. However, testing would be a much more worthwhile activity if the tester actually found errors in it, since by finding and correcting errors, the quality of the piece of software has been enhanced, and so the testing activity has really achieved something.

A definition of testing which reflects this view is given below:

Testing is the process of executing a program with the intent of finding errors.

(Myers, 1979)

The objectives for a particular testing phase should be documented so that the customer and the developer are clear about what the exercise is intended to achieve. Where at all possible, this must be stipulated in measurable terms, since otherwise it will be difficult to show conclusively that a testing phase has accomplished its aims.

Criteria determining when testing should stop

Determining when a particular test phase is complete is difficult. Since testing can never hope to prove that a piece of software is totally correct, you can never be sure that all errors have been detected. Therefore, it is difficult to say when testing should be stopped.

SAQ Suggest three criteria which might be used to decide when to stop unit testing. (Think of practical reasons for stopping as well as technical reasons.)

SOLUTION The following three criteria are the most common ones used in practice:

1. The time allotted to unit testing is over.

2. All test data specified in the test procedure has been used, and any resultant errors have been corrected.

3. All possible paths through the program have been tested.

The first criterion listed in the answer to the SAQ is arbitrary and clearly inadequate. The problem with the second criterion is that the adequacy of the testing depends on the quality of the test data in the test procedures. Of course, if the system of quality assurance is working properly, one would hope that the test data is adequate. The third criterion sounds hopeful, but this does not address the problem where the programmer or the designer have misunderstood the program unit's specification. All possible paths through a piece of software may execute correctly, but if a path is missing then the unit is still defective. Also, except for the smallest application, testing all the paths is impossible.

It is, of course, possible to develop a combination of the above criteria which determine adequately the completion of a set of tests, but you can see that it is not as easy as it first seems.

Test schedule

A schedule of testing activities should be drawn up as soon as possible in the project so that the project manager can see clearly how and when project completion can be attained. A PERT network should be used for documenting the time sequencing of testing activities. The approach to be used for integration testing must be specified before an integration testing schedule, or test plan, can be drawn up, since the list of relevant tasks must be identified first, and this cannot be done until the integration strategy is known.

The integration test plan specifies the order in which program units are to be added to the system being developed and the tests which are to be carried out after an integration. Normally the order of integration is determined and the individual test procedures are specified in outline during the initial stages of detailed design.

The main body of the project plan lists the tasks to be completed for the entire project, and their time scheduling, but detailed information relating to testing activities may be contained in the test plan instead.

Individual responsibilities

The responsibilities of each member of the quality assurance team and the project staff within the particular project must be specified. The use of a work breakdown structure like that introduced in Chapter 6 encourages such responsibilities to be identified, since each task shown in the structure must be associated with someone. For testing activities, responsibilities include the preparation of validation tests, participation in the reviews associated with testing and the auditing of documents produced by staff carrying out testing. Individual responsibilities for designing, writing, executing and verifying test cases and test procedures must also be identified.

It is always beneficial to avoid having a programmer testing his or her own work. Since testing is the process of finding errors, this will be accomplished much more effectively if the person trying to 'break' the software did not produce it. This is why many large organizations have a separate group of people whose sole job is to test other people's programs.

Resources required

In order to plan the testing activity, it is important that the project manager should know what resources are required, both hardware and software. Obviously, these estimates will be refined throughout the life of the project, as will the resourcing estimates for the rest of the project.

Testing strategy

The testing strategy includes the methods used to review test activities and test procedures, to check on the successful execution of tests, to correct errors discovered in tests, to report the results of tests and to determine the software's readiness for acceptance testing. It also specifies the type of testing to be used. For example, one form of testing known as *volume testing* involves subjecting the software to heavy volumes of data to see how it performs. Another form, called *recovery testing*, tests how the system recovers after a system crash, measuring how much data is lost, how long it takes to return to its original state, and so on.

SAQ Name three other forms of testing which could be conducted on a software system.

SOLUTION There are many other categories of testing; you might want to test the required software functions, performance, response time, quality of the user interface, etc.

Six more testing categories are listed below.

1. *Function testing* This is the most obvious form of testing and is used to determine whether the software provides the functions described in its specification.
2. *Stress testing* This is similar to volume testing, only it involves ensuring that a peak volume of data can be processed within an acceptable response time.
3. *Performance testing* This form of testing concentrates solely on the efficiency of the software. In particular, response times would come under scrutiny.
4. *Usability testing* This form of testing explores the human–computer interface of the system and attempts to discover any problems relating to the use of the system.
5. *Storage testing* This form of testing ensures that the software does not use more storage space than its specification stipulates.

6.   *Documentation testing* A software system may meet its specification exactly, but if the documentation accompanying it is inadequate, then the system is as good as useless to its users who do not know how to use the system so as to achieve their aims.

The techniques, methods and approaches to be taken for all these forms of testing, and more, must be stipulated in the test plan.

Documentation produced

Both the customer and the developer will require evidence that the prescribed test has been performed and the desired results achieved. The best way of producing this assurance is by providing documentary evidence of the tests and their results. For example, the unit development folder contains evidence that tests have been conducted on a program unit.

Test procedures

Test procedures contain a description of each test that is to be carried out including the software and hardware to be provided, the test data to be used, the special software tools needed, a list of instructions for running the test, and the expected test results. For system tests and acceptance tests a description of each requirement to be tested, and a reference to the system specification should also be specified.

15.3 DERIVATION OF THE SYSTEM AND ACCEPTANCE TESTS

The main aim of quality assurance activities is to ensure that the system developed meets the customer's requirements, and this is tested during acceptance testing; when the developer demonstrates the use of the system to the customer. Before acceptance testing is performed, the developer will carry out a series of system tests; normally, the acceptance tests are a subset of the system tests which have been agreed to by the customer. The derivation of adequate system and acceptance tests is therefore an important activity in the software project.

It is one of the many jobs of quality assurance staff to ensure that the test procedures associated with system and acceptance testing have been carried out correctly. Quality assurance staff should therefore be the main participants from the developer's organization in deriving and performing system and acceptance tests.

During the later stages of the requirements analysis phase, quality assurance staff will examine the system specification and extract a series of verification requirements. Using these, the developer will then proceed to specify, in outline, a series of tests which will eventually evolve into the set of system tests. These tests represent checks on the behaviour of the system and will ensure that the developer has full confidence in the software meeting its requirements. Initially, outline descriptions of the tests and their purpose will be produced from the system specification.

Consider the following section of a system specification:

1   The effect of the REPORT command is to display on the originating VDU the state of a chemical reactor. The name of the reactor should be typed after the REPORT keyword.

2   The effect of the ERROR command is to display on the originating VDU the number of monitoring errors that have occurred on a particular thermocouple for a particular reactor. The name of the reactor and the name of the thermocouple should follow the ERROR keyword.

.
.
.

7   Any error in a command should be reported on the originating VDU.

8   The response to any command should be no more than 10 ms.

.
.
.

17   A maximum of 10 reactors and 40 thermocouples will be connected into the system. No more than 3 VDUs will be online at any one time.

The tests that need to be written down for these verification requirements include testing each command under the following conditions: for normal execution when reactor and monitors are correctly specified; when an error has been made in specifying a reactor and a monitor; at peak processing load when the maximum number of reactors, thermocouples and VDUs are connected to the system; and with incorrectly specified thermocouples or reactors at peak processing load. Two test descriptions are given below:

Valid 23

This test checks the correct functioning of the REPORT command at peak processing load. The reactor name typed will be a valid reactor. The test will be carried out with 10 reactors, 40 thermocouples and 3 VDUs attached to the system. The test will check that the command has been executed correctly and that the system response is less than 10 milliseconds.

Valid 24

This test checks the REPORT command with an incorrectly specified reactor name at peak processing load. The test will be carried out with 6 reactors, 40 thermocouples and 3 VDUs attached to the system. The test will check that an error message has been displayed and the system response is less than 10 milliseconds.

SAQ Provide two further test descriptions relating to the system specification extract given above.

SOLUTION There are many other tests which could be derived from this system specification abstract. Choosing which ones should go forward to be system tests is a skilled task. It would be impractical to expect that all possible situations can be covered, but the spread of test cases must be adequate. The descriptions obtained from this system specification should be of the same form as those in the following list:

Valid 25

This test checks the REPORT command with a correctly specified reactor name at peak processing load. The test will be carried out with 10 reactors, 40 thermocouples and 3 VDUs attached to the system. The test will check that the state of the specified reactor has been displayed and that the system response is less than 10 milliseconds.

Valid 31

This test checks the ERROR command with a correctly specified reactor name and thermocouple. The test will be carried out with 10 reactors, 40 thermocouples and 3 VDUs attached to the system. The test will check that the correct number of monitoring errors that have occurred on the specified thermocouple has been displayed and that the system response is less than 10 milliseconds.

Valid 32

This test checks the ERROR command with an incorrectly specified reactor name and a correctly specified thermocouple. The test will be carried out with 10 reactors, 40 thermocouples and 3 VDUs attached to the system. The test will check that an error message has been displayed and that the system response is less than 10 milliseconds.

Tests such as those described above will be expanded during the project with more detail being added during the system design and detailed design phases. During system design, the tests derived from the verification requirements are expanded into test procedures. At the start of system design the verification requirements will have been extracted and a series of tests specified. Both of these will have been approved by the customer. The task of the quality assurance staff is to take each test and express it as one or more test procedures.

Consider the following test description, which will have been derived directly from the system specification:

Valid   1237

This test should check that if the RECALL keyword is mistyped then an error message will be displayed by the system.

This test may give rise to the following three test procedures. Note that these procedures are only in outline form. The test data to be used and the other elements of the test procedure will be added as the procedures are refined.

TEST PROCEDURE ACC 1237.1

The tester should load the system from file FULLBLD.OBJ. The commands in the file SYSBATCH.BAT should then be executed. The system will respond with the message

SYS READY

COMMAND?

When this prompt is received on the terminal the tester should type the keyword RECALL with a missing letter followed by the parameter monitor1. The following message should then be displayed on the VDU:

*** COMMAND NOT RECOGNIZED ***

TEST PROCEDURE ACC 1237.2

The tester should load the system from file FULLBLD.OBJ. The commands in the file SYSBATCH.BAT should then be executed. The system will respond with the message

SYS READY

COMMAND?

When this prompt is received on the terminal the tester should type the keyword RECALL with two transposed letters followed by the parameter monitor1. The following message should then be displayed on the VDU:

*** COMMAND NOT RECOGNIZED ***

TEST PROCEDURE ACC 1237.3

The tester should load the system from file FULLBLD.OBJ. The commands in the file SYSBATCH.BAT should then be executed. The system will respond with the message:

SYS READY

COMMAND?

When this prompt is received on the terminal the tester should type the keyword RECALL with an extra letter added to the end of the command, followed by the parameter monitor1. The following message should then be displayed on the VDU:

*** COMMAND NOT RECOGNIZED ***

These test procedures are vital as they represent the concrete manifestation of the verification requirements. They should be thoroughly reviewed internally by quality assurance staff and, preferably, be reviewed in conjunction with the customer. In order to assist the customer in accepting test descriptions or procedures, these are often written so that they include references to the customer's own statement of requirements, the verification requirements and other project documents with which the customer is familiar.

The extract below represents some verification requirements for a system which provides information on stored items in a warehouse. Each requirement is labelled with a unique number:

12 The RETRIEVE command, when executed, will display the stock availability for items specified by the order clerk.

13 All commands should incorporate error-checking.

14 The response time to all commands should be less than 2 seconds.

Some acceptance tests corresponding to these verification requirements are shown below.

Valid 102

Database 12 should be loaded and the RETRIEVE command typed with one item which is contained in the database. The system will respond with the availability of the item.

Validation requirement(s) 12

Valid 103

Database 12 should be loaded and the RETRIEVE command typed with five items which are contained in the database. The system will respond with the availability of the items.

Validation requirement(s) 12

Valid 104

Database 12 should be loaded and the RETRIEVE command typed with twenty items which are contained in the database. The system will respond with the availability of the items.

Validation requirement(s) 12

Valid 105

Database 12 should be loaded and the RETRIEVE command typed with one item which is not contained in the database. The system will respond with an error message

Validation requirement(s) 13

.
.
.

Valid 118

Database 12 should be loaded and the RETRIEVE command typed with twenty items which are contained in the database. The results should be displayed within 2 seconds.

Validation requirement(s) 14

Notice that this excerpt specifies references to the verification requirements to help the customer check that the acceptance tests are adequate. The customer would be able to examine the acceptance tests and check that the tests adequately cover the verification requirements, for example, by counting references to them.

During the period when the tests are developed, quality assurance staff will ensure that the tests conform to the format specified in the quality plan, and that any outstanding points from review meetings are followed up and dealt with. During the later stages of the process of establishing the verification requirements, the quality assurance staff will, in conjunction with development staff, be able to predict any need for special testing software during system and acceptance testing. At this stage in the project this software may be ordered from an external contractor or specified for internal development.

15.4 SUMMARY

Testing is the most common form of validation which is conducted for a software system. It is also the most visible form. The test plan is that part of the quality plan which documents matters relating to the testing of a system. This includes the strategy to be used for testing the system, the criteria determining when testing should stop, the schedule for testing activities, the responsibilities of individual project team members and the test procedures themselves.

System tests and acceptance tests are derived directly from requirements expressed in the system specification. These requirements, called verification requirements, are extracted from the system specification at the end of the requirements analysis phase and must be approved by the customer as being adequate for the purposes of acceptance testing. It is therefore important that the verification requirements reference both the system specification and the statement of requirements, where possible.

BIBLIOGRAPHY

Myers, Glenford J. (1979) *The Art of Software Testing*, John Wiley and Sons, USA.

16

AN EXPERIMENTAL APPROACH TO QUALITY ASSURANCE

AIM

- To describe an advanced method of ensuring quality in a software system.

16.1 INTRODUCTION

This section looks at an experimental approach to quality software development, called the Cleanroom Experiment. We shall reproduce an interview with the man behind this novel approach, Mike Dyer, but first of all, we shall give you some background to the experiment.

The cleanroom approach to software development was pioneered at the IBM Federal Systems Division at Bethesda. The technique gets its name from the clean room in a semiconductor manufacturer's factory which is an extremely clean area where semiconductor circuits are constructed and where specks of dust are not allowed to intrude. The intention of the experiment was to place software development under statistical quality control, and to emphasize error *prevention* through stringent verification of designs, rather than error *detection* through repetitive testing. The main focus of the experiment was software reliability.

There were two novel aspects to the cleanroom approach:

1. The developer used a formal method of software development based on verification. Program units were developed using a process of data refinement and then stringently reviewed. The developers felt so confident that their approach would lead to high-quality software that *no* unit testing was carried out.

2. Statistical techniques were used to predict the reliability of the software system that was being constructed. The development team developed a statistical distribution which characterized the data that was to be processed by the system, randomly generated test data which followed this distribution and observed the behaviour of the system to see whether it passed or failed the test. They then timed the duration between each test failure and used statistical theory to calculate the reliability of the product in terms of the mean time to failure, i.e. the average length of time that the system would execute in its operational environment before it failed.

While you read the interview, identify reasons why reliability was the main consideration for this project, and note how successful the experiment was.

According to Mike Dyer, the customer is more interested in having a system which is reliable than one which is correct. Although this may seem surprising, if you think that some organizations rely so heavily on their computer systems that they cannot operate without them, it is little wonder that so much emphasis is placed on reliability. This point of view is underlined by considering the application of the cleanroom ideas to the avionics problem which Mike Dyer described.

The cleanroom approach was used to develop an avionics application which supports the pilot of a helicopter. Test samples were generated after a profile of input data was obtained from the customer, so that test input matched the kind of data which the system would be expected to handle in real operation. One surprising aspect of the approach which Mike Dyer emphasized while describing this application was that the specifications were written in English text, rather than in a mathematical notation.

Verification was based on a set of correctness proofs each of which related to one design construct such as an IF...THEN...ELSE construct. Each design construct used to build the software was associated with specific proof steps which had to be completed. To give you an example of the kind of proof steps used, the correctness proof for the IF...THEN...ELSE construct is reproduced from Dyer (1986) in Fig. 16.1. The verification output for a program unit containing this structure would therefore include the two correctness considerations shown on the right-hand side of Fig. 16.1, together with justifications for why the answers to these questions are both 'yes'.

```
CORRECTNESS PROOF EXAMPLE FOR THE IF...THEN...ELSE CONSTRUCT
[Z := Max(X,Y)]            State the intended function
IF
   X ≥ Y
THEN
   Z := X     First correctness consideration is that
              'For the case X ≥ Y
              Does Z := X satisfy Z := Max(X,Y)'
ELSE
   Z := Y     Second correctness consideration is that
              'For the case  X ≤ Y

              Does Z := Y satisfy Z := Max(X,Y)'
FI
```

Figure 16.1 Correctness argument for IF statement.

The results from the cleanroom experiment have been heartening. Software developed conventionally was being delivered with, on average, 10 to 20 errors per 1000 lines of code. Software developed using the cleanroom approach was delivered with well below 1 error per 1000 lines of code. The use of statistical prediction has also given IBM an excellent tool for enabling them to predict when to stop testing. This was done by recording when a particular release of a system failed and by statistically predicting the mean time to failure (MTTF)—a measure of the time between failures. As the MTTF rises with new (corrected) versions of a system, the time between failures should increase and the system should be observed to be more reliable. When the system reaches a point of development at which the MTTF is sufficiently high, testing can stop.

SAQ Why is an increase in the mean time to failure rate, i.e. an increase in the time between failures, more indicative of an improvement in the reliability of the software than an increase in the number of errors found?

SOLUTION The number of errors found in a piece of software is a relatively useless piece of information regarding the reliability of that software, when taken in isolation. If that number is high, you cannot tell whether the method of detection is working well, or if there were simply a great number of errors to start with. If the number of errors detected is low, you cannot tell whether the method of detection is not working properly, or the software was relatively error-free to start with.

If the input data is representative of the data which the software will encounter when in operation, the mean time to failure is a better indication of the software's reliability since it reflects more accurately the user's experience of the system.

16.2 THE CLEANROOM EXPERIMENT

A colleague of the authors, Benedict Heal, talked to Mike Dyer.

Benedict: Why was there a need for a change in your software development practice? Hadn't software been produced perfectly satisfactorily using conventional methods?

Mike: What we were finding was that while we were delivering software that was acceptable to our customers, when his users, in turn, started using it in the field, they were running into problems. So what we did was we invented the so-called 'cleanroom' process; this is an attempt both organizationally and technically to get a handle on software reliability.

Benedict: Can you tell us briefly what this 'cleanroom' experiment is? And what led you to the rather curious choice of name?

Mike: Basically, what we were trying to do is avoid the introduction of any faults or errors into software as we were developing it. We looked around for a name, and we saw that in the manufacturing hardware arena, people built these elaborate pressurized rooms in which they developed components and kept contaminants from getting into the rooms.[1] So what we thought was: well, this would be a good idea to use in the software arena as well.

Benedict: Can you spell that out? How does the analogy compare with software, what's the equivalent of dirt particles?

Mike: Dirt particles in software tend to be errors, design errors basically. What we tried to do was introduce more formal methods[2] into the design development process which we think will come up with a better quality product, a different way to address

---

[1] This is a reference to the practice adopted by semiconductor manufacturers who use expensive filtering systems to exclude dust and other particles from their integrated circuit manufacturing area.
[2] The term *formal method* refers to the use of mathematics as a specification medium.

testing. Which is, actually testing the software by addressing how it's being used by the user rather than just trying to root out errors—which is the typical way people test software. And what 'cleanroom' has tried to do is several things. First, it is an attempt to come up with a better way of specifying software, introducing more formal methods. Second, it introduces the notion of developing usage statistics as part of the specification, which would subsequently be used in the functional testing of the piece of software.

Benedict: Could you give us an example in practice of how your development method would differ from other people's?

Mike: We introduced formal methods into the design process, and then brought in the ideas of formal correctness proving, which we would use in lieu of any unit testing by the developers, so that the programmer would implement a design without actually executing that design.[3] Once this was completed it would be passed to an integration and test function.[4] The difference here is that we would create statistical samples based on the usage data for the testing.

Benedict: So you're really handing over untested code that's never been executed to staff who carry out integration testing?

Mike: That's right. What we do is we actually rely on verification[5] to do the same kinds of testing that we would normally get with a conventional unit test.

Benedict: One of the projects you applied this technique to, I believe, was something to do with the aircraft industry. Can you tell us something about that?

Mike: The avionics application was for the operational software in a helicopter system that we were developing. This is the software that would interface directly with the pilots and allow him to monitor the status of all the systems on the aircraft. So it was the main way that the pilot would fly the helicopter.

The systems engineering group put together the set of specifications for that job. When we started the actual cleanroom development, those specifications were not at a level that we felt we could get started with. So what we did was we asked the systems engineering people to work a little longer on it; they did, and we got it to a level where the software developers felt that they were probably somewhere about 80 per cent accurate.

Those specifications, then, were the basis for the developers to actually go off and do the design. When we started trying to do the design we wanted to use the formal methods that IBM had pioneered. We now had to figure out how to apply those to a real avionics programme. We thought that it would result in about 40 to 50 thousand lines of code.

---

[3] Dyer describes the fact that programmers in the cleanroom project do not carry out any unit testing, but prove a module correct and then hand it over for system testing.
[4] This is a reference to the staff who carry out subsequent system testing.
[5] Mathematical verification.

And what we did then was step through and start defining state machines[6] that represented the high-level subsystems in our system, and use the stepwise refinement process which is part of the formal method to expand the design to lower level details. As we stepped through the design process we applied verification to make sure that the originators of the designs did, in fact, come up with correct designs for the specifications that they were working with. And then we used a modified inspection[7] process to bring in other people to check their correctness arguments. We have to use a one-on-one approach, namely, that each designer was assigned an inspector, and it was the combination of the inspector and the designer which made sure that they came out with the correct design.[8]

We were using a non-standard computer, which was going to host the software. So we could control access to execution and therefore we knew that our developers could never execute their code, because they were not allowed access to the computer.

So we ran the inspections, we allowed them to do their design, and when somebody got to a point where their code had been inspected, and it seemed to be at the right level of quality, then we would pass that off to the integration and test group. As we collected code for increments, we had six increments to deliver the 40 000 lines;[9] so we were delivering somewhere about 8000 lines at a time. We put all the 8000 lines on this non-standard computer and turned on the machine and saw what happened. To our delight, the software always cycled, it just didn't sit there and look at us, so we knew that at least the software was in a form that you could start testing it, and therefore we could actually go into the integration and test process.

What the testers had been doing the whole time that the software people were doing their design and development was trying to define this representative input sample.[10] So they spent around four to six months identifying what were the inputs to this avionic system, you know, what kinds of commands that went from pilots, co-pilots, etc. What kind of data values were we talking about? What were the more normal kinds of inputs that would be coming in versus other portions of the flight? And we started building up this body of data on what are the inputs. What are the ranges of data values for the input? And then what are the probabilities of those inputs occurring?

Since the testers had to be completely familiar with the operation of the proposed helicopter the testers went to the operational engineering people, and actually back to the customers to get a better handle on what is the real profile of how this helicopter is going to be used in the real world. We think it was a very good distribution or representation of how the input traffic would look to the software.

---

[6] A state machine forms part of the formal method used by the developers, essentially it represents a system design.

[7] The term *inspection* is used in IBM to refer to technical reviews.

[8] Dyer describes technical reviews with only two members of staff doing the reviewing.

[9] Dyer is describing a gradual integration of the system in terms of versions which increase by 6000 lines of program code at a time.

[10] A sample of data for integration and system testing.

Once we had that, it would allow us to do a generation of test samples. Once you go through the work of collecting the distributional data, collecting all the input data, the actual generation of the samples is sort of trivial.

So once the code has started to be delivered, the testers had this database of information about inputs, they could create their samples automatically, run the samples against the code that was delivered, and check for failures. Now the only thing the testers did differently was they collected the time of execution of every test case. Since the 'time between failures' were based on representative projections of how inputs were derived from the system, we would then take those 'time between failures', feed them into a reliability model and come up with a mean time to failure.[11]

The real proof of the pudding on whether or not you're doing this development correctly is that when you actually take something like the helicopter and fly it, and record what kind of data you have in terms of software failures. In this particular case we were fortunate in that some time had elapsed, the helicopter has been built, has been flown in flight test, and we had a set of data on what the results of the flight test were that we can extrapolate back to our projections. We were within 10 to 15 per cent in terms of reliability projections that we had made two or three years earlier. And this says two things: first, it says that the models we're using are reasonable, they give reasonable results and, second, and probably more importantly, that our insight into what the inputs to the system and the distribution would be was fairly accurate when we got started. The key here is that the verification process that we go through forces us to look closer at the specifications. So, since we're trying to verify the design from the top level down, we have to ask the questions about the specifications to make sure that we can, in fact, prove their correctness of the design. So we are continually challenging up-front the systems engineering people who are writing the specifications to get clearer and more precise and more accurate specifications to us, so that we can, in fact, do our verification.

16.3 SUMMARY

This chapter has been an introduction to a development technique which, over the next decade, should become increasingly popular. The main impact on the project manager is that using mathematical notations on a software project makes it easier to monitor and control the project than if looser notations such as natural language were used. For example, using a mathematical notation for specification means that the project manager can easily relate how much programming has been carried out as a function of the amount of specification that remains to be implemented.

Also, since mathematical techniques give greater validation, the documentation associated with validation is able to give the project manager much more confidence that the final system will be the one that the customer requires.

---

[11] What is being described is a technique whereby data, based on the time period between errors in system testing, is used to calculate the reliability of the software.

BIBLIOGRAPHY

Dyer, M. (1986) Software development under statistical quality control, in *Software Design Methods*, edited by J.K. Skwirzynski, Springer-Verlag.

QUALITY STANDARDS FOR SOFTWARE SYSTEMS

AIMS

- To describe the nature of software quality standards.
- To describe the relationship between software quality standards and software quality assurance.
- To examine briefly four draft software quality standards.

17.1 INTRODUCTION

Many products on the shelves nowadays are governed by a standard of some kind. The reassuring BSI Kitemark symbol[1] informs the potential buyer that the item in question has been tested and that it conforms to the relevant standard. However, there are, as yet, no equivalent standards which refer directly to software production; such standards are currently being developed.

Quality standards for software systems would be useful for two reasons:

1. They provide an independent yardstick for both the developer and the customer to resolve quality issues for the project.
2. They can be used as a guide for setting up a developer's own quality system.

This section investigates some of the main activities in the attempt to provide standards for the software industry, and examines the concerns addressed by these activities.

17.2 ONE VIEW OF SOFTWARE QUALITY ASSURANCE

This section contains an interview with John Souter, who is head of the Software Engineering Department of BSI Quality Assurance. This interview will give you an idea of current software quality assurance practices.

Helen: Could you tell me something about the BSI and its role?

John: BSI is the national standards body. We started around the turn of the century. Over the years it's developed into a commercial entity in its own right. And now there are three autonomous divisions. And where I work, which is BSI Quality Assurance, we are a commercial entity offering quality assurance services to industry.

---

[1] Every product certified by the British Standards Institution (BSI) carries this mark.

Helen: When someone claims that a product conforms to standard does that actually mean that BSI have tested it then?

John: No, it doesn't. Standards—British standards or international standards—are public documents and anyone is free to claim conformity with the standard, providing they themselves feel that that claim is accurate. And of course it's very much easier to make a claim of conformity than it is to actually verify it, and so what is really needed is for the users to demand more evidence that a claim is an accurate one.

Helen: So just because it has a line on the bottom saying that this conforms to BSI standard, it doesn't necessarily mean that it does.

John: No that simply means that that's the claim that the vendor makes, and of course your only recourse is the Trade Descriptions Act. And you can imagine how difficult it would be to take a compiler to your local trading standards officer and say, 'I just bought this and it claims to comply with ISO 7185 and when I use variant records in this particular way, it doesn't seem to work'. You'd be very lucky if you can find a trading standards officer that would be able to understand that, never mind about taking the action on it.

Helen: What sort of quality assurance activity might you be concerned with then?

John: We offer a certification of products and registration of conformity of companies' quality systems to a national quality system standard. And so when you see the kite mark on a product you'll know that BSI has tested it for conformity and also checked the process of production to ensure that it's consistent.

Helen: What kind of activities might you be concerned with in testing the process for something like a toy or a bed?

John: Well, we use one common standard whether it be software or hardware which is BS 5750. This is the national standard for quality systems. It also is the international standard because it's international standard number item ISO 9000. And that's a very general standard that applies to good housekeeping practices whether they be production of services, goods, software or whatever.

Helen: So, you'd go into an organization and observe what they're doing, would you?

John: Yes, but it's not just an observation, the quality systems standard requires the manufacturer to have a documented quality system, and that that system itself must cover the aspects determined by the standard. We check to see that they actually carry that out in practice. And we do that by an initial assessment that covers all aspects of the business and then by surveillance visits which pick up the whole scope of what they are doing over the course of a year. And those visits are unannounced so that it gives the manufacturer the discipline to continue to conform. Usually you don't need to be a detective. Our greatest allies, in fact, are the people who work for the companies, who themselves want the discipline of an outside assessor to ensure that they can have an effective quality system.

Helen: So do you also apply some kind of quality tests to the product itself?

John: If it's a Kitemark it means that the product has been tested by an independent laboratory and found to conform to the standard. It means that we're monitoring the quality system as I've described, but it also means we'll continue to audit the quality of the product as well, by taking samples from time to time and again testing them. But if it's a registration scheme then that means we're simply checking the quality system of the manufacturer, and it's up to them to determine what testing is required for the goods or services they're providing.

Helen: How close have we come to getting the same sort of system for software?

John: Well, it's still early days yet. We've had a scheme for registering software houses for a couple of years and I think that we've got something of the order of 50 clients now, with probably twice as many waiting to be assessed.

Helen: So when you go into a software company what kind of activities would you assess?

John: There are three parts to the British Standard for quality systems: part one covers both the design and production of goods; part two covers only production; and part three is for systems where you can determine the quality by final inspection and test. And clearly with software, design is the essence of it, and so the assessment of the software company will cover all aspects of the design process. We take the analogues of those things that apply in hardware and apply the same good practice to software production.

Helen: So do you consider looking at the product, the actual software product itself, to produce certified software?

John: We take two approaches: we look top down by examining the managerial structure that the company uses to maintain quality to the standards they set. And we also look bottom up by taking particular projects and trailing around them, finding how they themselves produce evidence that they'd met the quality standards they set themselves. So, in a traditional software development plan we'd make sure that they were indeed producing statements of requirements, system specifications, design documents and they had test plans which were produced in the early stages, rather than thinking about them late, and so on and so forth.

Helen: So how would you make sure that these things are actually produced as part of the software development process?

John: We'd expect the company to show us everything, certainly all documentation, and we would expect to see the quality system documentation in advance of going to do the assessment on site.

Helen: Do you then consider looking at the product, the actual software product itself, to produce certified software?

John: In the strict ISO-standard definition of the word 'certification' there are no software certification schemes as yet. Certification means both testing of the product to a standard and assessment of the quality system used to produce it, and it's a conjunction of those two things that hasn't been achieved by any organization yet.

There is work going on at international level on producing a companion part of the ISO 9000 series that specifically applies to software but it isn't published yet.

Helen: Do you have any idea what that might cover?

John: Yes, it will obviously try and make a mapping between the sort of terminology that's used for hardware quality control or quality assurance, and the same things that apply in software. Clearly one isn't so concerned about the routine production aspects preserving the quality of goods after they've been made—warehousing type of issues—those are not applicable to software. But there are similar things, and there are analogues of most of the things that the companion document will have to cover.

Helen: Can you maybe now talk a bit about what your department does?

John: I work in the Software Engineering department of BSI Quality Assurance. And we offer two types of services. One is for the registration of the quality system of software houses and the other is for software product services, and they breakdown into a number of categories including things like validation and evaluation services.

Helen: What validation services do you offer?

John: Well, we started out with compilers, which, although in many senses, is the hardest area to tackle, it also happens to be the one we can approach because there are standards in that area. And validation, in our use of the term, means that we have tested the product and found that it conformed to a standard. We differentiate that from certification, because we haven't assessed the method of production of that compiler, merely that it complied with the standard at one particular time.

Helen: So these standards you're talking about now are standards for the programming language?

John: Yes, although the better programming language standards cover two distinct things. First of all, the abstract concept of the language, and secondly, the requirements for conforming processors. And we firmly believe that without the two things, that you can't have any kind of validation service for compilers.

Helen: So when you talk about the abstract concept of the language, do you mean the sort of facilities that it will offer a programmer?

John: Yes. Taking the language at a conceptual level as opposed to the product that instantiates it.

Helen: Right. And conforming processors?

John: We deliberately use the word 'processor' because it could be a compiler, a cross-compiler or an interpreter.

Helen: And you would make sure that that was true to the language?

John: We would make sure that it conforms to the relevant requirements of the standard, and that usually means checking all the syntax and semantics.

Helen: So how do you go about validating a compiler then?

John: Well, we use test suites. These are large sets of test programs usually addressing the extremes of conformity. So for example, we won't bother to see whether the compiler can add one and one and get two; we'd be much more interested in seeing what happens at the limit case.

Helen: So do you have pieces of software to test the compilers?

John: Yes. An example would be the Pascal validation suite, which is something like 800 test programs which are usually run using scripts to take each test in turn: try to compile it, then try to execute it and then try and log the results to a file, so that we can analyse them later.

Helen: By scripts you mean a high-level command language?

John: Yes, whatever is available on that particular computer.[2]

Helen: How do you go about generating test data for these kinds of tests?

John: Well in the case of a compiler the data is a program, and I'll give you the example of Pascal. What we did is we searched the standard for every occurrence of the word 'shall' implying a requirement, and then tried to produce both a positive test and a negative test to check both aspects of handling that requirement. So the positive test would be a conforming Pascal program that would execute in a predictable way using the semantics defined in the standard. And the negative program would be something that looked awfully like Pascal but actually wasn't, and therefore was, in effect, a trap for the compiler. If the compiler compiled it, because there would be no semantics, there could be no correct execution, and therefore we'd know that the compiler was wrong in some sense.

Helen: How did you go about generating these things that looked like Pascal?

John: They're mostly done by hand and take a long time, although over the years we've developed a number of generative techniques. For example, to check the error handling facilities, we've now got programs that will seed conforming programs with errors so that we can exercise all aspects of the error reporting of a compiler. We also know that deviance tests are very powerful in that there's empirical evidence that they find twice as many compiler bugs as the conformance tests.

Helen: Could you explain what you mean by deviance tests and conformance tests?

John: Yes. A conformance test is something that is strictly conforming Pascal or whatever the programming language is that we are testing. And a deviance test is something that isn't, so, in theory, you could give a FORTRAN program to a Pascal compiler and that would be a deviance test, but it would be a pretty poor Pascal compiler that couldn't spot it. The programs will look awfully like Pascal, certainly to the eye, but sometimes they may contain errors say only in the declarations and then the

---

[2] Such high-level command languages are often part of a computer operating system. The best example is the UNIX shell.

only executable part of the test will be something that writes a message to the screen or the file which records the fact that it was able to compile those declarations.

Helen: So are there any other kinds of tests apart from deviance tests and conformance tests?

John: Well, usually, the tests breakdown broadly under those two categories, but sometimes there are subtleties below that. So, for example, one of the reasons why you might detect an error in a program is that you haven't implemented that construct. And so to check that that isn't occurring we have a pretest which is guarding against the compiler giving what seems like the right answer but for the wrong reason.

Helen: What do you generate at the end of your testing procedures?

John: Well, we try to write the executable log of the testing into a file, and then we have some tools which parse those files and generate a first draft of a test report from there. There's a small amount of hand editing to finish it.

Helen: So the end product is a report?

John: That's correct.

Helen: Which will say whether the compiler conforms to standard or doesn't? Does it also follow up the points about when it doesn't conform? What sorts of things it cannot do?

John: In general, all of the test programs that we use are self-checking, and so they will make some effort to diagnose what is wrong, if there is something wrong. And we do that because that means that we can rely on our log files being relatively complete. If the compiler did nothing when it failed then it would sometimes be hard to tell the difference between having done nothing and having failed the test.

Helen: So can you give an overview of how you go about validating a compiler?

John: The test suite will have to be moved to the computer where the compiler is to be tested. And since we can't have all possible computers here at BSI this often means we have to go to the compiler manufacturer's own site to do the testing. Our more sophisticated test suites have a harness which enables us to automate the testing process, and so the first task will be to get that harness running on whatever machine the compiler is being tested upon.

Helen: And what do these test harnesses do?

John: Well, when we're validating usually they just simply automate the repetitive testing of possibly thousands of tests, but in our evaluation services the test harnesses have to do much more work than that. So in our Ada test suite, for example, we have a harness which will dynamically modify the tests, when we are trying to find a capacity limit of the compiler in some area of other. So we use techniques like binary chop to ensure that we can generate a lot of test cases quickly to find the actual limit.

Helen: Would you explain what you mean by binary chop?

John: Yes, we'll take usually two extreme values and check if the compiler can handle those extremes, and if it can't then we'll half the range and then retest in either the upper or lower half, and then keep moving in whichever direction is indicated until we find the actual value that the compiler can handle. It saves us having to have a large set of static tests covering all possible eventualities, because on a small machine a lot of those tests will be inapplicable, maybe on a large machine we won't have a large enough set to find out what the actual limit is.

Helen: So does the test harness actually modify the sections of code that you've fed in?

John: Indeed, it has a preprocessor that understands the grammar of the language in question, and is able to either generate more lines of source text or to delete parts of the program depending on which way the particular test is performing.

Helen: How do you cope with the fact that ultimately a compiler may be running on different machines with different operating systems?

John: It very much depends on the test suite in question. But our more sophisticated suites can handle a compiler that perhaps runs on one machine which we would call the host and produces code that will execute on a different machine which we would call the target. And sometimes we even use a third machine which monitors the host and the target and drives the process, generates each new test and keeps the log file.

Helen: What's the advantage of having a third machine?

John: Well, we write our test harnesses in the standard language and therefore we assume that there'll be at least one compiler available that will be able to compile our test harnesses and so far that has worked.

Helen: Roughly how many tests would you expect to do on a compiler that you were given to validate?

John: Well, usually, it's related to the size of the language. So Pascal is quite a small language, and we have something like 800 tests that we run. The Ada validation suite has over 4000 tests and it's by no means finished yet either.

Helen: This must generate an awful lot of test data?

John: It depends if the programs are elegantly self-checking; no, they don't have to. However, it can certainly soak up a lot of CPU time.

Helen: I assume nobody is sitting watching this?

John: No, again if the programs are well designed you can have it automated and pretty well the only thing that can go wrong is if the test causes the entire system to crash —which is not unknown.

Helen: I assume then the compiler is thrown out?

John: Well, it certainly wouldn't get a validation certificate under those circumstances.

Helen: Can you explain why we go through this process at all?

John: It's the key part in many ways of the software development process. It's all very well to have a good design and an elegant implementation in the source code of whatever application you're trying to develop, but if the compiler then converts it into something else altogether, you will be understandably cross. And I think that all the efforts that we can put into analysing the source code of applications software to check that it does meet its statement of requirements, loses its point if the compiler doesn't compile it correctly. So the validation process is very important indeed. In fact also these bugs can be rather subtle and may be in portions of code that aren't executed very often or need some kind of extreme conditioning before they're provoked. And so, just like any piece of software, it's important that the compiler itself is meeting its statement of requirements as expressed in the language standard.

Helen: Who produces these language standards?

John: Well, they are set by committees who work very hard to try to define both the syntax and the semantics precisely. A number of techniques have been used over the years, the early standards were all written in English, which is something of a paradox when you consider the technicalities of defining a language using an informal language. But the more recent ones are produced using formal methods. The Modula-2 standard, which is being written at the moment, is being produced using a formal method called VDM.

Helen: Does this mean that the standards for older languages are harder to validate against?

John: Yes indeed, not only are they weaker technically, but they quite often omit the requirements clauses that give the real power to the validation process. So, for example, the FORTRAN and COBOL standards don't entitle the validator to use deviance tests, and that means that quite a powerful testing technique is ruled out from the beginning.

Helen: So do you see that the validation of compilers is where the future of software quality assurance should go?

John: Oh no, it's only one tiny part of it. It's an important part but some of the techniques that have been developed in this area can be applied to other kinds of software. For example, we can try to apply negative testing techniques to all kinds of software and again I think we'll find in practice that that's a very powerful method.

Helen: So where do you see the future of quality assurance heading then?

John: I think what we need to do next is to look at combining the best of current validation techniques with assessment of the quality system and the processes used. So, what we would get out of that is not just an assurance that a compiler or piece of software conformed once, but that each new release of it would also be conforming, and that we could rely on that based on the testing that the vendors themselves would do.

Helen: So do you feel that we need standards for the actual process of producing software?

John: I think that what we're missing in software engineering is a big shelf of standards, in the same way that the general engineering industry has built up over the years its own infrastructure and comes to rely upon subsidiary standards. And so there'll be a place for lots of different kinds of standards, not just standards which contain requirements for actual products but process standards, glossaries, methods of testing and so on. It's been mooted for example that a unit test standard be devised, whereby conformity with that would tell you at what state the software was, up to the point where it was starting to be integrated with other modules. And so I'm sure there's a place for all kinds of standards of that type.

Helen: So you would like to see those coming out in the future?

John: Well we would, and I think in general the community will benefit from that. But what complicates it is that a lot of the methodologies that are used in software development are proprietary ones and it's somewhat harder to see how they can become standards in the true sense. That is, that not just the producers have control of them but also users have a say. The word *standard* is misused in the information technology area because people talk about things like MS DOS being a standard; it certainly isn't, because it's controlled by the producer of the goods and the user really has no say at all.

Helen: But it was the first one on the market and therefore it has become a standard?

John: Yes, you have this dreadful term *de facto standard* which usually means it isn't a standard at all. It is, in fact, enshrined in BSI's constitution that standardization should involve all the interest groups. And so a standard that was made only by the manufacturers of the goods would be regarded as entirely inadequate or inappropriate.

Helen: How do you think we are going to be able to validate safety-critical systems in the future?

John: Well, first of all, I think we have to retrench to a very, very conservative approach to all aspects of the development process. We need to use formal methods right from the very first stages, we need to formalize the process of hazard analysis, and how that applies to requirements capture, we need to ensure that each of the steps of the process are kept in line, we need to ensure that the process of refinement is done in very, very small increments, so that we can be completely confident that some kind of error hasn't crept in as each transformation takes place. And we need to use a conservative approach to implementation which means avoiding esoteric languages and certainly sticking to the mainstream areas of the languages that we use.

Helen: What are you not doing now that you would like to see being done?

John: Well, we are starting to analyse source code. I think this comes naturally out of providing services for testing compilers, because you start to get into the intricacies of the grammars of the languages, and then starting to analyse source code comes naturally from that. I think we feel strongly that software engineering standards need to be enforced by tools. If you haven't got tool support for whatever methodology or standards you are using, then it's so easy to deviate from them and perhaps not even know. So one of the things we hope to market in the future is a set of tools that will check source code of programs for strict conformity to the standard. That won't necessarily mean they are right, but it will be a good check to ensure that you're not using exotic features or you're misusing the semantics in some way, that are likely to cause problems during compilation and execution. And I think that if we can provide such tools then they'll be seized upon by people who share our view about tool support for standards and methodologies.

The main standard which is used by the BSI to ascertain quality in software systems is BS 5750: Part 1.[3] This is a general standard for quality systems and therefore does not relate specifically to software. Two schemes operate using this standard—*certification* and *registration.*

A registration scheme for software houses is run by the BSI, but no certification scheme for software has yet been devised, although work on producing a standard for software is under way.

A major area which John Souter mentioned during his interview is that of validating programming language implementations.[4] This work is based on standards which have been produced for specific programming languages. Such standards cover two aspects of a programming language.

Programming language standards and the validation of their implementations are of interest to us for two reasons. First, as case studies in quality assurance and, secondly, as tools for the implementation phase of software development. Programming language standards are very detailed system specifications which are widely available; national or international standards for Pascal, Ada, FORTRAN, COBOL, BASIC, PL/1 and APL have been published, as have drafts of standards for Modula-2, C, Prolog and Extended Pascal. Validation suites for Pascal, Ada, COBOL, FORTRAN, Modula-2 and C all exist, and others are under development. These test suites are object lessons in software quality assurance.

The second point of interest, the choice of programming language and language implementation, is important, notwithstanding the importance of the early phases of software development. All the care and attention paid to early activities will have been in vain if an ill-chosen compiler generates code for a program text which does not conform to the language standard for the compiler and that code subsequently fails to properly control a landing aircraft.

SAQ   Consider the following text. Is it a Pascal program?

```
program m355test;
var x, y: integer;
begin
    x := y
end.
```

SOLUTION   No! It looks like one; indeed, it is of the correct form, as defined by the syntax rules of Pascal. However, if compiled and executed (and most compilers would accept it), it would immediately violate the dynamic semantics rules of Pascal by

---

[3] The BS 5750 series of quality assurance standards is the British version of the international and European standard series, ISO 9000 and EN 2900.

[4] In the interview, John Souter referred to language implementations as language processors.

attempting to access an undefined variable: y is never given a value, so it is meaningless to give y's 'value' to x.

The above SAQ raises an important question: when a 'program' violates the semantic rules of a language, what should happen? The general answer is that it depends on the language and on the violation. For Pascal, and most languages, in most circumstances the executing code enters an undefined state and its meaning thereafter cannot be determined. Thus y in the SAQ might be given a random value, or 42, or might shut down a factory; the specification (of Pascal) does not specify what should happen and so anything might. For complex, possibly safety-critical, systems it would be foolish to allow such a situation and a validated language implementation is a vital tool for quality assurance.

17.2.1 Conformance testing

When validating implementations of programming languages (usually compilers), the test data used must be a program, or a document which closely resembles a program. John Souter mentioned the Pascal validation suite, and the program in Fig. 17.1 is an example of the data used for a *conformance test*, i.e. a test which checks if a system (e.g. a compiler) conforms to its specification (a programming language standard). We reproduce, in full, a short test which checks that the scope rules of Pascal have been properly implemented. In Clause 6.2.2–7 of the Pascal standard these rules are specified as follows:

> When an identifier or label has a defining-point for a region, another identifier or label with the same spelling shall not have a defining-point for that region.

(BS 6192)

The program CONF031 checks that an implementation correctly distinguishes the two types called *colour*; the type of the variable *c* is the type defined in line 19—(*red, amber, green*)—and the type of *paint* is the type defined in line 24—(*purple, red, blue*).

By introducing a new type in line 24 (but one with the same name and structure as used in line 19) the test checks whether the language implementation sees it as a new type. The body of the procedure, *nested*, checks (in lines 28–32) that the values of the two types called *colour* are different, and that the value denoted by the first *red* can be assigned (using the predecessor function in line 10) even though the identifier *red* refers to the value in line 24 within the procedure *nested*. The final check (lines 36–39) tests that the value of *c* is the first *red*, as it should be.

Do not be tempted, at this point, to think 'so what?'; although the test is simple and the code obscure, and seemingly unlikely, the scope facilities of Pascal are fundamental to the language. Indeed, since Standard Pascal does not have separate compilation facilities (like UCSD or Turbo Pascal, Ada, or Modula-2) scope is vitally important to large projects where different programmers are likely to choose the same identifiers. Experience has shown that if an implementation does not handle scope properly, it is likely to be poor in many other respects.

Note that a standard form of heading is used for the test program (lines 1–16). This is used by BSI support tools for configuration management and automatic result checking and report generation.

```
 1    {                    Pascal Validation Suite   Version 5.2 }
 2    {
                                                    }
 3    {(C) Copyright 1982, A J H Sale and British Standards Institution}
 4    {
                                            }
 5    { TEST 6.2.2-7, FILE=CONF031, CLASS=CONFORMANCE, LEVEL=0        }
 6    {
                                                    }
 7    {:This program hides part of a type while leaving other parts
      }
 8    {:accessible.}
 9    {
                                            }
10  {
                                        }
11  { Modification History :                              }
12  { V3.0:Comment revised and writes rewritten. Was previously }
13  {        6.2.2-10.}
14  { V5.2:    File header comments reformatted and file name added to}
15  {          TEST line and output lines.                      }
16  {
                                    }
17  program CONF031(output);
18  type
19    colour = (red, amber, green);
20  var
21    c: colour;
22  procedure nested;
23  type
24    colour = (purple, red, blue);
25  var
26    paint: colour;
27  begin
28    c := green;
29    paint := red;
30    c := pred(amber);
31    if (ord(c) <> 0) or (ord(paint) <> 1) then
32        writeln(' FAIL...6.2.2-7 (CONF031)')
33  end;
34  begin
35    nested;
36    if (c <> red) then
37        writeln(' FAIL...6.2.2-7 (CONF031)')
38    else
39          writeln(' PASS...6.2.2-7 (CONF031)')
40  end.
```

Figure 17.1 A conformance test.

17.2.2 Deviance testing

We conclude by briefly examining a *deviance test* which is a test which verifies whether a language implementation can detect something which is *not* standard Pascal. Consider the 'program' in Fig. 17.2.

```
 1    {                     Pascal Validation Suite   Version 5.2
                    }
 2    {
                                            }
 3    {(C) Copyright 1982, A J H Sale and British Standards Institution}
 4    {
                                    }
 5    { TEST 6.8.1-4, FILE=DEV193, CLASS=DEVIANCE, LEVEL=0 }
 6    {
                                    }
 7    {:This program attempts to jump into the middle of a for-statement}
 8    {:by means of a goto-statement.}
 9    {
                                    }
10 { Modification History :                              }
11 { V3.1: Test renumbered was 6.8.2.4-5                 }
12 { V5.2:    File header comments reformatted and file name added to}
13 {          TEST line and output lines.                }
14 {
                              }
15 program DEV193(output);
16 label 100;
17 var
18    i,  j: integer;
19 begin
20    j := 0;
21    for i := 1 to 0 do
22    begin
23 100:
24        j := 1;
25        writeln(' DEVIATES...6.8.1-4 (DEV193)')
26    end;
27    i := 0;
28    if j = 0 then
29        goto 100
30 end.
```

Figure 17.2 A deviance test.

SAQ Examine the 'program' in Fig. 17.2, and explain why this is a good deviance test for a Pascal compiler.

SOLUTION The text in Fig. 17.2 is not valid Pascal because of the jump into the for loop. A for loop is meant to execute a fixed number of times, as determined by the start and finish expressions at the head of the loop (in this case the start value is greater than the finish value and the loop body should not be executed); jumping into the loop avoids evaluating them and so no meaning can be given to continued execution.

The test 'program' *DEV193* is a good test because it looks like Pascal; all the declarations and statements are individually correct. It is the combination of a jump (from line 29) and the placing of the target label inside a for loop (at line 23) which invalidates this 'program'. Furthermore, this style of coding, though generally deprecated, is common with programmers who habitually use languages like BASIC and FORTRAN, and they often reproduce the style when writing in languages similar to Pascal.

17.3 ISSUES IN QUALITY STANDARDS FOR SAFETY-CRITICAL SOFTWARE

One area of software development which is becoming increasingly important is the production of systems which entail a safety element. In the context of safety, software quality assurance becomes vital, literally. In 1989–90 a number of initiatives brought to the fore questions on how safety should be accounted for in a software project. This increase in concern about safety is due to the fact that more and more safety-critical software systems are being developed, and they are also becoming very complex.

In this section we consider the impact of safety considerations on quality assurance by looking at four draft standards produced during 1989, two by the Ministry of Defence (MoD) and two by the International Electrotechnical Commission (IEC), through BSI. Although these standards have now been developed beyond draft stage, the extracts included here illustrate well the type of issues covered by such documents.

To begin our discussion we introduce two very similar terms, which are generally used interchangeably, one of which the MoD documents use and the second of which the IEC documents use. This divergence represents a difference of emphasis rather than fundamental disagreement. We discuss aspects of all four drafts in this section.

The MoD documents define *safety-critical software* to be software that implements a function which, if it fails, could risk human life. Their documents are primarily concerned with software for military purposes, but the term can be applied, for example, to systems which control nuclear reactors, chemical processing plants, engine controllers, braking suspension systems, systems used by air traffic controllers and systems used in hospital operating theatres to monitor the condition of a patient. The two documents are *Interim Defence Standard 00-55: Requirements for the Procurement of Safety Critical Software in Defence Equipment*[5] (Ministry of Defence, 1991a) and *Interim Defence Standard 00-56: Requirements for the Analysis of Safety Critical Hazards* (Ministry of Defence, 1991b).

The starting points of the IEC documents are the notions of (a) programmable electronic systems (e.g. computers) and (b) the equipment under the control of the former (e.g. plant

---

[5] All references to Defence Standard 00-55 and 00-56 are Crown Copyright 1991.

machinery). The IEC documents refer to *safety-related software* which is defined to be software which ensures that a system does not endanger human life, economics or environment. As well as safety-critical software, safety-related software includes the likes of systems which automatically shut down a chemical plant if emissions of sulphur dioxide higher than the recommended limit are detected, or systems which monitor world money markets for unusual trading activity. The drafts issued by the IEC (as BSI drafts for public comment) are *Functional Safety of Programmable Electronic Systems: Generic Aspects. Part 1: General requirements* (BSI document 89/33005) and *Software for Computers in the Application of Industrial Safety-related Systems* (BSI document 89/33006).

In order to give you an idea of the issues addressed by quality assurance standards, we shall concentrate on the MoD documents in this section.

17.3.1 The procurement of safety-critical software

The first of the MoD interim draft standards, 00-55, addresses the requirements for the procurement of safety-critical software. In particular, it proposes the adoption of formal specification and design techniques.

As you might expect, the role of project information which is important for management of any kind of software is emphasized even more for safety-critical software. Every decision and every development step taken must be documented and checked. Twenty-one documents are listed in the 00-55 draft standard some of which, such as a configuration management plan and source code, would be produced for most systems. Other documents are specific to safety-critical software; these include the safety plan and the hazard analysis report (see Sec. 17.3.2).

The 00-55 draft standard's recommendations can be divided roughly into three main areas:

1. safety management which relates to the project management practices needed to plan, monitor and control safety;
2. software engineering practices which specify the methods, techniques, languages and tools required to develop safety-critical software;
3. the project life-cycle.

Safety management, as the name suggests, addresses the management of the production of safety-critical software. The main purpose of safety management is to ensure that all stages of the design and creation of safety-critical software are adequately documented so that the development can be checked by independent assessors. The standard specifies the roles and associated responsibilities of all those involved in producing a safety-critical piece of software. The standard in its current form does not specify detailed qualifications and experience, but it is expected that something of the status of a chartered engineer would be required.

Safety management is based on a safety plan which relates specifically to how the project will ensure that the safety requirements of the software will be met by the final system. A safety plan will be developed at the beginning of every phase of development, documenting concerns relevant to that phase. All safety plans must be approved by the project manager and by the independent software safety assessor.

SAQ What kinds of information would be included in a safety plan?

SOLUTION The safety plan should detail anything that is relevant to safety assurance: the responsibilities of staff and necessary qualifications, the methods, tools, techniques and languages to be used, and it should name the design authority, the independent assessor and the verification and validation team.

Part of the safety plan defined by the 00-55 draft standard is shown below:

The safety plan for the hazard analysis and safety risk assessment shall contain the following:

(a)   A definition of the purpose and scope of the plan, including those safety goals that are expected to be achieved by adherence to it.

(b)   Definitions and references.

(c)   A definition of the Design Authority's responsibility for ensuring that the requirements for safety are met and, if appropriate, a definition of those responsibilities formally delegated to contractors, subcontractors or suppliers.

(d)   Details of the management of hazard analysis and safety risk assessment activities, including:

    (1)   the identification of the organizations and key personnel required by this standard including:

        (a)   Design Authority;

        (b)   Project Safety Committee;

        (c)   Project Safety Engineer;

        (d)   Independent Safety Auditor;

        (e)   relevant contractors, subcontractors or suppliers;

    (2)   a description of the interfaces between the MOD(PE),[6] the Independent Safety Auditor, the Design Authority, the MOD Safety Assurance Authority and their respective contractors, subcontractors or suppliers, and the interfaces between teams concerned with hazard analysis and safety risk assessment of related systems;

    (3)   the definition of the circumstances under which matters concerning hazard analysis and safety risk assessment shall be referred between the Design Authority or its relevant contractors, subcontractors and suppliers and the Independent Safety Auditor, the MOD(PE) PM[7] and the MOD Safety Assurance Authority;

    (4)   details of adequate resource planning, including, but not limited to, finance, personnel, equipment and tools;

    (5)   details of the way in which evidence of application of the plan is to be recorded throughout the project lifecycle;

    (6)   details of the deliverable items to be produced containing the essential details defined in **7.11** of this Standard;

    (7)   reference to the Configuration Control Plan;

---

[6] The United Kingdom Ministry of Defence Procurement Executive, the body responsible for the purchasing of defence systems.
[7] Project management.

(8)   details of the organization and CVs of individuals who will carry out the analyses;

(9)   specification of the qualifications required of key staff;

(10)   details of the certification process;

(11)   specification of the criteria for tools approval and limitations on the use of certain tools;

(12)   the procedures for evaluating hazards and risks from previously developed or purchased systems.

(MoD 00-55)

The methods, tools, techniques, languages, verification activities, milestones, staff qualifications and other items of information contained in the safety plan will vary from phase to phase.

The safety plan must reference several documents, including one which specifies the software engineering practices allowed or disallowed on the project. Some unacceptable practices are listed in the standard, which should be discouraged for safety-critical software:

> SCS shall be designed so that it is easy to justify that it meets its specification in terms of both functionality and performance. This requirement may restrict the length and complexity of the software and inhibit the use of concurrency, interrupts, floating-point arithmetic, recursion, partitioning and memory management.

(MoD 00-55)

Floating-point arithmetic is inherently imprecise and so the results of floating-point calculations have to be used with caution. Modern floating-point chips have different modes of use which affect the way in which they perform calculations, and what the result of a given calculation will be. Furthermore, many hardware devices which provide floating-point arithmetic containing bugs have been sold on the market.

Despite these concerns, the inconvenience caused by prohibiting floating-point arithmetic is probably not justified since standards for floating-point units exist and chips can be validated against such standards. Floating-point arithmetic can be specified using formal methods and hardware or software floating-point implementations can be formally proved.

Recursion causes concern because each recursive call results in storage being consumed for the local data of the recursive procedure. Thus, storage can rapidly become exhausted, resulting in the failure of the software. It is impossible to predict how much storage is needed when a recursive procedure is first called because the depth of recursion (and rate of consumption of storage) depends on dynamically calculated values.

Although it is feasible to have a language or language implementation which permits the availability of storage to be checked prior to each procedure call, failure to complete a recursive algorithm due to storage exhaustion, maybe leaving a partially updated data structure, could be just as dangerous as an unexpected failure. Therefore, this proposed prohibition is justified.

The proposed standards also address the project documentation to be produced, and issues relating to the conduct of design reviews, implementation, static code analysis, verification and validation testing and tool support. The tool support specified by the various draft standards is quite extensive and includes configuration management tools, validated compilers, static code analysis tools, simulators and test coverage monitors.

Clearly, verification and validation of the software is paramount. Therefore the generation of test cases is important. The interim draft standard specifies dynamic testing as follows:

Tests shall be monitored with a test coverage monitor. Testing shall continue until at least the following have been exercised:

- All statements.

- All branches for both true and false conditions, and case statements for each possibility including 'otherwise'.

- All loops for zero, one and many iterations, covering initialization, typical running and termination conditions.

(MoD 00-55)

17.3.2 Safety life-cycle model

The model for software development is somewhat different to the traditional phase-oriented model presented in Chapter 1. The crucial difference between the safety-oriented model and the traditional model is that hazards must be identified and their risk assessed, taking into consideration factors such as legislation, standards relevant to the application and regulations imposed by safety regulatory authorities. Any piece of software may be considered to be potentially safety-critical, or to contain a safety-critical component until it is proved otherwise. The assessment of the level of safety-criticality for a system is performed initially during the feasibility phase, and in full during project definition. The process of identifying the level of criticality is called *hazard analysis*. A *hazard* is a condition which can lead to an accident. Hazard analysis consists of identifying all possible hazards, and the conditions which lead to the hazard, and determining their risk.

Risk is defined as 'The combination of the frequency, or probability, and the consequence of the specified hazardous event'. The concept of risk always has two elements; the frequency, or probability, with which a hazard occurs and the consequences of a hazardous event.

(BSI 89/33005)

Another result of hazard analysis and the assessment of risk is the determination of the *safety integrity level* of the software system which is a metric that can guide the choice of methods and tools; for example, for requirements analyis, system design and programming language. In general, the more safety-critical the system, the more rigorous the methods and tools should be.

In any particular application there will be a level of risk (the risk level) that can be deemed 'tolerable'. For a situation where the level of risk, without precautions, is not tolerable, there is a need to ensure that the applied [safety-] related systems reduce the risk to an acceptable level....

(BSI 89/33005)

Risk may be specified as a quantified probability or a combination of quantified probabilities but it is not possible to specify the software safety integrity in the same manner:

Software safety integrity is specified as one or more of five levels:

1   Very High

2   High

3   Medium

4   Low

5   Normal   (BSI 89/33005)

It should be noted, however, that although a process for deciding on the safety level is appealing, there is not yet enough experience of applying one to decide how useful it is in practice. We should maybe be ultra-cautious and consider all systems to be at level 1. Nevertheless, simply performing the type of analysis described may be in itself of great benefit in assuring the quality of safety-related systems.

17.3.3 The analysis of safety-critical hazards

The MoD interim draft standard on the analysis of safety-critical hazards describes a number of risk classes. Class A risks are intolerable, class B risks are undesirable and should only be accepted when risk reduction is impracticable, class C risks are only tolerable with the endorsement of a body known as the Project Safety Review Committee and class D risks are tolerable with the endorsement of the normal project reviews. Where possible, the risk of a hazard should be reduced.

SAQ How could the level of risk associated with a hazard be reduced?

SOLUTION Since the level of risk depends on the category of accident and the likelihood of the hazard occurring, either the category of accident should be altered, or the likelihood of the hazard occurring should be reduced. The latter is probably easier in practice. This can be achieved by redesign of the system, the incorporation of safety or warning devices, or the development of operating and training procedures.

Preliminary hazard analysis should be conducted during the feasibility phase of the project. This involves establishing the boundaries of the system with its environment, producing block diagrams to show the system's overall architecture and identifying the hazards and accident sequences together with their severity categories. All items relating to hazard analysis must be recorded in the hazard log. Even if risks no greater than class C are identified for the system, the hazard log must be continued throughout the whole project life-cycle, since changes in requirements or in the system's environment could result in further hazards developing.

The findings of preliminary hazard analysis are expanded during full system hazard analysis, and this is then translated into a risk analysis by considering the risks associated with each hazard identified. The safety requirements for the system are produced from the results of this analysis, and safety-critical components of the system are identified using this information. If a system or subsystem is deemed to be safety-critical, then the standard described above relating to the procurement of safety-critical software applies. In some organizations, the level of risk attached to a project is used to determine the contingency which must be added to the cost of the project. For example, if hazard analysis identifies a risk category of class A, then the safety-integrity level will be high and the cost of achieving this high level will be great.

Identifying the risk classification for a system is really the most difficult part of identifying safety-critical systems, i.e. deciding on whether a system is safety-critical or not. A more subtle, and a very much more serious problem is that although it may be possible to identify the integrity levels of components of a system, it may not be possible to decide the level of the entire system; its complexity may defy analysis, and there is no calculus for deriving the overall integrity level from the levels of the components.

SAQ Why is the classification of systems as safety-critical difficult?

SOLUTION Whether a system is safety-critical or not depends on the risk classification of hazards associated with that system. Identifying the risk classifcation is currently based on tables which involve the use of fuzzy terms such as 'occasional' and 'improbable'. In short, the classification is difficult because of the degree of subjective judgement.

17.4 ISSUES IN QUALITY STANDARDS FOR OTHER SOFTWARE SYSTEMS

The importance of quality software when it is of a safety-critical or safety-related nature is obvious, but software which has no direct safety implications should also be expected to reach a certain standard of quality, no matter how banal the consequences of its failure might be. After all, the customer has every right to expect that the software paid for should be of good quality. In other words, the quality of software should be appraised in the same way as other goods or services.

The standard currently employed by the BSI for quality systems governing most hardware (such as microwave ovens, radar systems, and so on) is BS 5750, which is the basis of a series of international standards, commonly known by the first, ISO 9000. BS 5750 is a general standard addressing quality systems, and is therefore not specifically tailored towards software. As John Souter mentioned in the interview in Sec. 17.2, attempts to produce a document which relates to software the general good practices described in this standard are underway. In fact, we quoted earlier in this chapter from a draft version of this document.

The emerging standard on quality systems for software projects concentrates on the quality system of the organization; it addresses issues such as the supplier's, (in our context the developer's) responsibility, and the purchaser's (i.e. customer's) responsibility. For example, the following extract specifies the responsibility and authority of the developer's organization:

Responsibility and authority

The responsibility, authority and the interrelation of all personnel who manage, perform and verify work affecting quality should be defined; particularly for personnel who need the organizational freedom and authority to

a)   initiate action to prevent the occurrence of product nonconformity;

b)   identify and record any product quality problems;

c)   initiate, recommend or provide solutions through designated channels;

d)   verify the implementation of solutions;

e)   control further processing, delivery or installation of nonconforming product until the deficiency or unsatisfactory condition has been corrected.

(BSI DPC 89/97932)

This extract is generally applicable to quality systems; it is, in fact, identical to the one in BS 5750. Other items in the draft standard relate solely to software.

Joint reviews

Regular joint reviews involving supplier and purchaser should be scheduled to cover the following aspects as appropriate

a)   continued fitness of the software items to meet purchaser needs;

b)   conformance of the software to the agreed requirements specification;[8]

c)   verification results;

d)   acceptance test results;

The results of such reviews should be agreed and documented.

(BSI DPC 89/97932)

SAQ What other areas would you expect to be addressed by the section in a standard relating to the framework of quality systems for software development?

SOLUTION Such a standard should address a software developer's organizational structure, the responsibilities of the developer, and the procedures, processes and resources by which the developer carries out quality management.

17.5 SUMMARY

This chapter has looked at the activities currently being undertaken to produce standards for quality assurance in software development. The importance of such standards is that they provide guidance on the implementation of quality systems to software developers, and provide an independent yardstick by which to assess the capability of developers to operate an adequate quality system. The BSI currently runs a scheme under which software developers may have their software development procedures registered with them. This does not approve their quality system but registers their capability to operate one. There is no scheme as yet which certifies the software produced. This registration scheme is based on the existing standard for quality systems, BS 5750, which is the basis of an emerging standard on quality systems for software.

In Sec. 17.2 you read an interview with the head of the BSI Quality Assurance's Software Engineering Department, John Souter, who described their registration scheme which uses BS 5750. He also described their services for validating programming language implementations, particularly Pascal implementations. We then looked at what is meant by conformance and deviance testing by examining tests from the Pascal validation suite.

National and international standards for software systems are being developed. Currently, activity is greatest in the area of safety-critical systems. Draft standards from the International Electrotechnical Commission propose how systems should be classified as safety-related, how

---

[8] 'Requirements specification' is what we call statement of requirements.

their risk should be assessed, and how the safety integrity level of the software should determine the possible methods and techniques for producing it. The interim draft standards from the Ministry of Defence cover both the procurement of safety-critical software (00-55), i.e. the development of the software, and the analysis of hazards associated with the software (00-56) i.e. the safety classification of the software. One of the emphases which is clearly stated in these standards is the need for independent assessors and verification and validation teams.

BIBLIOGRAPHY

(Ministry of Defence, 1991a) *Interim Defence Standard 00-55: Requirements for the Procurement of Safety Critical Software in Defence Equipment* (MoD 00-55).

(Ministry of Defence, 1991b) *Interim Defence Standard 00-56: Requirements for the Analysis of Safety Critical Hazards* (MoD 00-56).

(BS 5750: Part 0): Section 0.1: 1987/ISO 9000-1987. Quality Systems Part 0 Principal Concepts and applications. Section 0.1 Guide to selection and use.

(BS 5750: Part 0): Section 0.2: 1987/ISO 9004-1987. Quality Systems Part 0 Principal Concepts and applications. Section 0.2 Guide to quality management and quality system elements.

(BS 5750: Part 1): 1987/ISO 9001-1987. Quality Systems Part 1 Specification for design/development production, installation and servicing.

(BS 5750: Part 2): 1987/ISO 9002-1987. Quality Systems Part 2 Specification for production and installation.

(BS 5750: Part 3): 1987/ISO 9003-1987. Quality Systems Part 3 Specification for final inspection and test.

(BS 6192: 1982) Specification for Computer Programming Language Pascal

(BSI 89/33005). Functional Safety of Programmable Electronic Systems: Generic Aspects. Part 1: General requirements, (BSI document 89/33005).

(BSI 89/33006). Software for Computers in the Application of Industrial Safety-related Systems, (BSI document 89/33006).

(BSI BS 4778): Part 1: 1987/ISO 8402 - 1986, Quality vocabulary Part 1. International Terms.

(BSI DPC 89/97932) Guidelines for the Application of BS 5750: Part 1 to Software.

INDEX